CW00324186

Italy

COLLIER
WORLD TRAVELER
SERIES

Italy

Editors:
Philippe Gloaguen and Pierre Josse

Translated by
Mark Howson

COLLIER BOOKS
Macmillan Publishing Company
NEW YORK

Collier Macmillan Publishers
LONDON

Macmillan Publishing Company
866 Third Avenue, New York, N.Y. 10022
Collier Macmillan Canada, Inc.

Library of Congress Cataloging in Publication Data
Gloaguen, Philippe.
Italy.
(Collier world traveler series)
Translation of: Italie.
1. Italy—Description and travel—1975-   —Guide-
books.   I. Josse, Pierre. II. Title. III. Series.
DG416.G56313   1986   914.5′04928   85-31377
ISBN 0-02-097720-4

Macmillan books are available at special discounts for bulk purchases for
sales promotions, premiums, fund-raising, or educational use.
For details, contact:

Special Sales Director
Macmillan Publishing Company
866 Third Avenue
New York, N.Y. 10022

10 9 8 7 6 5 4 3 2 1

Printed in the United States of America

CONTENTS

Italy

ITALY

Admirable that the Italians, blessed as they are with a superabundance of talents, should have preferred to be ruled by passion rather
than reason; the getting of wisdom and the whole question of how
one *ought* to behave oneself they prefer to leave as a puzzle for other
races. In fact, renouncing specialization altogether, they've gone on
to perfect themselves in the basic arts of living. Keep your eyes wide
open, and you might find out how it's done.

Getting There

If you are going to Italy, chances are you either have a short time
(two weeks to a month) or a long time (part of an exploring *wander-
jahr*). If you have the time, check out going standby on Peoples Express or Virgin Atlantic, 2 unorthodox airlines with incredibly cheap
flights to London (would you believe $300 roundtrip?). From there, it
is easy to hop a train, boat, or bus for Italy.

For short trips, a straight flight to Italy is almost mandatory. Happily, there are many charters and special discount flights available
year-round. Just check *The New York Times* travel section for the
most up-to-date prices and existing organizations, or use your trusty
local travel agent. Some recommendations:

CIEE: This solid and time-trusted charter company has flights
from all over the U.S. straight to Rome. Telephone (800) 223-7402.

TFI Tours: 34 West 32nd Street, New York, NY 10001. Telephone
in NYC (212) 736-1140; Southwest U.S. (512) 477-6500; or (800) 2
FLY-TFI.

Access Europe: 250 West 57th Street, Suite 511, New York, NY
10107. Telephone (212) 333-7280.

Apex Travel: 230 Park Avenue, New York, NY 10169. Telephone
(212) 661-1606 or (800) 428-8848.

Useful Addresses

Compagnia Italiana Turismo/Italian State Railways/Alitalia: 666
Fifth Avenue, New York, NY 10103. Telephone (212) 397-2667. A gov-
ernment-sponsored travel agency with offices in Chicago, Los Ange-
les, San Francisco, and in most major European cities.

Italian Government Travel Office/ENIT: 630 Fifth Avenue, New
York, NY 10111. Telephone (212) 245-2822; 360 Post Street, San
Francisco, CA 94108. Telephone (415) 392-6206. An official tourist
information agency that also has numerous European branches (for
example: 23, rue de la Paix, 75002 Paris. Telephone 266-66-68).

Italian Cultural Institute: 686 Park Avenue, New York, NY 10021.
Telephone (212) 879-4242. Good for info on language programs for
foreign students in Italy and other questions not involving train fares
or similar nuts-and-bolts issues.

Transalpino: 16, rue Lafayette, 75009 Paris (no U.S. office). Telephone 247-12-40. For info on BIGE rail tickets. Likewise, *Wasteels,*
31, quai des Grands-Augustins, 75006 Paris. Telephone 329-50-50.

Both have numerous branch offices and affiliates in the U.K. and on the Continent.

Formalities

All you need to get into Italy (and back into the U.S. or Canada when you're through) is a valid passport with an international vaccination certificate (typhoid and tetanus are especially recommended). If you're planning to stay for 90 days or longer, you'll need a visa as well. Contact your local Italian consulate for even *more* specific info than this guide offers.

If you're planning to do any driving (in a car not your own), a valid driver's license (domestic or international) and an international insurance certificate (green card) will also be required. If, for reasons best known to yourself, you have your own car over there, you'll need an international registration card (gray card) as well.

Where to Sleep

Youth Hostels: 75 of them altogether, most in interesting places and very well kept as a rule. An international hostel card can be purchased at these establishments; also obtainable in the US from American Youth Hostels, Suite 800, 1332 I Street, NW, Washington, D.C. 20005. Telephone (207) 783-6161. Or from Metropolitan New York Council of American Youth Hostels, 132 Spring Street, New York, NY 20005. Telephone (212) 431-7000.

Casa dello Studente: There's one in most of the larger cities, and you can get your meals in a university dining hall. Unfortunately, they don't always stay open during the summer.

Religious Communities: Monasteries, to be more precise. Large-sized monkish cells sleeping 5 or 6, available (especially in the summer) to persons of every (or no particular) religious persuasion who are prepared to comport themselves in a reasonably decorous manner. Some are located in especially attractive settings, of course, notably the thirteenth-century monastery in Assisi or the seminary that's attached to the Salute in Venice. The only inconvenience, a minor one, is that you can expect to be awakened at 5 or 6 A.M. by the ringing of bells and the chanting of the morning liturgy (in Venice, a spectacular experience in itself). Also, the gates may be locked at a specific time, not to be opened again until the next morning; no problem, since you're going to be getting up at 6 in any case. Rates vary but tend to be very modest; info on local facilities is available at the diocesan offices in any fair-sized town. Also, every parish has a *presbytery* (equivalent of the parish house) where they may be able to put you up as well.

Fanatical campers and minimalists may prefer to sleep out, absolutely free of charge, in the rest areas and service areas on the *autostrade*.

Hotels: No less expensive than elsewhere in Europe (perhaps only a bit less so than in the U.S.), though there may be more of a gradation. The *autostelli* and *AGIP motels* are the top of the line (from the standpoint of price, at any rate). Hotels come in 4 different categories and *pensioni* in 3, plus the *locande* (boardinghouses). Comparison shopping is made somewhat more difficult by the fact that not all *pensioni* require you to stay for a minimum number of days or to take all (or any) of your meals on the premises; some of them don't even serve breakfast *(prima collazione)*. A *locanda* may be cheaper than either a fourth-class hotel or a third-class *pensione* (and the latter two may not differ from one another in any important respect), and the truly memorable accommodations—the "great little place I found for only X thousand lire a night"—are almost certain to be in a *locanda*. The system, like most manifestations of the Italian organizational genius, seems needlessly complex but is ultimately workable. When you get to town, you can pick up the *lista dei alberghi* (list of hotels) at the Tourist Office and take it from there.

Alpine Shelters: During the summer, most have a caretaker on the premises and furnish basic services. For info on the others, open only by request, contact the Italian Alpine Club, via Ugo Fescolo 3, Milan.

Hitching

Is pretty easy due to the native courtesy and compassion of the Italians, the relative compactness of the country, and the *autostrade,* which allow you to really lap up the miles. Note, however, that as in most places hitching on the highway itself is illegal (violators are subject to a fine). Don't hesitate to take advantage by asking drivers for a *passagio,* a look at the landscape—admittedly a bit nervier than asking a bus driver for a transfer but frequently productive of memorable results. If your driver takes a turnoff that you're not interested in pursuing, don't get out right away; wait until the night service area. A few kilometers are wasted, perhaps, but you'll acquire a tremendous savings in time and effort over the long haul.

Beware of suburban beltways, ring roads, or whatever you care to call them, surrounding large urban agglomerations (like the one around Bologna), especially when they run parallel to the *autostrada* and are consequently monopolized by short-haul local traffic. Slow death for hitchhikers.

Working the highway service areas is highly recommended. Useful phrases: *Dove andate? Andate in direzione de ... ?* (Where are you going? In which direction are you headed?) The tollbooths at the end of an *autostrada* and at individual exits are also possibilities. You won't get rousted from the former but you may from the latter if you try to hitch right by the tollbooth. Regional peculiarities: There are no tolls on the *autostrada* that runs through Calabria, and there are no service areas in Sicily.

The AGIP superhighway map is unfortunately no longer available, but almost any one will do. The ACI map, for example, is admirably detailed. You can pick one up when you cross the border.

When you make your sign for hitching, it's best to use the standard city abbreviations to show you know what's what—the same ones found on license plates, so you can preselect useful prospects at a highway service area. Thus, Livorno = Li, Pisa = Pi, Siena = Si, Verona = VR or VN; larger cities have a single letter followed by a numerical suffix: Bologna = BO, B1, B2; Florence = F1, F2, F3; Milan = M1–M8; Naples = N1–N4; Rome = R2–R8; Turin = T0–T5; Venice = V2, V3. . . .

Women hitching in Italy will soon discover that Italians are eager to live up to their reputations as so many Don Giovannis or Mastroiannis. . . . Everyone hitching in Italy will discover that Sunday traffic consists largely of Mama, Papa, and in fact *tutta la famiglia* stuffed into a tiny little Fiat, with hardly any room left over for a large-sized foreigner, especially if heavily encumbered.

Driving

If you're driving a car registered *outside* the country, you're entitled to purchase gas coupons (the equivalent of 200 liters per annum) at a reduced rate, plus a bonus book of coupons redeemable at tollbooths on the *autostrade* north of Rome-Pescara. (Additional coupons for the southern *autostrade* will be made available later on, along with coupons entitling you to a discount on an additional 200 liters of gas if purchased in the south *plus* reduced rates on auto repair and wrecking services.)

This automatically makes you a member of the *ACI* (Italian Automobile Club), with all the various perquisites that that involves. You can buy the coupons with any currency except lire on presentation of a valid driver's license or proof of ID plus the car's registration at any Italian frontier post of ACI office outside the country. One important benefit of ACI membership: If you have an accident or a breakdown anywhere in Italy, you can summon an ACI towtruck simply by dialing 116. There's a small charge for the call (not much); ACI imposes a strict ceiling on any repair bills that you might subsequently incur.

There are plenty of authorized repair shops (called *officina meccanica* or just *meccanico*) along the highways, especially in the south; they'll readily lend you the tools so you can finish the job. Major repairs are accomplished much less readily, often at some expense. If you're driving an off-brand of car (that is, anything but a Fiat or an Alfa-Romeo), you'll probably be better off if you find your way to a dealership in the next big town.

Gas stations in urban areas are frequently closed between 11:30 A.M. and 4 P.M., and they close for the day at 7 P.M. A good thing to keep in mind.

Autostrade are numerous and tolls are minimal, sometimes nonexistent. National roads are generally in pretty good shape and give you a better sense of the landscape. It's best to make sure the lights of your car are in good working order—one thing the cops along the highways tend to be fussy about. A high-visibility distress signal (the plastic triangular kind) is something that every car should have.

There's usually a small charge for parking at archeological sites and other tourist attractions, and while you can generally count on parking for free somewhere down the line, this generally can be regarded as a false economy (due to the multiple uncertainties involved in parking in the public domain).

Trains

They're fast and very comfortable. You're even allowed to put your feet up on the seats, as long as you put down a newspaper or something first. Before you get on, make a careful study of the diagrams on the platform illustrating the makeup of the train; different sections of the train are most likely going to end up in different cities. Failure to observe this simple rule can have very disconcerting results.

Fares are the cheapest in Europe, plus tickets for journeys of more than 250 kilometers remain valid for another day for every additional 200 kilometers traveled (up to a maximum of 6 days), with unlimited stops permitted along the way. Clearly, if you're planning a series of consecutive hops, it makes more sense to buy a single ticket for the entire journey. A BIGE railpass (available in Europe through numerous Wasteels and Transalpino travel agencies) entitles travelers under 26 years of age to as much as a 50 percent reduction on certain trains. The famous Eurailpass is more expensive and somewhat more restrictive in its terms than the Inter-Rail pass that is (theoretically) available only to Europeans. Other interesting discount fares include:

Round-trip Ticket: Available at a 15 percent discount for journeys of fewer than 250 kilometers or for any distance between regional and provincial capitals. Valid from 1 day (for journeys of 50 kilometers or less) up to a maximum of 3 days.

"Circular" Ticket: Unlimited stops over a total distance of more than 1,000 kilometers provided that no single leg of the journey is repeated more than twice. Valid for 60 days if the ticket is issued outside Italy, otherwise just 30.

"Italian Tourist Ticket" (or BTLC): Available to foreign nationals for unlimited travel on all Italian trains (even the superchief *rapido*, on which an extra charge is required) for a period of 8, 15, 21, or 30 days. (All but the first of these can be converted to a shorter-term ticket with partial refund). Free reservations, extra charge for sleeping cars *(wagon-lits)* and couchettes *(cuccette),* and half-fare for children.

Kilometric Ticket: An especially good deal. Valid for up to 20 one-way trips and/or a total of 3,000 kilometers over a period of 2 months. Can also be used by more than one person at the same time (maximum of 5); children's fares are computed at a rate of .5 kilometer for every kilometer traveled.

Family Ticket: 30 percent discount for family groups of 4 or more members (with documents to prove it). The journey must begin or end at the Italian frontier; tickets remain valid for 60 days. May be purchased at travel agencies outside Italy *(CIT, 666 Fifth Avenue, New York, NY 10103 or your local branch office),* or in any Italian railroad station.

In puzzling out your itinerary, note that Italian trains, like prunes and canned black olives, deal exclusively in superlatives. Starting at the bottom of the list, the *accelerato* makes virtually all local stops, the *diretto* and the *direttissimo* not quite so many, the *espresso* fewer still, and the *rapido* stops for nothing less than a major metropolis.

The Siesta

The custom dates back to the days of ancient Rome. The word itself is a corruption of the Latin *sexta hora,* "the sixth hour" (that is, after sunrise), and the expression "mad dogs and Englishmen go out in the noonday sun" may have made lots of money for Noel Coward but is said to have originated as a popular Roman proverb. Nowadays, especially in the summer, stores close at noon, traffic slows down, and all public and private life comes to a virtual standstill. Perhaps the smartest thing for the sensitive visitor to do is simply play along and participate in a ritual that is said to have a markedly restorative effect on both body and mind. The siesta has recently been suppressed in certain quarters, in the interest of productivity; this stern directive emanates not from the Communist Party or the Club of Rome but from John Paul II, the first non-Italian pope since the Renaissance, who has strongly encouraged his co-workers at the Vatican to learn to do without.

The Italians/Background Reading

Suffice it to say that the Italians are really first-rate, even if their attitude toward women leaves something to be desired (actually, their attitude toward women leaves practically no one *not* to be desired). The blood runs hot, but the Church keeps the lid clamped down tight. The language is about as mellifluous as you can get without actually bursting into song (though that does happen from time to time), and people tend to speak pretty much the way they think, a legacy of the Renaissance perhaps. . . . This subject is explored at greater length in *The Italians* by Luigi Barzini; Francophones are directed to a wonderful book called *Les Ritals* by Cavanna (Livre de Poche), a comic masterpiece in its own right. Strictly English speaking readers interested in a more serious deep background might be better off with the regional approach: *The World of Venice* by James Morris is one of the best travel books ever written. Not quite in the same league but still very fine are Eleanor Clark's *Rome and a Villa,* Mary McCarthy's *The Stones of Florence,* Lawrence Durrell's *Sicilian Carrousel,* and Christopher Hibbert's *Rome* (unfortunately available only as an expensive hardback). Lastly, D. H. Lawrence's travel writings on Italy (now collected in a single volume), though a little lacking in topicality these days, can still give you a pretty good idea of what is really at the bottom of it all.

Points of Interest

In theory, museums are open from 9 to 2, and from 9 to 1 on Sunday (also free admission) and closed Monday. Student discounts are very hard to come by except in a few private establishments, happily including the Vatican. In practice, of course, this simple rule is subject to endless modifications; some of them may seem almost rational (to those familiar with the application of alternate-side parking regulations in most of our major cities, for example), others less so. An example of the former type: A museum may be closed on Sunday the thirtieth because Tuesday (the first) is a holiday. Churches and other points of interest are even more likely to be closed (*chiuso,* a good word to know) for reasons of the latter kind— basically supernatural, transcendental, and so forth. On the other hand, it's comforting to know that a church or museum in Italy will almost never be open when it's supposed to be closed. Churches are generally closed between noon and 3 P.M., just to start with; the papal interdict against the siesta has yet to trickle all the way down to the lower echelons.

General Knowledge

Before you can be admitted to St. Peter's (for example), you have to go through a kind of small-scale dress rehearsal for the Last Judgment; this time, however, the decision on admission or exclusion is based entirely on what you're wearing. The *dress code* is not always so stringently enforced in other churches, but it's best to adhere to it in any case. The following are absolutely *out:* shorts (for men and women), skirts above the knees, backless dresses, and halter tops (or worse).

Letters for general delivery/poste restante should be addressed as follows:

Signore/a/ina _____
Fermo Posta
Posta Centrale di [name of town]

You can pick up your mail on presentation of a piece of ID (and upon payment of a modest tax).

American Express has offices in 16 different cities.

Telephoning the U.S. and Canada: 001 is the dialing code. Direct-dialing from a public phone booth is possible only in Rome, Naples, and Genoa; elsewhere you'll have to go to a phone company office and follow a slightly more complicated procedure. Note that a very hefty surcharge is usually tacked on if you place an overseas call through a hotel switchboard.

Thievery: Really endemic only in Naples and Rome and organized by highly cost-conscious professional criminals who tend to be much more interested in a handsome Louis Vuitton with gold-plated catch, lovingly rubbed with saddle soap every day, and even a hand-stitched correspondent's shoulder bag from L. L. Bean than the grimy olive-drab duffel you picked up at Cousin Vinnie's bankruptcy sale in 1973. This is not to say that grubbiness is to be regarded as some sort of protection. On the contrary, the Italian cult of personal attractive-ness, another legacy of the Renaissance perhaps, is as well devel-oped as the Italian fascination with beautiful objects, and you'll be much better off striking some sort of compromise—poor but not unmindful of the elements of style is the basic look to strive for. Women and/or photographers are especially cautioned to keep one arm tightly clamped around their shoulder bags as a precaution against bag snatchers. Otherwise, it's best to console yourself with the reflection that there are plenty of other pigeons much riper for the plucking and simply not to fret about this sort of thing too much.

Bargaining may be attempted even in the better shops, but possi-bly at the risk of some small unpleasantness since it isn't always appreciated all that well.

A fair number of cafés and *trattorie* don't have bathrooms or even urinals. It's best to know about things like that in advance.

Money

Coin slots in public telephones accept only tokens *(gettoni).* These are widely acceptable as change in other transactions (current value L200) and are much prized as a form of currency that's conve-niently indexed against inflation (residents of New York City and other disadvantaged areas in the U.S. should not be too surprised by this).

Banks are open Monday to Friday from 8:20 A.M. to 1:20 P.M. They close at noon on the day before a holiday. That's it. The Italians invented banking, and these are the original banker's hours. If you run out of lire on a Sunday, you may be able to break a traveler's check by buying a little item of some sort at a service area on the *autostrada.* Note that traveler's checks denominated in lire are not so easy to dispose of (at least in return for value or services rendered).

Food

Just as the early universe was divided into matter and antimatter, Italian food, for the most part, is divided into *pasta* and *antipasto.* Both of these having become staples of cuisine in North America, it may surprise you to find these items cheaply and plentifully available in the most nondescript of Italian restaurants. A real food meal generally costs L10,000 and up in any restaurant worthy of the name, but on the other hand, more than one sit-down restaurant meal a day is surely excessive. It would be best to eke out the rest of your requirements in pizzerias and grocery stores, bearing in mind that the latter are generally closed on Thursday; travelers on a fanatical budget are advised to hit the bakeries when the current batch of freshly baked bread goes on sale, generally around noon and 5 P.M. (pizzas likewise in certain establishments).

Basic Pasta Terminology
Bedouin Arabic has hundreds of different words for different brands of camel; Eskimo languages are notoriously capable of making quite subtle distinctions between various types of snow; and the culture that devised such things as the aria, the arioso, and the arietta has shown hardly less self-restraint in classifying the almost infinite varieties of their staple foodstuff. Thus, any menu item you order that includes one of the following terms is bound to involve some sort of pasta. Bear in mind also that in Italy pasta is not served as an accompaniment to a main dish but rather as a kind of appetizer (which for picky eaters and cheapos may well be sufficient).

Long form: Apart from the obvious spaghetti and lasagna, we also have *fettuccine* (long and flat), *tagliatelle* (same but narrower), *bucatini* (fat, small-bore spaghetti), *tonnarelli* (square spaghetti, green or yellow), and *margherite* (little daisies).

Short form: *Rigatoni* (little pillows), *penne* (smooth, quill-shaped), and *conchiglie* (shells).

Stuffed form: *Cannelloni* (pillows), *ravioli* (cushions), *tortellini* (rings), and *tortelloni* (same, in a slightly larger size). Also *gnocchi* (plus the diminutive *gnocchetti*), little pasta dumplings.

In a soup: *Quadrucci* (like *fettuccine*), *capellini* (little hairs), *occhi de pernice* (bird's eyes—those of a partridge, to be precise), *puntine* (little dots), and *farfalle* (bowties/butterflies).

Specialties
Pizza and spaghetti are the cheapest items on the menu, but going into a restaurant and ordering only spaghetti is not generally regarded as a very classy maneuver. Italian pizza, which began as the traditional midday meal of the Neapolitan dockworkers, is refreshingly different from the North American variety (especially the West Coast and Midwestern franchise), with the crust folded over at times, and all sorts of interesting stuff baked inside. Italian salamis, sausages, and related products are diverse, flavorful, and often very spicy. *Coppa,* a kind of sausage with an enormous amount of pepper in it, is truly delicious.

Here are a couple of Roman specialties to start with, as served not only in the better restaurants and *trattorie* but also in those dinky little hole-in-the-wall-type places that this invaluable guide is only too pleased to direct you to.

- *Stracciatella:* Italian egg-drop soup (sort of) is omnipresent (and practically impossible to get off your clothes, should you happen to misplace a drop or two).
- *Saltimbocca:* Little veal cutlets wrapped in prosciutto and sautéed in marsala. In the following 2 dishes and elsewhere, the phrase *alla Romana* means "with mint" (though this is not the case with *pizza alla Romana,* you may rest assured): *trippa* (tripe) and *carciofi* (artichokes) *alla Romana;* the *carciofi* are fried in oil with plenty of garlic. Both are very tasty.
- *Abbachio:* Roast lamb.
- *Carciofi alla giudia:* Artichokes fried until they've completely lost their curl.
- *Cipoline in agro dolce:* Onions in sweet-sour sauce.
- *Coda alla caccinara:* Oxtail stew.
- *Coratella:* Fried lamb kidneys (and other selected entrails).

Note that meat dishes in restaurants are generally served without vegetables.

Where to Eat

Keep an eye out for the little no-name places featuring home-style cooking (variously styled *cucina della mamma, di biduli, casalinga*); there may not even be a sign in many cases. Broccoli (called *brocoli* over here for short) is a staple of home-style Italian cuisine, and it is used in lots of great dishes, while it is rarely found on North American restaurant menus. Eateries are divided into 2 basic categories: restaurants, where you pay afterwards, and all others where you pay in advance *(tavola calda, rosticceria, pizzeria, trattoria, hostaria,* snack bar, milk bar, *caffè).* The last 3 mainly have sandwiches and pastries. In principal, the *rosticceria* sells hot dishes to go and the *tavola calda* sells hot dishes—a pizza or a plate of spaghetti—to be consumed on their countertop, in the manner of the neighborhood pizza-by-the-slice places in the U.S. Nowadays, a modest establishment of this kind is just as likely to be called a *pizzeria-bar* or a *rosticceria,* and a *tavola calda,* so-called, has been upgraded into something like a *trattoria,* a sidewalk café with tables where food and drinks are served. *Pizzerie* are about evenly divided between the sit-down and stand-up varieties.

Note that, in general, breakfasts served in restaurants tend to be on the stingy side whereas the sandwiches and pastries in the *caffè* are both ample and abundant. A service charge should be included in the prices in the fast-food and self-service places and in the better-class *trattorie,* though of course there's no shortage of scoundrelly restaurateurs who live off the vigorish (a 20 percent *servicio* not included or an equally outrageous *coperto,* or cover charge) on an otherwise reasonably priced menu. Pass 'em by.

Drink

Italy leads the world in absolute production as well as per capita consumption of wine, some of which is about as good as you can get and some of which is pretty rotten. No one gets too excited about vintage years, and since grapes are grown practically all over the country, most regional varieties, even the very good ones, tend to stay pretty close to their place of origin. It's considered bad form, in fact, to order a frascati in Venice or a valpolicella in Naples. Here, reading from north to south, are a few notable wines of Italy:

Asti spumante: Asti, 40 miles east of Turin, is conveniently located right near the *autostrada.*

Valpolicella: Comes from Verona and *Lambrusco* from Modena, near Bologna. The latter is a lightly sparkling red table wine and a bit of an acquired taste. It's best to try a glass or two before you invest in a barrel.

Chianti: From the region between Florence and Siena, it is one of the few Italian wines that gets a whole lot better with age (5 years maximum). A mediocre Chianti is best for adding the occasional color accent to the tablecloth, but a good one, in our opinion, is up there with the very best Italian reds.

Frascati: Good white table wine from Rome that still doesn't compare with its lesser-known compatriot, *Est! Est!! Est!!!,* which is also the subject of a fairly sweet story. During the ninth century a German prelate who was planning a pilgrimage to Rome sent his steward on ahead of him with instructions to stop in at all the *tavernas* along the way and sample the local product. He was further instructed to chalk the Latin word *est* on the door of the *taverna* if the local vintage was particularly distinguished and *non est* in the opposite case. The vintage that went completely off the charts in the manner alluded to above is produced in the Montefiascone district, not far from Rome.

Lacrima Christi ("the tears of Christ): Comes from grapes grown in the volcanic soil of the region south of Naples. The distinctive, delicate taste of this wine and the wines of the nearby islands of Capri and Ischia is alleged to have something to do with the high sulfur content of the soil, but since a certain amount of sulfur creeps in during the production of all white wines, this explanation is not likely to be the correct one (merely the most prevalent). An all-purpose remark, which can readily accompany one's first taste of any Italian wine (after taking a healthy swig and swishing it around your mouth for a moment or two): "Hmm"—slight, thoughtful frown— "the vineyards are too close to the trolley-car tracks." This never fails to impress.

Marsala: From Sicily, this wine is always accompanied by an egg chaser *(marsala all'uovo)* . . . first one, then the other. The order is important.

Even the tiniest towns have a decent *vino locale* (in about 9 cases out of 10). Naturally you'll want to know whether it's *rosso* (red) or *bianco* (white), and which is better *(il melio).* It is always cheaper than the stuff that comes in bottles and often it is just as good.

Considering the Italian flair for all-inclusive nomenclature, it's not surprising that hardly anyone ever orders a mere *espresso.* It's much more likely to be a *ristretto* (strained), if not *ristressimo* or *machiato* ("stained" with just a splash of milk, either hot, cold, or lukewarm). There are about a dozen possibilities in all. We favor the *cioccolato,* a smooth, creamy beverage that's delicious to scarf up with the aid of one of those long spoons; the world-renowned *capuccino* often cannot be distinguished from an ordinary *caffè a latte* (coffee with milk).

The Commedia dell'Arte

Italy's other great contribution to the dramatic arts (apart from the opera, of course) began in the mountainous northern district of Bergamo, whose inhabitants were celebrated for their shrewdness and rusticity; it is also the home of the character Arlecchino (Harlequin). A number of the other commedia characters are associated with particular cities; for example, Pantaleone (Pantaloon) with Venice, and Pulcinella (Punchinello, Mr. Punch) with Naples.

The commedia was pure theater, highly improvisational, with plot restricted to a handful of basic scenarios—typically involving the young lovers' efforts to outwit the heavy father who has promised his daughter's hand to an elderly mugwump like the *Dottore* or the *Capitano,* or to forestall the villainous intrigues of pirates, sorcerers, wicked fairies, and the like. The stock characters, the *masks* as they were called, were also highly stylized in their behavior—the *zanni* (whence "zany") such as Harlequin, Brighella (another Bergamo boy), and Coviello, sociopathic scroungers who were always willing to assist the lovers in their intrigues against the more respectable elements (Tartaglia, the dithering old man; Pantaleone, the stuffy old capitalist; and the Capitano, the narcissistic soldier of fortune, a direct ancestor of Colonel Flagg on *M*A*S*H.*

The commedia was also primarily an actor's theater, with all other elements minimized or highly stylized, and with nothing to animate this fairly restricted repertory of very basic material but the vitality and virtuosity of the performers themselves, including such modern drama-school staples as juggling, fencing, and mime. *Lazzi,* verbal or physical gags and bits of business, came to be collected in prompt-books for the actors to study, but the action on stage was highly spontaneous, encouraging the actors to take full advantage of the gestural and verbal possibilities of every situation without losing track of the tangled and very slender narrative thread provided by the scenario. The commedia remained enormously popular in Western Europe for three or four hundred years and exercised a very considerable influence on the later development of the theater, the opera, and the ballet, as well as on a variety of artists all the way from Shakespeare, Molière, and Watteau to Stravinsky, Prokofiev, Marcel Marceau, of course, and further to a whole generation of mimes, whitefaces, bozos, rock stars, and real-life scroungers of the present day.

Basic Vocabulary

yes	*si*
no	*no*
yesterday	*ieri*
today	*oggi*
tomorrow	*domani*
where?	*dove?*
how much?	*quanto?*
to the right	*a destra*
to the left	*a sinistra*
enough	*basta*
too much	*troppo caro*
what time is it?	*che ora è?*

tourist office	*ufficio di turismo*
train station	*stazione*
bus station	*fermata*
post office	*l'ufficio postale*
the police	*la polizia*
the bank	*la banca*
hello	*buon giorno*
good evening	*buona sera*
how are you?	*come sta?*
good-bye	*arrivederci*
please	*per favore*
thanks	*grazie*
I don't understand	*non capisco*
campground	*campeggio*
youth hostel	*albergo della gioventù*
hotel	*albergo*
restaurant	*ristorante*
to drink	*bere*
to eat	*mangiare*
sleep	*dormire*
more	*più*
water	*acqua*
coffee	*caffè*
milk	*latte*
bread	*pane*
cold	*freddo*
hot	*caldo*
good	*buono*
bad	*cattivo*
toilet	*gabinetto*
one	*uno*
two	*due*
three	*tre*
four	*quattro*
five	*cinque*
six	*sei*
seven	*sette*
eight	*otto*
nine	*nove*
ten	*dieci*
twenty	*venti*
thirty	*trenta*
forty	*quaranta*
fifty	*cinquanta*
sixty	*sessanta*
seventy	*settanta*
eighty	*ottanta*
ninety	*novanta*
one hundred	*cento*
one thousand	*mille*

Amateur philologists take note: *Bibite* means not so much "a drink" in general as a nonalcoholic apéritif in particular.

Mileage Chart

	Ancona	Aosta	Bari	Bologna	Bolzano	Florence	Genoa	Milan	Naples	Palermo	Rome	Turin	Trent	Trieste
Aosta	370													
Bari	303	673												
Bologna	130	241	432											
Bolzano	297	282	600	129										
Florence	158	497	461	66	240									
Genoa	307	150	609	177	242	165								
Milan	265	116	567	135	166	202	91							
Naples	251	614	173	380	547	325	464	515						
Palermo	763	1,125	490	928	1,058	836	975	1,026	515					
Rome	175	470	298	247	421	181	320	380	1,026	655				
Turin	337	78	640	208	255	268	101	90	567	1,078	423			
Trent	260	245	562	136	37	203	205	129	510	1,021	384	218		
Trieste	303	291	606	194	204	260	334	257	553	1,064	441	347	174	
Venice	211	291	514	102	133	169	242	175	461	973	350	264	95	102

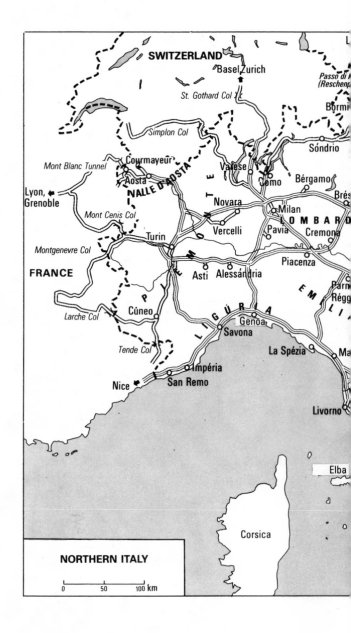

NORTHERN ITALY

0   50   100 km

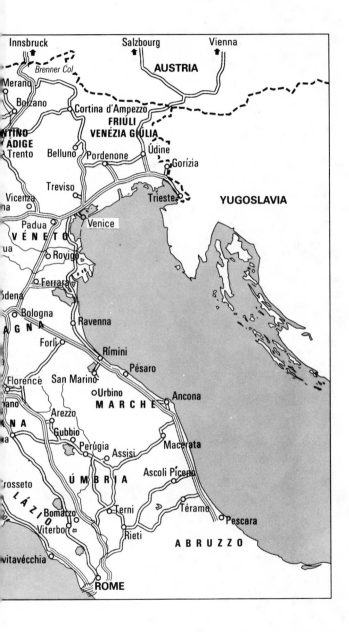

Sample Itinerary

Miles

Aosta–Ivrea–Vercelli–Novara–Milan	115
Milan–Brescia	57
Brescia–Verona	41
Verona–Vicenza–Padua–Venice	167
Venice–Ravenna–Rimini......................................	141
Rimini–Fano–Foligno–Terni–Rome	205
Rome–Terracina–Gaeta–Naples	142
Naples–Sorrento–Amalfi–Salerno	62
Salerno–Auletta–Cosenza	184
Cosenza–Catanzaro–Reggio di Calabria	144
Total	1,258

Messina–Catania–Syracuse...................................	95
Syracuse–Ragusa–Agrigento	134
Agrigento–Palermo	103
Total	332

Palermo–Naples (by car, via the Straits)	558
Naples–Rome...	142
Rome–Siena–Florence	189
Florence–Pisa–Genoa.......................................	162
Genoa–Ventimiglia	112
Total	1,163

Total: Palermo to Naples by boat	2,196
Total: Palermo to Naples by car.............................	2,754

THE NORTHWEST

VALLE d'AOSTA

The gastronomic specialty of this high valley, up by the Great St. Bernard Tunnel, is the link sausage, about as thick as your thumb and truly delicious. There are some great campsites around the town of Aosta, especially on the road to Ivrea. Tuesday is market day, when you'll find clothing as well as foodstuffs in abundance. If you don't have a car, there's a campground at Sarre that is quite hospitable and has a decent restaurant; it's 10 minutes out of town on the No. 3 bus.

A modest (12-mile) detour to the south to *Breuil-Carvinia* will enable you to check out the Matterhorn (known around these parts as *Cervinia* or *le Cervin*), one of Europe's most spectacular peaks. It is a good place to end up around sunset. Mont Blanc (Monte Bianco), the tallest mountain west of the Caucasus, can be viewed from nearby Courmayeur (22 miles from Aosta). Schedules for the excellent local bus service are posted at the Chamber of Commerce.

Gran Paradiso National Park: One of the most beautiful in Europe, a collection of 5 mountain valleys to the south of the Mont Blanc Tunnel. The most prominent mammalian species include ibex (European version of bighorn sheep), chamois, and marmots. You'll also find numerous campgrounds with hiking and climbing trails in all possible degrees of difficulty. In our opinion, *Val de Cogne* and *Valsavaranche* are the nicest valleys. There's a splendid campground out at the end of the Valsavaranche road; it gets pretty cold at night, though (altitude 6,200 feet). There's another campground at around 5,000 feet, near the village of *Bien de Valsavaranche,* where food and other essentials are quite a bit less expensive.

LANS-LE-BOURG

A rather small youth hostel on the banks of a rushing Alpine torrent, just a couple of kilometers over the border in France. Primarily of interest to those who are heading through Mont Cenis Pass, the most direct route to Turin. Note that the pass is often closed, except during the height of summer, in which case you'll have to try the auto-train tunnel at Modane.

LA SACRA DI SAN MICHELE

Can be found 8 miles northwest of Turin. The road climbs upward to a sharp rocky pinnacle (2,980 feet), revealing a spectacular downside panorama. Site of a Benedectine abbey, a kind of Mont St. Michel in miniature that dates back to the year 998. Open from 9 to 12 and from 2 to 7 (5 in the winter).

A city of 1 million inhabitants whose collective personality seems solemn, austere, and even downright chilly. In our view, anything more than the briefest stopover would be an act of kindness.

Useful Addresses

EPT (Regional Tourist Information Office): Via Roma, 226, and at the Porta Nuova station.

Post Office: Via Alfieri.

American Express: c/o Ventana, via Gobetti, 10. Open from 8:30 to 12:30 and from 2:30 to 6:30 on weekdays; from 8:30 to 12:30 on Saturday.

Bank of America: Via Arcivescovado, 7. Telephone 510-800. They'll advance cash money against your VISA card.

Medical Emergency: Via San Domenico, 260.

Transalpino: Piazza CLN, 260, near via Roma.

Where to Sleep

Youth Hostel: Corner of via Alba and via Gatty. Take a No. 52 bus from the Porta Nuova station. A brand-new one, it's quite comfortable.

There are quite a number of little hotels off to the left of the Porta Nuova station (as seen from Via Roma).

Pensione San Carlo: Piazza San Carlo, 197. Telephone 553-522. A little expensive but otherwise quite acceptable.

Hotel Verna: Via Galliari. Expensive. No showers. Notable for the '50s decor of the entrance hall.

Pensione Lux: Via Galliari, 9. Telephone 657-257. A lot cheaper than the foregoing. Nice atmosphere.

Pensione San Marco: Via Gotto, near the station. Telephone 659-419. On the expensive side.

Pensione Italia: Via Mecci, 17. Telephone 553-888. A very cheap, hospitable establishment. The proprietor collects foreign coins, and a few more will always be welcome.

Le Petit Hôtel: Via San Francisco d'Assisi. Telephone 537-619. Centrally located (walk up via Roma from the station and turn left at Piazza San Carlo; it's the fourth on the right). A little expensive. Bar and restaurant.

Albergo Verdi: Via Vanghiglia, 8. Comfortable and fairly cheap.

Camping Riviera sul Po: Corso Moncalieri. Campground on the edge of town. Take a No. 67 bus.

Where to Eat

A couple of Piedmontese specialties: *Agnolotti* are a kind of ravioli stuffed with rice, ground beef, cheese, and egg. *Gnocchi alla fontina* are little cubes of cheese and pasta that have been breaded and fried. Salads are traditionally served with *bagna caoda,* a dressing with garlic and anchovies. As noted earlier, *Asti spumante* is only the best known of several first-rate local wines. A kind of chocolate caramel called *gianduliotti* is no less justly celebrated.

Cucina Toscana: Via Galliari, 16. Near the station. A couple of tables set up in a little dining room. The menu is both extensive and inexpensive. *Agnolotti al ragù* is a specialty.

Trattoria Messico: Via Galliari, 8. Same basic concept. Yellow frosted glass in the front window casts a bit of a pall, but there's nothing wrong with the food.

AGM Self-Service: Via Lagrange, 43. Student hangout. Food is good, cheap, and plentiful.

La Nuova Lapara: Via Andrea Doria, 21. A very good seafood place that is far from expensive.

A whole flock of worthy family-style *trattorie* can be found just beyond via Nizza (notably at the corner of via Saluzzo and via Giotto), where you can sit and munch your *agnolotti* and watch it all go by.

The Sights

Egyptian Museum: Piazza Carignano. Generally agreed to be the second best of its kind in the world (right after the Cairo Museum). There are 2 enormous sculpture galleries on the ground floor, specializing in works of the Tutankhamen era, plus a collection of grave objects, tomb models, and figurines that give a remarkably complete, even an intimate picture of the ordinary life of the Egyptians. The small funeral chapel and the famous Book of the Dead are especially worth checking out. The famous erotic papyri may come as something of a disappointment to us jaded moderns. The very respectable fine arts museum is housed in the same building.

Duomo San Giovanni Battista: This cathedral houses the celebrated Chapel of the Holy Shroud, a sacred relic that has recently become the object of intensive scientific study and a great deal of publicity, notably in light of one physicist's assertion that the Resurrection was an exothermic reaction accompanied by an instantaneous temperature flare-up of several thousand degrees. The shroud displayed in the sacristy of the chapel is a detailed replica of the original.

National Film Museum: Piazza San Giovanni, 2, near the royal gardens. Turin was the center of the Italian film industry during the silent era, before Mussolini built Cinecittà outside Rome. Early film-related artifacts on display include eighteenth-century magic lanterns, nineteenth-century stereoscopes, a couple of patent-model Kodaks, plus a highly evocative array of vintage film posters. Classic films are shown on the premises, of course. Closed Monday and Thursday. Take a No. 15 trolley and get off at piazza Castello.

National Mountaineering Museum (Duca degli Abruzzi): Monte dei Capucini abbey. For those who already miss the Alps. You'll see models of the Mont Cenis dam, Alpine villas and farmsteads, plus exhibits of furniture, traditional tools and farm implements, pre-twentieth-century costumes, and miscellaneous (memorabilia of the Umberto Nobile polar expedition of 1907 and an extensive collection of skis from 1800 to the present). Open every day. Take a No. 15 trolley from the station, then a No. 13 across the bridge.

Automobile Museum (Buscaretti di Ruffia): Corso Unità d'Italia, 40. South side of town. Star of the collection is undoubtedly the Itala touring car that won the Peking-Paris race in 1907, though the '94 Peugeot and the '99 Panhard also have their admirers. Closed Monday.

Palazzo Madama: This squared-off fifteenth-century castle has an

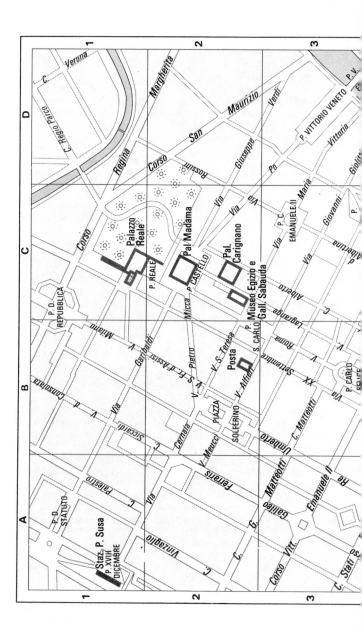

TURIN

0 100 200 m

Staz di Porta Nuova F.S.

Pal. d. Esposizioni

ITALY • 21

add-on neoclassical west wing with a very lovely façade. Home of the municipal museum, whose treasures include one of the most beautiful of illuminated manuscripts, *Les Très Belles Heures de Duc de Berry.*

Borgo Medioevale: In the Parco del Valentino. Elaborate replica of a medieval village (itself over a century old) and a castle in the center. Take bus No. 16, 50, 52, 59, or 73. Paid admission.

LAKE MAGGIORE

In spite of the numerous spas and other settlements along its shores, Maggiore has still preserved a great deal of its wild and unspoiled beauty and is especially famous for its luxuriant flora.

• Stresa
Best-known lakeside resort with lots of hotels and no shortage of summer visitors. Site of a memorably futile 1930s peace conference. There's still not much point in lingering here, in our opinion, except to catch the boat out to the islands.

• Borromean Islands
Isola Bella contains the ancestral headquarters of the Borromeo family (famous for having produced at least one pope, one saint, and numerous cardinals and archbishops), surrounded by formal gardens. The boat fare doesn't include the price of admission to the palace and grounds, which is a bit of a ripoff but basically worth it. Lots of restaurants and cute little stores adjoining, but these can profitably be ignored. Island #2, *Isola dei Pescatori* is, as the name implies, the home of a perfectly genuine fishing village with narrow streets (not many) and considerable charm. Provides a temporary refuge from the tidal flux of tourism that afflicts its sister island. Island #3, *Isola Madre,* is recommended if and only if you'd like to visit a world-renowned botanical garden—with another slightly exorbitant admission charge. On the other hand, you get a break on the price of the boat ticket if you spring for all 3 islands.

Back on shore, there's a funicular railroad that takes you up to the summit of *Mottarone* (4,620 feet). Lovely view of Stresa and the islands in clear weather.

• Angera
A small lakeside resort on the southeastern shores of the lake, opposite Arona. The town is overlooked by a massive fourteenth-century castle that is open for inspection between April and October.

Camping Città di Angera: Via Bruschera al Lago, right by the lake. On the expensive side (like most Italian campgrounds) but has all the amenities—lots of shade, hot showers, swimming pool, tennis court, restaurant-bar, and a couple of little stores.

• Baveno
Features relatively cheap accommodations. A convenient point of departure for excursions on the lake itself or up into the mountains. More specific info is available at the Tourist Office, piazza Dante. There are 11 campgrounds in the immediate vicinity, plus hotels and furnished rooms. The cheapest of the former is *Camping Diverio,* via Gramsci, 31, located in a peaceful, shady spot.

Pizzeria da Michele: Via Garibaldi. Moderately priced and otherwise thoroughly commendable. There's also a little place on via Gramsci that makes excellent fresh pasta (especially lasagna). Place your orders in advance.

Presence of numerous dead fish will alert you to the fact that the municipal harbor is not quite suitable for swimming. *Villa Fedora,* with access to the lakefront, has been acquired by the town for that purpose; the water is quite refreshing, though you probably wouldn't want to swallow a whole lot of it.

• *Lake Orta*

About 10 miles to the southwest of Maggiore. One of the smallest and less frequented of the lakes of northern Italy. *Orta San Giulio* is a very nice village, with boat service out to Isola San Giulio, where it's possible to go swimming (subject to the same disclaimer as in the previous entry). There's also a church, a seventeenth-century abbey, and a couple of handsome villas. Makes for a very pleasant outing.

PAVIA

All in red brick, particularly the narrow streets in the old quarter of town where the play of the afternoon light brings out all sorts of earth-toned subtleties. Pavia is the home of one of Italy's oldest and largest universities, supplying an unexpected animation to the streets of this handsome medieval city (a pace that's naturally somewhat abated during the summer months).

EPT office: Corso Garibaldi, 1.

Where to Sleep

Practically nowhere that's reasonably priced. Most hotels are closed in August.

Camping Lido: Via Varrazze. A pleasant, shady spot by the river. Basic necessities on site, plus a bar that's open in the evenings and horseback riding (200 meters away).

The Sights

Duomo: An important monument of the Lombard Renaissance, it's the work of several architects (including Leonardo). The interior of the cathedral is in the form of a Greek cross (4 arms of equal length), and the dome is the third largest in Italy (right after St. Peter's and Novara Cathedral). The round pulpit is particularly bizarre.

San Michele: The most impressive of Pavia's churches. Charlemagne was crowned king of Lombardy in the original basilica (built in 661) and the emperors Frederick Barbarossa and Henry II in the present Romanesque structure, which is especially notable for the decoration of the facade (especially the carved monsters and demons) and right-hand doorway.

Ponte Coperto: The almost 700-foot covered bridge over the Ticino was completely destroyed during World War II, but its successor should lose that raw, unfinished look in a few hundred years.

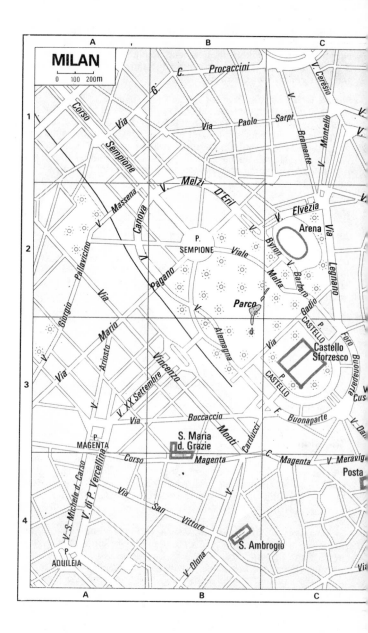

MILAN

0 100 200m

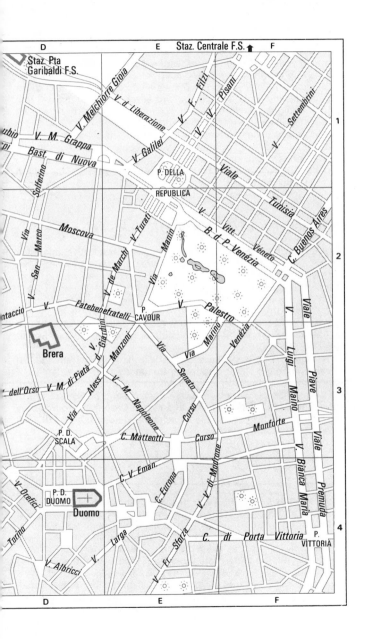

The Outskirts

Certosa di Pavia: The Charterhouse, about 6 miles north on the road to Milan. Probably the most spectacular achievement of the Lombard Renaissance. Founded in 1396 to assure the salvation of the Visconti family, the local magnates, many of whom are buried beneath the church. The entryway is decorated wtih fifteenth-century frescoes, and in the interior courtyard is *Foresteria,* the guesthouse, and old apothecary shops (now dispensing liqueurs and other monkish delights; the place is run by Cistercians). At the rear of the courtyard, the facade of the church contains several kinds of marble from various regions of Italy. Closed Monday (religious holidays excepted). Open from 9 to 11:30 and from 2:30 to 6.

The nearby plain of Certosa was the site of the so-called battle of Pavia (1525) in which Francis I was disastrously defeated by the Emperor Charles V (and was afterwards confined in the Charterhouse as a POW). Culture seekers who have gotten as far as the first paragraph of Proust may remember something about this.

THE DRIVE FROM VALLE d'AOSTA TO MILAN

The highway runs along the edge of the Gran Paradiso National Park for some distance, then right through Ivrea (principal product: typewriters), and down the valley to Vercelli. Right between, on the fringe of the mountains, you'll find the pleasant lakeside town of Viverone and a very good restaurant:

Il Corsario: Via Provinciale, 50. Telephone (01-61) 984-91. Right on the *nazionale* in the center of town. Trout grilled over a wood fire, veal Milanese (the real thing), all kinds of pasta and succulent sorbets. . . .

Habitués of college film societies will instantly be reminded of Sylvana Mangano, sloshing around the paddy fields in *Bitter Rice,* when they reach the agricultural outskirts of Vercelli. The town itself has some nice old streets, a lovely Romanesque basilica *(San Andrea)* with Gothic afterthoughts, the piazza Cavour, surrounded by handsome arcades, and a little museum devoted to the productions of local Renaissance masters.

MILAN

Italy's second city (after Turin in population, after Rome in other respects) and the design capital of the universe sits like a tasteful spider at the center of a vast web of industrial parks and suburbs. The pace of the city traffic—cars, trucks, buses, and streetcars—is impressively frenzied, as befits the former headquarters of the Futurist movement. The blare of their horns and the roar of their engines are no less impressive (as befits the current headquarters of Italy's neo-expressionist avant-garde). . . . On a slightly more prosaic note, there are 2 separate subway lines. Subway tickets are valid on all surface transportation for 75 minutes after purchase, a system clearly devised with the commuter rather than the tourist in mind. It's not absolutely clear that Milan is a beautiful city, but it's certainly interesting enough (Stendhal's last request was to be buried here), and there's always a lot going on.

Useful Addresses

EPT Offices: In the Stazione Centrale and the Palazzo del Turismo, piazza del Duomo. Free maps of the city and the region.

American Express: Via Vittorio Pisani, 19, near the Stazione Centrale. Open from 9 to 6 from Monday to Friday, and from 9 to 12 on Saturday.

Bank of America: Via San Prospero, 2. Telephone (2) 88-76. Another convenient VISA card liquidation station.

Posta Centrale: Via Corbusio, 4, near the piazza del Duomo. Branch office in the Stazione Centrale.

Telephone Office: In the Stazione Centrale. Open 24 hrs.

U.S. Consulate: Piazza della Republica, 32. Telephone 65-28-41.

Canadian consulate: Via Vittorio Pisani. Telephone 857-04-51.

Where to Sleep

Ostello per la Gioventù Piero Rota: Via Martino Bassi, 2 (on the western edge of town). From the central station, take the green line (subway) to Cardona, change for the red line (toward San Leonardo), and get off at a station called QT8. Go up the stairs to via Salmoiraghi. It's only about 200 yards from there. (If you're driving, ask for directions to the Stadio San Siro.) A spacious, modern hostel. Inexpensive. Somewhat handicapped by its remote suburban location. Still, it's often full in the summer. It's best to phone ahead—367-095. Open from 7 to 9 A.M. and from 5 to 11 P.M. There's a little *pizzeria* on the square nearby.

Several cheap hotels can be found in and around viale Tunisia, near the central station, including:

Pensione Vivarelli: Piazza Cirque Giornale, 6. Telephone 450-248. Very moderate prices. A cordial welcome is assured.

Pensione Arno: Via Lazzaretto (the cross street off via Tunisia), 17. Telephone 271-56-74. Not great, but one of the cheaper places in the neighborhood.

Where to Eat

Bar-Pizzeria la Cuccuma: Via Pacini, 26. Near the Piola subway station. Neopolitan specialties. Closed Monday.

Rosticceria Pech: Via Cesare Cantu, a little street off via Torino (a big street off piazza del Duomo). A memorable little eatery with very nice decor and wonderful sandwiches (*panini,* actually) stuffed with sausage and sauerkraut or burger meat, plus deep-dish fruit pies and various hot dishes to go. Closed Monday. Open from 8:30 to 2 and from 2:30 to 7.

Al Panino: Via San Paolo, in back of the Duomo. Features hamburger à la provençale and beer, plus an inexpensive daily special.

Il Duomo: On the piazza. Somewhat upscale in price and appearance. You may want to fall back on the *menù turistico.*

Restaurant Omero: Via Lazzaretto, near the viale Tunisia. A nice respectable establishment.

Restaurant Linus: Largo Corsia dei Servi, 21 (also corso Vittorio

Emanuele, 26). Typical Italian specialties. Great *gnocchi,* but on the expensive side. Closed Monday.

The Sights

If you feel like putting in a few solid hours of sightseeing in Milan, we can recommend the following highly compact itinerary: Starting in *piazza del Duomo,* stop off at the Tourist Office and load up on literature, then head over to the *Duomo.* A stroll down *galleria Vittore Emanuele II* takes you to *La Scala.* Next, head for the *Castello Sforzesco* and finally over to *Santa Maria delle Grazie* for a look at Leonardo's *Last Supper.*

Duomo: Construction was begun in 1393 at the behest of the current Visconti, who was determined to beat the Florentines at their own game. Nicknamed the Marble Hedgehog on account of the flamboyant Gothic excesses of its façade, the cathedral's interior is disappointingly normal. There's an elevator that takes you up to the roof for a stroll around and a better look at the 2,245 carved figures up aloft, backdrop for a memorable scene in *Rocco and His Brothers,* an early film by Visconti (a direct descendant of Milan's medieval warlords).

Right by the entrance you'll see a line traced on the floor that points to a tiny aperture in the vault (in the first bay over the right-hand aisle), which allows a single ray of sunlight to shine through at midday. You should definitely come back for a second look when the Duomo, with its multitude of prickly little spires, is brilliantly lit up at night.

Galleria Vittore Emanuele II: A far from pedestrian mall. Completed in 1877, it's arranged in the shape of a cross and is lined with cafés, restaurants, and chic shops. Cool in the summer, unbearable in the winter, and always packed with people. The first café on the left (as you go in) has some remarkable mosaics inside.

Teatro alla Scala: The Vatican of the opera world. Tickets are on sale every day but Monday from 10 to 1 and from 2:30 to 5:30. With luck you may even be able to pick up an unclaimed or standing-room ticket for that day's performance (starting at 5:30 P.M.).

The museum entrance is in front of the building, to the left. Contains an astounding collection of operatic and theatrical costumes, plus relics of the great voices of the past. Open from 9 to 12 and from 2 to 6. Around the corner and down the street at via Manzoni, 29, is the house where Verdi died. During his final illness his admirers covered the street outside with straw so that the maestro's last hours would not be profaned by the rattle of carriage wheels.

Castello Sforzesca: The Sforza family castle is a massive brick structure with cylindrical turrets at its 2 front corners. It now houses a museum of painting and sculpture; notable among the latter is Michelangelo's unfinished *Rondanini Pietà,* his last work, a kind of 3-minute sketch in stone with the figures just beginning to emerge from the imprisoning marble. On the second floor you'll find furniture, a vast collection of ceramics, and historic musical instruments. Open from 9:30 to 12 and from 2:30 to 5:30. Closed Monday (except holidays).

Santa Maria delle Grazie: The dome, formed of 16 triangular panels and surrounded by an exterior gallery, and the interior cloister are both well proportioned and attractive, but the *Last Supper* is what you're here to see. Entrance is on the left-hand side. Admission is fairly steep. Leonardo's incredible fresco occupies one wall of what was once the refectory (dining hall) of a Dominican abbey. Nitre deposits on the walls, numerous nearby detonations during World War II and repeated, ruinous cleanings and restorations in the past have leached out or chipped off quite a bit of the original pigment, but the current ultra-high-tech restoration is expected to undo a great deal of the damage. The subject of the painting is, of course, the highly charged moment just *after* Christ has announced to his Disciples, "One of you shall betray me," to which the Disciples exhibit a variety of reactions while Christ remains impassive, almost indifferent. Using an original and not very successful fresco technique, Leonardo worked on the *Last Supper* for 2 years. There are those who have suggested that, obsessed as he was by the imperfect and ephemeral nature of all human endeavor, he deliberately ensured that the greatest of his masterpieces would begin to deteriorate even before its completion.

Pinacoteca di Brera: Via Brera, 28. A first-rate collection of old masters, thoughtfully assembled for your viewing pleasure by Napoleon. 40 rooms of Rembrandts, Rubenses, Titians, and Van Dycks, plus Mantegna's the *Dead Christ,* the *Supper at Emmaus* by Caravaggio, the *Flagellation of Christ* by Donato Bramante and, finally, the Montefeltro altarpiece, consummate expression of the genius of Piero della Francesca.

The *Stazione Centrale,* built at the beginning of this century at the behest of King Victor Emmanuel III, never fails to get a reaction.

Hitching Out of Milan

A No. 84 bus will take you out to the *autostrada* heading south.

Toward Turin: Take bus No. 42 or 47 from the *stazione,* then walk for 1 kilometer.

LAKE COMO

Mountains and water meet in innumerable tiny gulfs and inlets; the villas and towns along the shore look exactly the way they're *supposed* to look, though you may come across a factory or a concrete apartment block the moment you stray from the highway that hugs the shore. The landscape looks particularly fresh and clean in the evening and early morning when the fog lifts off the lake. A favorite haunt of Chopin, George Sand, Edward Lear, and other nineteenth-century artists who required a large amount of cheering up.

• *Como*

Getting a bit too big and industrial to qualify as a bona fide resort. The narrow streets of the old town are worth a brief reconnaissance; pause for a moment to admire the svelte, secular-looking characters swaggering around in their doublets on the façade of the Duomo—an early instance of Lombard fashion-consciousness (bitterly protested at the time by God-fearing local citizens who were still, as they say, back in the Middle Ages).

At the western edge of town, by the lake, have a look at the *Villa Olmo* and its gardens. The path that leads down to the shore will bring you back to the center of town, past a number of inhabited villas in a thoroughly charming setting. There's an outdoor *public pool* near the Villa Olmo. Swimming in the lake is out of the question. In the center of town you can take the funicular up to *Brunate,* on a high (2,220 feet) wooded plateau with a wonderful view of the town and the lake.

Youth Hostel: Right behind the Villa Olmo, the entrance is off the main road. The building is a former gamekeeper's cottage, recently restored and surrounded by beautiful shade trees. Very nice indeed.

EPT Office: On the piazza, across from the boat landing. Has a great map of the region with points of interest, campsites, trails, and roadways, all clearly marked, and complete schedules for the excursion boats that stop at all the little beauty spots around the lake. Bear in mind that the bus does the same and costs only about a third as much, and the stretch between Como and Donato (33 miles) is by far the prettiest.

If you're hitching out of Como toward Milan, take the bus out to Ponte Chiasso (the last stop for 3 different bus lines) and walk over to the highway entrance from there. If there's nothing doing, try walking a little farther on (1 kilometer) to the parking lot by the border crossing. Lots of tourists and truckers. Show no mercy.

• *Cernobbio*
3 miles from Como. Full of attractive villas and formal gardens; a trysting place of international renown. The *Villa d'Este,* transformed into a hotel in the last century, is definitely worth visiting, as are the gardens, notable for a double waterfall surrounded by lofty cypresses and magnolias.

• *Lenno*
17 miles from Como. The beginning of the *Tremezzina,* a narrow band of very rich soil that runs along the shore; often called the "garden of Lombardy." In fact, the parks through here are so lush and numerous that they do appear to be a single continuous formal garden, dotted here and there with some of the most elegant villas in the entire region.

• *Azzano*
18 miles from Como. A little bit downhill from the tiny village called Giulino di Mezzegra where Mussolini and his mistress, Clara Petacci, were executed by partisans for their high crimes and misdemeanors and strung up by their heels (outside the doorway of No. 14).

• *Villa Carlotta*
Just outside Tremezzo, 19 miles from Como. Now a museum. The caliber of the artworks displayed suggests a remarkably high standard of vacation-cottage decor. The gardens may be a bit of a disappointment, especially considering the price of admission—and there are no student discounts.

• *Menaggio*
21 miles from Como. A pleasant little resort town with a long promenade along the lake. The *youth hostel,* right by the highway to the south of town, is in a kind of bilious yellow (to put it politely) modern building. Great view of the lake. Try not to get a room that faces the highway.

There are 2 campgrounds: The *Lido* is closer to town than the

Europa, plus you're entitled to swimming privileges at the adjacent beach-and-pool complex. The *Europa*'s beach is tiny, pebbly, and noisy (lots of outboards zooming around right offshore). The excursion-boat dock is not far away.

• *Rezzonico*
25 miles from Como. An inexpensive campground. Nice view, nice beach, and clean water. Also, there's a good and inexpensive restaurant in town, not much frequented by tourists: *Trattoria dei Platani,* via Statale, 41.

• *Domaso*
33 miles from Como. Best view of the entire lake; you can see as far as Bellagio, where the 3 separate lobes of Lake Como converge.

Also has the best *hostel* around these parts. It's right on the lake. The restaurant serves fresh-caught fish and excellent wine (wine of any kind being a great rarity in hostel restaurants). There's also a bar, pool table, and color TV. *La dolce vita. . . .*

• *Lecco*
66 miles from Como. A fair-sized town with some historic buildings. The appearance of several brand-new metallurgical plants has somewhat tarnished its old-world charm.

There's a 50-bed *hostel* about 2 miles from the center of town, at the foot of a mountain, in a nondescript building with a garden. It's a little bit hard to find. Start by taking bus No. 2 or 8 to the Germanedo district.

Camping Riva Bella: Right on the edge of town, on the road to Bergamo. Follow the signs. In a pleasant, shady spot on the lake, with hot showers, a bar, and a little store.

BERGAMO

Bergamo Bassa, the newer, lower city, is noisy, industrial, and not too interesting. We suggest, however, that you take the funicular (on viale Vittore Emanuele) up to the older, upper city, perched on top of a hill and surrounded by massive Venetian ramparts, and spend a few hours exploring.

EPT Office: Viale Vittore Emanuele, 4.

Where to Sleep, Where to Eat

Youth Hostel: In the Lonteroso district on the northeastern edge of town. An unabashedly modern building with a view of the surrounding countryside. Doesn't stay open for the whole summer.

Albergo San Giorgio: Via San Giorgio, 10, not far from the station. Clean, cordial, and one of the cheaper places in town.

Trattoria Bernardo: Right behind the Museo Civico. One of the cheaper places in Bergamo Alta. Nice vaulted ceiling. Pizzas are served in the evening. Closed in August.

Pizzeria Zaro: Passagio San Bartolomeo, 6. A fairly posh-looking place in the lower city. Prices are really quite reasonable. The pizzas are beyond reproach, with copious portions.

The Sights

The narrow streets of Bergamo Alta, redolent with medieval mystery, are guaranteed to captivate even the most jaded traveler. Stop for a drink in *piazza Vecchia,* a spot that Le Corbusier was particularly fond of and a fine example of unplanned city planning—the surrounding buildings, in many different architectural styles, have a peculiar harmony all their own. Along the main street there are a couple of bars that serve very good wine and excellent ham sandwiches (both local products, of course).

LAKE GARDA

The largest of the Italian lakes. Very mild climate. A popular weekend resort since Roman times. Salò, one of the larger towns on its banks, was the capital of a short-lived "social republic" presided over by Mussolini (1943) after the Allied advance had stripped him of most of his former domains.

Camping del Vo: In Dezenzano del Garda, at the lake's southern tip. Great location, with access to a little beach. There is a bus from the train station every hour.

THE NORTHEAST

VERONA

Our favorite city in northern Italy (except for Venice). Has an extra-high density of classical, medieval, and Renaissance monuments, a number of which the Veronese have thriftily and tastefully recycled. The Roman amphitheater, handsomely restored during the Renaissance, is now one of the world's most beautiful opera houses; Shakespeare's plays are performed in Italian in the old Roman theater outside town. It's ironic that Verona, a lively and attractive city with many stylish buildings, a river, and a range of hills (suitable for inclusion in a Renaissance painting), a city that, as the travel books like to put it, "has served as a source of inspiration for many artists over the centuries," owes much of its romantic reputation to Shakespeare, who was working from secondary sources and never even set eyes on the place. He is also largely to blame for the fact that Verona is completely packed with googly-eyed tourists and backpacking culture seekers during the summer months.

Useful Addresses

Tourist Office (Azienda Autonima di Turismo): Via Dietro Anfiteatro. Open from 8:30 to 12:30 and from 3:30 to 5:30. Closed Sunday and Saturday afternoon.

Telephone Office: In the train station. International calls (including collect) are a specialty. Closes at 10.

Where to Sleep

Take a No. 2 bus from the station to get to piazza delle Erbe, where most of the more affordable hotels are to be found.

Albergo Rosa: Vicolo Raggieri, 9. Telephone 286-93. Near via Rosa, right behind piazza delle Erbe, in a tiny little street where you half expect to bump into Tybalt and the boys going the other way. Decor leans heavily on the *rosa* motif.

Locanda Catullo: Via Catullo, 1 (second floor), near via Mazzini. Telephone 227-86. Entrance on the side street. Quite centrally located, fairly cheap, and not the least bit shabby (though some of our readers have reported problems of one kind or another).

Albergo Mazzanti: Via Mazzanti, 6. Telephone 591-370. Inexpensive and thoroughly adequate.

Albergo Posta: Piazza Viviani, 14. Telephone 268-21. Right behind the post office. Inexpensive; the shower is included. A handsome façade that looks a bit like a set for an operetta. A little restaurant with a terrace right next door.

Pensione Marina (currently *Marin,* since the *a* has fallen off); Via Ponte Nuovo, 5. Telephone 259-68. Near the above. Not so cheap and rather shabby besides. For those who value a convenient location above all else.

Istituto Don Bosco: Via Antonio Provolo, 16, near Castelvecchio (see map). Telephone 591-300. For the buget-conscious; the shower

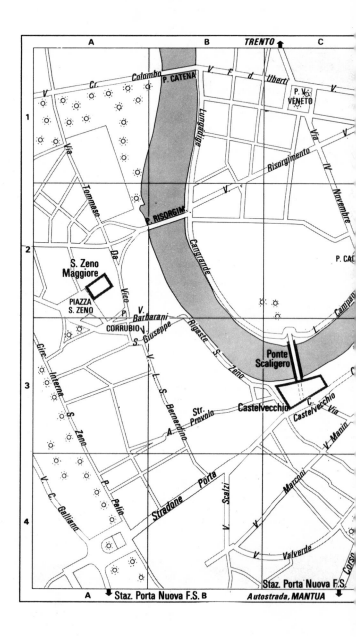

34 • ITALY

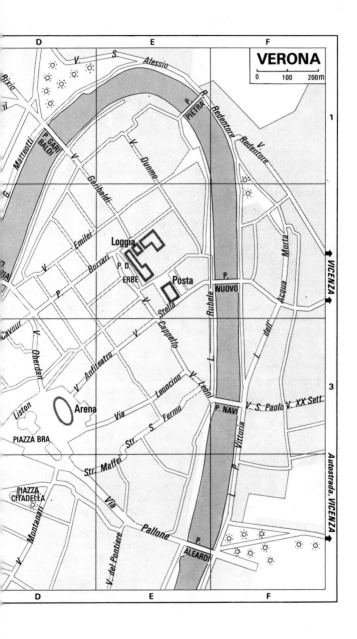

is included. The school converts to a low-rent hostelry between June 1 and September 30. There are 2 large dormitories; sexual segregation is strictly enforced. Register after 6 P.M. Free 24-hour baggage check, but dorms are kept locked between 8:30 A.M. and 6 P.M. Lights out at 10:30 P.M., but this is sometimes indulgently extended to midnight. Very clean. Plenty of hot water.

Casa delle Giovane: Via Pigna, 7 (second floor). Telephone 249-78. *Women only.* Very cheap and very well maintained, but a little noisy.

Casa della Studentessa: Via Tezza. Likewise, although the atmosphere is a bit less frenetic than the above.

Camping Romeo e Giulietta: Via Bresciana, 54, about 2 miles out toward Brescia (the exit on the *autostrada* is Verona Norte). Has a brand-new swimming pool but otherwise not so great. The management seems single-handedly determined to resolve Italy's foreign-exchange crisis. Not very convenient if you don't have a car.

Where to Eat, Where to Drink

Osteria Cucina: Piazzetta Pescheria, near the Ponte Nuovo, in the heart of the old city. Fine old place with wooden tables. Our best bet in Verona. Great food, reasonably priced, and a bar at the back where the proprietor has been serving up a first-rate *vino locale* for over 25 years. Closed Sunday and sometimes for the entire month of July.

Vina e Cucina da Luciano: Via Trotta, 3A. Not far from the preceding. Look for a rusty sign with a picture of a fish on it. The interior has recently been redone, more's the pity, but the kitchen is still in excellent working order. Especially recommended: *spaghetti alla matriciana* and *vitello tonato,* a classic Italian version of surf 'n' turf—veal smothered in a sauce made with tuna and capers. Theirs is one of the best we've tasted anywhere.

Saionara: Via Santa Maria in Chiavica, 5 (near piazza dei Signori). Not much for atmosphere but gives good value for the money. The *pizza della casa* is especially tasty. Closed Monday.

Ristorante Brunelli: Via Leoni, 15, near the river. Serves food only at lunchtime. Limited selection but quite good. The bar, generally crowded with neighborhood folk, serves first-rate local wines at any hour. Closed Sunday.

Trattoria alla Pontanina: Piazetta Chiavica. A little expensive, but the terrace looks out on a wonderful little piazza (that unfortunately does double duty as a parking lot).

Spega: Head down the porta Nova from Piazza Bra (the one with the Arena) until you see round windows with wood trim. Good, inexpensive, with great lasagna and hot dishes to go.

Piazza delle Erbe: The main market square, this is a great place to go food shopping. Lots of little stalls selling prepared food are clustered around the tall medieval tower that dominates the square.

Despar: Piazzetta Pescheria, right opposite the Osteria Cucina. A well-stocked supermarket installed in a very old building. Lots of interesting local products.

Osteria del Duca: Via delle Arche Scaligere. There's no sign or anything, but you shouldn't have any trouble finding this first-rate neighborhood bar. Excellent wines of the region.

There's a bunch of cafés on *via Capello,* near piazza delle Erbe. Popular with the younger crowd. Fresh fruit juice, some with a modest alcoholic content. Most are very tasty. Fig juice is recommended only for its startling medicinal properties.

The Sights

The Arena: One of Italy's best-preserved Roman amphitheaters and second largest (right after the Colosseum); about 470 feet long by almost 400 feet wide. A few rows of columns from the outer wall (Doric, Ionic, *and* Corinthian) are still in place; the inner oval is practically intact. Inside there are seats for 22,000 spectators and plenty of room for the grandest of operas. Closed from 11:30 to 2:30. For information about tickets and current program, you can write or call *Ente Lirico Arena di Verona,* piazza Bra, 28, Verona 37100. Telephone (045) 235-20. (Some of the CIT national tourist offices overseas have also been known to handle advance ticket sales.) Opera has been a popular art form in Italy since the nineteenth century rather than the preserve of cultists and snoozing socialites as in other lands. Tickets aren't exactly cheap, but a pleasant, small-town-ballpark sort of atmosphere still prevails to some extent, and it's not uncommon to see the fans in the bleachers loading up on very old sausage and very young chianti during a lull in the action onstage.

The Arena is located on piazza Bra, one of Italy's broadest and most attractive piazzas, with plenty of crowded outdoor cafés around its outer rim. Head down via Mazzini, a lively, tree-lined pedestrian street with swanky stores, to *piazza delle Erbe,* the aforementioned market square, also the most beautiful in Verona. First of all, you'll note that a few buildings around the square are covered with frescoes. In the morning, the produce market supplies a great deal of activity and animation, and much of the square is covered by the distinctive wooden-ribbed sunscreens, like Japanese parasols, used by the vendors to protect their wares.

Next, head down via Costa ("Rib Street") to *piazza dei Signori;* as you pass under the arch, note that attached to it is an enormous rib (which once belonged to a whale or perhaps a diplodocus), for reasons that are no longer very clear. In contrast to piazza delle Erbe, piazza dei Signori is aloof, aristocratic, and collected. Several of these imposing structures on the piazza housed the city's administrative apparatus during the Middle Ages. The atmosphere is fairly sinister at night, after all the tourists are safely tucked in their little beds.

Casa de Giulietta: Via Cappello, 23. The building, also called *Il Capello,* dates from the thirteenth century and was (according to local tradition) the family seat of the Capuletti. Whether or not Juliet actually lived at all and, if so, whether she actually lived *here* is a moot point; the house does have a balcony, which pretty much clinches it for most of us. Shakespeare seems to have gotten the ideas for *R and J* from a popular novella of the sixteenth century, all about the feud between the Montecchi (Montagues) and the Capuletti (Capulets).

There's not much to look at inside (except starry-eyed couples walking around holding hands), but it's nice to see the young folks having such a good time. (The city of Verona has engaged a special operative, a charming young woman called Paola Sella, to handle all of Juliet's correspondence with the lovelorn. It's a full-time job.)

Sant'Anastasia: A huge Gothic church, the largest in the city. Opens at 4 P.M. Frescoes on the interior of the vault depicting stylized foliage and some nice trompe l'oeils on the walls (left unfinished, which kind of spoils the illusion). The 2 stooped figures supporting the holy water fonts in back are popularly known as "the Hunchbacks." Nearby *via Sottoriva* takes you over to the famous Ponte Pietra, which has a few house fronts and porticos dating back to the thirteenth and fourteenth centuries.

Ponte Pietra: Over the Adige. Built by the Romans, blown up by the retreating Germans in 1945, and completely restored in 1959 using the original materials. You'll see a great view out over the banks of the winding river from the middle of the bridge, a good place to end up at sunset.

Castelvecchio: A fortress built entirely of brick with an imposing crenelated tower that housed the garrison and the more palatial quarters of Verona's princely family, it is now the civic art museum, with a number of interesting works of the Venetian School. The adjoining *Ponte dei Scaligeri,* like the castle, was destroyed during the war and subsequently reconstructed (with bricks retrieved from the bottom of the Adige). The bridge's 3 arches are raised up on pillars and are provided with impressive fortifications.

San Zeno Maggiore: In the western part of town (see map). This is perhaps Verona's most distinctive monument (next to the Arena) and a masterpiece of Romanesque architecture. Its famous bronze doors depict scenes from the life of St. Zenas, first bishop of Verona. The amazing triptych over the high altar is Mantegna's *Virgin with Eight Saints* (now reduced to a diptych; one wing is in the Louvre). Walk through the left transept to the Romanesque cloister and the tombs of several members of the Scaligeri family (which produced numerous Renaissance warlords and a famous literary critic).

Tomba di Giulietta: South of town on via del Pontiere. It's quite far, but the backdrop is appropriately mossy and romantic—a Capuchin convent with a cloister and a Romanesque chapel. Closed on Monday.

MAROSTICA

19 miles north of Vicenza. Famous for its *living chess game,* played with human "pieces" in the appropriate Renaissance costumes: pawns dressed up as men-at-arms; knights as *condottiere;* rooks perched atop a telephone-booth-sized turret on wheels. This civic costume spectacular is comparable to Siena's Palio (see p. 96). The original game of chess (normal size) was played on September 12, 1454, by 2 rivals for the hand of the town belle, Lionara, daughter of the castellan of Marostica, who had persuaded them to settle their rivalry over the board instead of on the field of honor. It is reenacted with much pageantry on a gigantic chessboard on the Campo Grande, in front of the Castello Inferiore (now the town hall). These days the game is held on the first or second Sunday in September but only in *even-numbered* years. Check with the Tourist Office in Vicenza for details.

VICENZA

A quiet provincial city that, in the days of its glory, was defeated and colonized by the Venetians and finally turned into a kind of summer resort for those eager to avoid the summertime reeks and miasmas of the Mistress of the Adriatic. It has some splendid palazzos and imposing facades but can't match Venice for pomp and pageantry. It does have a kind of restful, semi-rural quality which Venice definitely lacks.

Useful Addresses

EPT Office: On piazza Matteotti, next to the Teatro Olimpico.
Post Office: Contrada Garibaldi, near the Duomo.

Where to Sleep

Pensione Venezia: Contrada Porti, 30. Telephone 322-24. Only 2 blocks from the architectural delights of corso Palladio. There's no sign; just confidently ascend the very dark staircase of this very old house. It's about the cheapest place in town; showers are included.

Albergo Due Mori: Contrada Rode, 26. Telephone 218-86. A first-rate establishment right next to piazza del Signori. Very clean, peaceful, and hospitable. The restaurant on the ground floor is satisfactory in every way.

Hotel Vicenza: Stradella dei Nodari. Next to the Caffè Garibaldi, in piazza dei Signori. Fairly cheap and a great location; often full in the summer.

Albergo Milano: Stradella dei Servi, 7, a little street off the east side of piazza dei Signori. Telephone 234-38. Very clean and fairly cheap; showers are not included.

Albergo Palladio: Via Oratorio Servi, 25. Telephone 210-72. Around the corner from the foregoing. Fairly cheap—don't be misled by the fancy entrance hall.

Where to Eat

La Taverna: Piazza dei Signori, 47. Under the steps that lead up to the basilica. The hokey Carlsbad decor with its bogus stalactites is hardly worthy of the heirs of Andrea Palladio (whom you'll be hearing a great deal about during your sojourn in Vicenza). The restaurant is on the expensive side. The *pizzeria* is much more affordable. Closed Monday.

Pizzeria CAB: Piazza delle Erbe, 9, right by piazza dei Signori. Downstairs in a vaulted cellar. The restaurant upstairs is quite a bit more expensive. Closed Wednesday.

Trattoria da Renato: Behind the Standa department store, on corso Palladio. A little place on a quiet square, a little bit off the beaten path. Has a great variety of tasty and inexpensive sandwiches. Serves food only at lunchtime. Closed Sunday.

The Sights

The Basilica: Piazza dei Signori. Not a church; the word *basilica* was used in this case in its original Roman sense of an all-purpose public building that housed the law courts and other public forums (as well as the stock exchange in this case). The exterior was completely rebuilt by Palladio, then just coming into his own as an architect. The stairway provides access to the immense Gothic interior, with a wooden hammerbeam roof like the keel and ribs of a ship turned upside down.

Teatro Olimpico: Palladio's last and greatest achievement (1580), reason enough for a visit to Vicenza. In many respects it's the last Classical amphitheater and the first modern theater. The seats are arranged in semicircular tiers, like a Roman arena; the design of the stage and proscenium is uncompromisingly modern. The painted trompe l'oeil maquette of ancient Thebes, its streets lined with marble palaces, though not the work of Palladio, is quite spectacular in its own right. Open from 9 to 12:30 and from 2 to 5:30 (from 2 to 6 in the summer).

Palazzo Chiericati: Opposite the Teatro Olimpico. An earlier work (1551) by Palladio and one of his finest. Inside, the *Museo Civico* with some Roman stuff, interesting works of the Venetian School (fourteenth to eighteenth centuries), and some amazing ceiling frescoes in several other rooms of the palazzo. Open from 9 to 12:30 and from 3 to 6:30. Closed Sunday and Monday afternoon.

The Outskirts

The Palladian Villas: From the fourteenth century on, the countryside around Vicenza became the playground and rural retreat of the Venetian nobility. During the last 3 centuries of the Republic (c. 1500 to 1800), over 2,000 of these villas were built, most of them quite luxuriously, and a surprising number were designed by Palladio himself (or inspired by his published designs). Artists of the caliber of Veronese and the Tiepolos supplied the interior decor; furnishings, fittings, and entertainments (receptions, theatrical performances, masquerades, dances—with concealed orchestras in the shrubbery playing airs by Vivaldi and Pergolesi—orgies, and all sorts of goings-on) conformed to the high standard of conspicuous luxury for which Venice was noted in those days. (According to J. Morris, the French king Henri III never completely recovered from a gala civic reception organized for him by the Venetians.)

Nouveau riche Venetian commoners began to get involved before too long, spurring the nobles on to ever costlier fits of extravagance (which they paid for by engaging in the popular Renaissance pastime of despoiling the monasteries). It all came to an end, however, in 1797 when Napoleon abolished the Republic and compelled the Venetian nobles to make restitution; many of them were compelled to sell off their estates on the mainland, causing a great many villas to become abandoned. What is surprising is that a fair number of them are still inhabited by old Venetian families who are making a commendable effort to keep the old places up in the style to which they were once accustomed; 2 of the most famous are quite close to Vicenza.

Villa Rotonda: About 2 miles southeast of town. Take bus No. 8 or 13. The prototype for dozens of little neoclassical copies in Europe and America (starting with Monticello and at least 4 English country houses). An elegantly simple Palladian arrangement of spheres and cubes, notable for the rotunda that gave it its name, its orientation to the cardinal points of the compass (some years before I. M. Pei) and, on a more practical note, a generous allotment of doors and windows to promote the circulation of fresh air. Open every day from 10 to 12 and from 4 to 6.

Villa Valmarana: Follow the path opposite the Villa Rotonda. Apart from the main house, there's also a guesthouse, stables, and so forth. According to local legend (which you're unlikely to hear about from any respectable guidebook) the original proprietor had a daughter who had stopped growing when she was very small. Her father decided to spare her from any unpleasantness that might result from this by raising her in the seclusion of this villa, with a pack of dwarfs for her only companions. One day she peeked over the garden wall and happened to spy a handsome young man riding by. In an instant she realized the truth and promptly did away with herself. Statues of the dwarfs can still be seen in the garden, providing incontestable proof of the veracity of this charming legend. There's also a splendid 360° view of the surrounding countryside, and the old couple who look after the place are truly delightful.

PADUA

A place of pilgrimage for devotees of Giotto and St. Anthony of Padua (finder of lost objects). Stores selling religious bric-a-brac are more numerous here than elsewhere, but it's also an important university town. The distant rumble of modern commerce is now distinctly audible amid the dim, religious hush of Padua's holy places, but for the most part the prevailing friskiness of the old city and the various infiltrations of modern life into this ancient sanctuary merely seem refreshing rather than incongruous or intrusive.

Useful Addresses

EPT Offices: Riviera Mugnai, 8, and at the train station.
Post Office: Corso Garibaldi, 25.
Telephones: Corso Garibaldi, 31. Stays open late.

Where to Sleep

There are a couple of relatively inexpensive hotels right off piazza del Santo (the Basilica). Take bus No. 3 or 8 from the train station.

Albergo Faggian: Via Luca Belludi, 37. Telephone 665-633. Quite decent and one of the cheapest we've come across thus far.

Pensione Bellevue: Via Luca Belludi, 11. Telephone 304-34. A kind of middle-class palazzo with an imposing reception hall and a Scarlett O'Hara staircase. Rooms are enormous, with parquet floors and high ceilings. A bit expensive, though.

Ristorante-Albergo "Al Santo": Via del Santo, 147. Also a bit expensive but otherwise entirely in order. Compulsory wakeup call at 6:45 A.M., when the bells of Sant'Antonio start tolling the *Ave Maria.*

Municipal Hostel (Ostello Città di Padova): Via A. Aleardi. Telephone (049) 283-69. The bus stop is Tito Livio, and then it's 5 minutes on foot from there. Plenty of room; showers and WCs. Curfew is 11 P.M.

The next 3 are more centrally located; the last one (the hostel) is way out in the boonies.

Albergo Moderno: Via Manin, 35. Telephone 244-32. Next to piazza delle Erbe. Okay but nothing special. Quite reasonably priced (if you don't take too many showers). Often full in the summer.

Albergo Pace: Via Papafava, 3. Also quite close to piazza delle Erbe. Rooms are clean and reasonably priced (but have no showers).

Hotel Sant'Antonio: Via San Fermo, 118. Telephone 246-09. Far from deluxe and more expensive than the preceding 2 but nicely situated (near the river and the Giotto chapel).

Ostello per la Gioventù de Montagnana: About 25 miles south of Padua, an hour by bus. Buses leave about every half hour; change at Montevice for Montagnana. A famous and highly atmospheric hostel installed in a fourteenth-century castle keep. Dorms occupy the first 6 floors. The top floor is a terrace with battlements and a circular walkway that enables you to survey the surrounding countryside and indulge in Machiavellian fantasies. Not much goes on in the town of Montagnana of an evening, but its splendid ramparts should make you feel awfully secure. It's a good idea to telephone ahead (810-76) since the hostel does tend to fill up and the registration desk shuts down pretty early.

Where to Eat, Where to Drink

Piazza delle Erbe, 40: A no-name bar in the marketplace with just a few tables and a fine assortment of sandwiches. The ones with Parma ham are the best.

Pizzeria Pontecorvo: Via Belludi, near piazza Pontecorvo. A college hangout with decent food that is not overly expensive.

Riviera: Via Rudena, 12. Telephone 665-413. A small family place with a good selection, copious portions, and moderate prices.

Ristorante Self-service: Via Matteotti, 17. Very cheap and not at all bad.

Caffè Pedrocchi: Piazza Cavour. Ornate neoclassical café modeled on the propylaea of the Parthenon) divided into several sections by an Ionic portico. Founded in 1831, it was the favorite hangout of Padua's coffeehouse radicals during the nineteenth century and even rates a mention in Stendahl's *Charterhouse of Parma.* Step up and have an espresso at the famous bathtub-shaped bar, which has mobile sugar bowls that run along a track like little railroad cars. Even setting aside its rich and varied historical associations, this is an obvious must-see.

The Sights

Piazza delle Erbe: An interesting produce market that is held every morning. The Palazzo della Ragione, on the square, is an enormous Gothic barn (complete with rafters) that once housed the law courts and popular assemblies.

The University (Palazzo Bò): Via VIII Febbraio. Noted in the Middle Ages as a hotbed of Aristotelianism, Arab learning, heresy, and other advanced notions. The present building dates from the sixteenth century and has an attractive courtyard with a portico, the oldest dissecting theater in Europe (quite interesting), and the "Galileo chair" (not an endowed chair or anything like that but an actual wooden one, intermittently occupied by Galileo when he was a professor here, c. 1600).

Piazza dei Signori: Lovely Venetian-style piazza dominated by the heraldic Lion of St. Mark perched atop a Roman column. The clock in the square, reputed to be the oldest in Italy, is a medieval high-tech masterpiece; when the thing finally broke down after a century, there was no one around who was smart enough to repair it. It depicts the motions of the planets and constellations as well as the time of day; the face is divided into 24 hours rather than 12.

Capella degli Scrovegni: Perhaps the most remarkable church in northern Italy, since its interior is almost entirely covered by Giotto's fresco cycle of the Redemption (1303–09). The chapel is quite persuasively transformed into an entire universe in microcosm, with scenes set in Heaven and on Earth (episodes from the lives of Christ and the Virgin Mary, allegorical figures of the Vices [over to the left] and Virtues), the 2 realms being separated by the Last Judgment. Feel free to just stand there and be amazed by the freshness and audacity of Giotto's discovery that a 2-dimensional surface can be made to *create* a 3-dimensional space (rather than merely representing it). Unless you're a recent art history major, still drenched in medieval iconography, you might also want to rent one of those little headsets to get the full story. Paid admission to the chapel.

Basilica di Sant'Antonio; In the southern part of town. Built to house the relics of *Il Santo* (in Padua, there's only one *santo*) shortly after his canonization in the thirteenth century. This was already some years after his death, of course, but the story is that his tongue (now housed in a handsome reliquary) was discovered at the moment of transfer to be supple and perfectly intact, an indication that he was still fully prepared to testify to the truth of the Gospels. The basilica itself is a mixed bag of architectural styles: a Romanesque facade, a couple of Byzantine domes (very popular around these parts), and Gothic spires and belltower. The interior is basically Gothic (not counting the smashing bronze sculptures by Donatello over the high altar) and impressively cluttered with an enormous number of ex-votos (votive offerings and testimonials) and found objects.

Monumento al Gattamelata: In front of the Basilica. Gattamelata was a veteran Venetian *condottiere,* and Donatello's bronze statue shows Mr. G., astride a massive bronze charger, as an old man but with an extraordinary expression of determination.

Prato della Valle: About 250 yards to the south of the Basilica. Originally a swampy meadow used as a fairground and marketplace, it was transformed during the eighteenth century into a very civilized park—an island planted with plane trees and surrounded by a canal, with the canal spanned by 4 different footbridges and its embankment adorned with statues of eminent persons of the day.

Orto Botanico: Right nearby. The oldest botanical garden in Europe, one of the world's most comprehensive collections (notably of orchids and carnivorous plants). Paid admission with a student discount.

The Outskirts

Excursion boat to Venice: Along the Brenta Canal, with brief stopovers at a few more Palladian villas. Tours are scheduled to begin at 8:10 A.M. every Monday, Friday, and Sunday at the Autostazione, via Trieste (between April 15 and September 30). It's a great trip, though far from cheap. See the Brenta Canal at the end of the next section for additional details.

VENICE

Venice is a bit like sex, at least insofar as there's no way you can adequately prepare yourself for your first on-the-spot encounter with

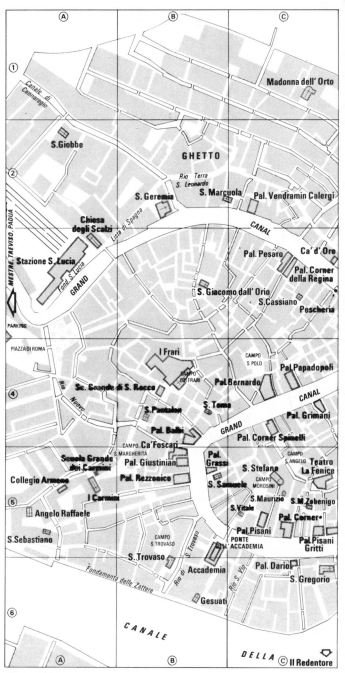

VENICE

0   100   200   300 m

Gesuiti

Fondamente

S.S.Apostoli

Strada Nuova

Ca' da Mosto

Pal. dei
Camerlenghi

S.Giovanni
Crisostomo

S.Maria dei Miracoli

Rio dei Mendicanti

Sc. di S. Marco

Nuova

Rio d. S. Giustina

S.Giacomo
di Rialto

PONTE
RIALTO

Fondaco dei Tedeschi

Teatro Malibran

CAMPO
S.S. GIOVANNI
E.PAOLO

CAMPO
S.BARTOLOMEO

S.S. Giovani e Paolo

S. Francesco da Vigna

Pal. Manin

Salizzada

CAMPO S.MARIA
FORMOSA

MERCERIA

Calle

S.Salvatore

S. Lio

S.M. Formosa

S. Lorenzo

Rio di S. Lorenzo

Sc. di S. Giorgio
dei Schiavoni

Pal. Loredan

CAMPO
S. LUCA

CAMPO
MANIN

Torre
Orologio

Fabbri

Pal. Querini-Stampalia

Rio di
Pal. Trevisani

S. Giorgio dei Greci

S. Zaccaria

Rio di S. Antonin

S. Giovani
in Bragora

S. Marco

Rio d. Palazzo

BACINO
ORSEOLO

Campanile

PIAZZA
S. MARCO

PONTE DEI
SOSPIRI

S. Fantino

S. Moisè

P.T.T.

PIAZZETTA

S. Martino

Rio d. Arsenale

C. Marga
XXII Marzo

Giardinetti

Pal. Ducale

Riva

degli

Schiavoni

S. Maria Pietà

Pal. Giustinian

BACINO

Museo Navale

Pal.
Contarini-Fasan

DI S. MARCO

Punta della Dogana

Dogana da Mar

S. Maria
della Salute

GIUDECCA

S. Giorgio Maggiore

the real thing (and in the case of Venice, you're virtually certain not to be disappointed). Be prepared to exist in a state of constant, abject astonishment from the moment you first set foot in the place, a state from which many first-time visitors (like the unfortunate Henri III) never quite seem to recover. If you've seen Nicholas Roeg's *Don't Look Now,* at least you'll be prepared for the eerie experience of being dogged by the echo of your own footsteps through the less frequented streets and piazzas of this wondrous "town without traffic."

Even if you go in July or August, when everyone else does, you won't be much the worse for it (assuming, of course, that you can find a place to stay) since the package tours and the coach parties rarely venture far from their twin beachheads on the Rialto and piazza San Marco. June and September are both thoroughly pleasant, though perhaps it's the spring and fall that really bring out the subtlest highlights in the cityscape. It should also be noted that May is the windiest and October the rainiest month in Venice. All the same, we'd also encourage you to come in the winter when the sky is gray, the air is a little cold, the fog adds an attractive note of mystery, and the city takes on the sort of morbid, Draculalike allure of a beautiful dead thing (a literally fatal attraction in the case of Browning, Wagner and, of course, Herr von Aschenbach, the hero of Thomas Mann's *Death in Venice*). Curious that most visitors who depart relatively unscathed from their first encounter with Venice seem all the more eager to return for more.

A Little History

Venice was founded in the fifth century by refugees from the Huns, Ostrogoths, Lombards, and other rapacious heathen (or, what was worse, heretics) who were currently making the Italian mainland inhabitable for decent Christians. A couple of centuries later these few inaccessible islands in the midst of a swampy lagoon had become a prosperous commercial seaport (nominally a tributary of Byzantium; if you've been to Istanbul, you'll note the close architectural resemblance between San Marco and the Hagia Sophia) and the principal conduit of trade between Europe and the Orient.

In 1215, the Venetians actually persuaded a charter party of Crusaders to take time off from their sacred mission and assist them in overthrowing the Byzantine emperor and sacking Byzantium itself. As part of the loot they brought back the bronze Horses of St. Mark that can now be seen in the Basilica. If they had been able to figure out a way to get the Hagia Sophia into the hold of a ship, they probably would have brought that back as well. In 1497, Vasco da Gama finally figured out a way to trade directly with the Orient without letting the Venetians in for their cut, and shortly after that the Most Serene Republic of Venice began its slow and irreversible decline, first into outrageous decadence and then into shabby gentility (which is pretty much its present condition). The Republic was remarkably lucky in its admirals, generals, and ambassadors, who managed to keep things going for exactly 300 years; as mentioned earlier, the coup de grace was administered by Bonaparte in 1797, at the head of the first foreign army in history to successfully attack the city. For 70 years Venice was part of the Austrian Empire, albeit a very sullen and rebellious part; in 1867, as a result of further diplomatic shenanigans, she was restored to the united kingdom of Italy.

Venice's oriental heritage is evident today in a number of other ways apart from the Byzantine domes and staring mosaics of its churches. First, the siesta is a sacred institution. Second, bargaining is definitely encouraged in certain shops, and in the less tourist-oriented quarters you'll find plenty of merchants who like to take their time working out a deal, Middle Eastern–style, and building up a relationship of trust with their customers. However, this is probably as good a place as any to mention that prices in Venice are about 30 percent higher than elsewhere in Italy and even higher in the shops and cafés around piazza San Marco.

Arriving in Venice

By Train: Don't get off at Mestre, even though the station is called Venezia-Mestre, which is still on the mainland. Hang on until you get to Santa Lucia station, which is right on the Grand Canal (see map). From here you can catch the *vaporetto* into the center of the city. Later on you'd be well advised to make sleeping-car reservations or get train tickets through a travel agent (American Express, for example) rather than wasting hours standing in line at the station.

By Car: The most convenient place to leave your car in the city is piazzale Roma near the station (see map), but you could probably wait for years before you'd find a space. Instead, follow the signs for *Tronchetto,* a vast municipal parking area on an artificial island. Here you have your choice of leaving your car in one of the cheaper, unsupervised lots and maybe coming back to find it without tires, radio, and so forth, or putting it in one of the more expensive lots. In fact, the only enjoyable thing about bringing a car to Venice is the last leg of the journey, which takes you right along the Brenta Canal for part of the way: Get off the *autostrada* from Verona at Dola and follow the signs for Mira, then Malcontenta, then Fusina. Note a couple of very fine Palladian villas en route.

At Fusina there is a parking lot, a tourist information office, and a campground with all the amenities. Stock up on foodstuffs in Malcontenta since the supermarket by the campground is about twice as expensive. Note that there are lots of mosquitoes around these parts, especially in the summer. If you're at all allergic, you'd do well to fall back on Mestre, which is further inland. You can take a No. 16 *vaporetto* from Fusina to the Zattere landing, then change for a No. 8 or walk to the center of the city.

By Plane: Quality folk will be touching down at Marco Polo Airport, east of Mestre. For purely esthetic reasons you'd be better off taking the boat than the bus; the boat provides you with a triumphal Doge's eye view of the city and docks right near piazza San Marco.

Useful Addresses

EPT Office: 3 in all: piazza San Marco, 71c; piazzale Roma; and in the train station.

U.S. Consulate: Via Roma, 9. Telephone 68-728.

Central Post Office (D4 on map): Salizzada Fondaco dei Tedeschi. On the same side of the Rialto as San Marco. Open from 8:30 to 7 from Monday to Saturday. *Fermo posta* (mail pickup) facilities. *Tele-*

phones for international calls are right next door. Open 24 hours. It's best to go very late or very early, when it's cheaper and less crowded.

Laundromat (B2 on map): Lavaget, Cannaregio, 1269, same section as the train station, near the ponte Guglie.

CTS (B5 on map): Dorsoduro, 3252, on the fondamenta Tagliapietra (embankment of the canal). Student travel information center. Discount airline and BIGE tickets.

Albergo Diurno: Ramo Primo, 1266, behind piazza San Marco near the corner with the EPT office. Showers and baggage check.

Getting Around in Venice

First of all, note that numbered addresses are arranged by *sestiere* (district) rather than by street, which means you'll need a very good map. About the best one we know of is called *Tabacco,* published by Edizioni Storti, which has a red cover; it's pretty complete (most of them only give you about a third of the street names). For all the undoubted splendors of its great monuments, Venice is still basically a city of neighborhoods, more so perhaps than any other Italian city, which means a city of textures and flavors and shifting subtleties. It's a great place to walk around in and, of course, a wonderful place to get lost in. Finding your way around in Venice is quite a bit like wandering through a series of sun-dappled woodland glades or, as some would have it, through a swamp: The appearance of a particular place is likely to change dramatically depending on the time of day, the play of the sunlight on a wall, the reflections on the water. (For obvious reasons, Venice was a great favorite with the impressionists.) In any case, it's best to blaze a trail of enduring landmarks (names of restaurants and shops, and public monuments), and bear in mind that in the last analysis one canal tends to look very much like another. Useful terms: *fondamenta* = embankment, a street that runs along the bank of a canal; *sottoportego* = a passage underneath a building.

As far as public transportation is concerned, the gondolas are pretty much out of the question (except for the occasional joyride; see below). The *motoscafo* (motor launch) is equally unaffordable. That leaves the *vaporetti,* the Venetian equivalent of the city bus. Fares are pretty cheap; remember to specify which line you want, since tickets are nontransferable. The No. 4 *vaporetto* goes all the way up and down the Grand Canal; if you can't think of anything to do at night, just hop on board. It's a great trip. The No. 1 follows the same route, making all local stops. The No. 5 makes the complete tour of the city, then heads out to the island of Murano. *Vaporetti,* like trains, come in 3 different varieties: *accelerata* (the slowest), *diretto,* and *direttissimo.*

For those especially enamored of this form of transport, there's a *biglietto giornaliero,* good for an entire day of *vaporetto* travel, for about the price of 5 or 6 individual tickets (plus, of course, you don't have to wait in line every time). If you're going to be spending some time in Venice, you might consider investing in the *Cartavenezia,* which is valid for 3 years and entitles you to various discounts. Provide yourself with a suitable ID photo and apply at *ACTV,* pontife San Angelo. Those who can't quite feature the price of a long-haul (50-minute) gondola ride will have to content themselves with the *traghetto,* a cheapo gondola shuttle-service (with gondolas propelled by 2 oarsmen) available at numerous points along the Grand Canal. For example, a good way to get over to see the Collezione Guggenheim from the vicinity of San Marco is to head for the Accademia (behind the Gritti Hotel), then follow the signs that read *Al Traghetto*.

The Gondola

In the old days, Venetian aristocrats vied with one another to see who could outfit the most lavishly appointed gondola. When a number of them went bankrupt in the process, the Republic sensibly intervened, decreeing that henceforth gondolas would be painted black and adorned only with the traditional *ferro,* the ferocious-looking metal ornament at the prow, which has no known function and whose prongs are said to symbolize the city's six districts: Cannaregio (out by the railroad station), San Marco, Castello (to the west), Dorsoduro (near the Accademia), San Polo, and Santa Croce. As a result, the gondola acquired its present air of sleek, funereal elegance, a craft seemingly designed to cleave the dark waters of the River Styx (or, for that matter, to shuttle tourists past the moribund beauties of the Grand Canal, which amounts to very much the same thing).

The gondola has a number of other design peculiarities. You can make it go forward by rowing on only one side (try this out with any other boat if you doubt us). This has a lot to do with the fact that the gondola is asymmetrical, one side of the hull being much less rounded than the other. You'll also note that the gondolier does not straddle the central axis of the gondola, as any sensible person would, but stations himself in 3 different spots, depending on whether he wants to propel the boat forward, turn to the left, or turn to the right. Each stroke of the oar really consists of 3 different movements: The first pushes the blade of the oar back into the water, the second is the power stroke that also turns the bow of the boat a little bit to the left, and the third brings the oar back out of the water and supplies the correction that keeps the boat on course. In the process the gondolier twists the shaft of the oar in such a way that the oarlock is standing straight out, ready to begin the next stroke. Gondoliers, in short, are skilled and licensed professionals, and their numbers (hence the number of gondolas on active service) are strictly limited by a fiercely monopolistic gondoliers' guild. Hence, fares are astronomical.

As noted above, the traditional circuit involves the Bridge of Sighs and the piazza San Marco (via the Grand Canal, of course). A brand-new gondola costs a few million lire, and while it may seem as though the average gondolier could easily recoup his investment with a good day's work, there are a few ways to keep the costs down: Remember that a gondola can handle as many as 5 passengers at once; bargaining is always an excellent idea; and if you show up early (before 9 A.M.), you may find plenty of gondoliers hanging around the landing with nothing much to do.

Love, Death, and Carnival in Venice

These topics have seemed to most observers to be closely linked for the last 3 centuries or so when the Venetians decided to distract themselves with a riot of mindless hedonism (the famous Carnival, in those days, sometimes lasted for a couple of months) from the depressing facts that their mastery of the seas had been irretrievably wrested from them and their city was slowly sinking into the bottomless ooze of the lagoon. (Nowadays, thanks to a massive infusion of funds and scientific expertise, it's beginning to appear that the day on which this will actually occur has been postponed indefinitely). Still, it's true that the city's great monuments have a kind of 2-dimensional pasteboard look to them when brilliantly lit up at night, and the Venice so much admired by tourists is not a living city but an exquisite corpse, miraculously preserved for the ages like the tongue of St. Anthony of Padua.

Several films may help you get into the proper frame of mind for your trip to Venice: The classic treatment of the love and death theme is Visconti's *Death in Venice,* inspired by Thomas Mann's novella. Fellini's *Casanova,* like its subject, frequently irritating and self-indulgent, has certainly caught the flavor of eighteenth-century Venice (though the same might be said of the scene in *Moonraker* that has James Bond riding around on a gondola Hovercraft). Best of all are the films of Comencini (especially the Carnival sequences), though you may have to wait until you get to Venice (or to Italy, at any rate) before you can see them.

You might also want to look at Casanova's *Memoirs*—at least the early chapters in which he describes the horrors of his imprisonment in the notorious dungeons of the Council of Ten, a circumstance that even the Prince of Liars found it difficult to exaggerate (as you'll be able to verify for yourself when you visit the Doge's Palace). Be warned that a more prolonged exposure to the *memoirs* is likely to destroy your interest in Venice for a considerable period of time thereafter.

Where to Sleep

Let's consider the worst-case scenario: It's spring or summer, and you don't have a reservation. There's a reservation center at the train station that may be able to fix you up with something. A long line forms almost the moment that the train pulls in, so try to be among the first. There's a similar reservation center on piazzale Roma (a 10-minute walk from the station) for those who arrive by car. (Closed Sunday). If you get in before 10 A.M., you may be so bold as to make directly for the hostel (see below), but under no circumstances should you join the hundreds of tourists who, as if driven by some obscure self-destructive instinct, head right over to piazza de San Marco in a frenzied and ultimately futile search for an empty bed.

If you arrive in Venice after 6 P.M., your chances of finding one are just about nil, so you have your choice of checking into a hotel over in Mestre or of checking your stuff at Santa Lucia station in Venice and looking around for a quiet place to crash. You'll find about 200–300 of your fellow travelers strewn over the vast expanse in and around the train station. Great atmosphere, lots of music, plus basic amenities (sinks, toilets, and even showers) are available in the *albergo diurno* in the station (open from 6 A.M. to 8 P.M.) You can also plan on being (gently) rousted by the cops at 6 A.M. No problem, however, since that's the very best time of all to start wandering around Venice.

A much more sensible approach is to make a selection from the following list of perfectly splendid little hotels and give them a call, taking into account the 8 to 11 hours of time difference, which makes the early morning a good time to try if you're in the eastern U.S. Call at least a month and preferably 2 months in advance. Most Venetian hotels will have someone on hand who speaks English; most will take your check for the equivalent of 1 or 2 nights' lodging as a deposit (which is what you should send them, posthaste, to nail down your reservation). If not, then you'll have to subject yourself to the modest hassle of securing an international money order, and then you're all set. The same procedure is effective in the case of hostels and the other nonprofit establishments listed in the following section.

• *Institutional/very cheap*

Ostello per la Giuventù: A youth hostel on the island of Giudecca. Cross the Grand Canal from the station and catch the No. 5 *vaporetto*. Get off at the Zitelle landing; it's about 200 yards off to the right. Registration begins at 5 P.M., but in the summer it's best to get there by 3 at the latest. The place is always packed, and the daily turnover is not that great; but it's still worth looking into since rooms are, as promised, very cheap and quite well maintained. A very nice atmosphere and a great view of the Doge's Palace. The principal drawback is the 11 P.M. curfew, which deprives you of one of Venice's greatest pleasures. We refer, of course, to the sight of the city at night. The hostel canteen is about twice as expensive as the little grocery store down the street to your left.

Istituto Cannóciane: Giudecca, 428. *Women only.* From the hostel, head to the left and cross 2 bridges. About a 7-minute walk. Run by a religious order. Spartan quarters (dorms with 7 beds in each) but well maintained. The office is closed between 8:30 A.M. and 4 P.M. The curfew is 10 P.M.

Fostiera Valdese: Castello, 5170, Venezia 30124. Telephone (041) 867-97. From campo Santa Maria Formosa (E4 on map), take calle Lunga Santa Maria Formosa. It's in the vine-covered, somewhat ramshackle-looking palazzo right after the bridge. The reception desk is open between 11 and 1 and between 6 and 8:30. Single or double rooms and dormitories. A bakery and a grocery store are right down the street.

Istituto Ciliota (C5 on map): Calle Muneghe, 2976, Venezia 30124, Telephone 704-888. Near campo Morosini. *Women only.* Run by a charming group of nuns, but curfew is at 10:30.

Domus Civica (B3 on map): San Polo, 3082. Telephone 243-32. To the east of piazzale Roma, corner of calle Chiavale and calle Campazzo. *Women only.* In an immense, gloomy-looking patrician building in a somewhat remote location. Also run by nuns.

• *Near the Accademia*

Locanda Montin: Fondamenta di Borgo, opposite the fondamenta Eremite. Telephone 271-51. A charming spot in our favorite part of town, just a few minutes' walk from the Accademia. An establishment favored by those who plan to spend a few months in Venice. Has a certain something about it that's very appealing. The proprietors are quite cordial. Great restaurant (see below). Reserve at least 2 months in advance.

Hotel Iris (B4 on map): San Toma, 2912, Venezia 30124. Telephone 228-82. Not far from the Church of San Toma. A lovely pink building overlooking a placid little canal. A very good restaurant with a tiny courtyard underneath a shady arbor. Moderately expensive.

• Near San Marco

Albergo-Pensioni Doni: Riva degli Schiavoni, Santa Zaccaria, 4656 (calle del Vin), Venezia 30124. Marvelous location, just 2 minutes from the Bridge of Sighs, overlooking a very attractive canal. Superb façade with authentic Venetian-Gothic windows. Abundant foliage. Moderately expensive.

Locanda San Samuelo: San Marco, 3358 (C5 on map), Venezia 30124. Telephone 280-45. On a little street between the Grand Canal and campo Morosini. A very nice neighborhood indeed. Don't let the wallpaper in the entrance hall give you the wrong idea. The place is very well run and not too expensive for Venice.

• Near the Grand Canal

Pensione Ca'd'Oro: Campo SS Apostoli, 4391A (strada Nova) (D4 on map), Venezia 30124. Telephone 347-97. Cheapest place we know of that's right *on* the Grand Canal, though it's still moderately expensive in absolute terms. It's also right near the Rialto and the Ca'd'Oro (both the palazzo and the *vaporetto* landing of that name). Try to get room 11 or 13.

Locanda Semenzato: Campo SS Apostoli, 4363, Venezia 30124. Telephone 272-57. From the Ca'd'Oro landing, take strada Nova to campo SS Apostoli (D3 on map). It's on a tiny little street called calle d'Oca. Rooms are clean enough but very gloomy.

• Near the Santa Lucia station

As you leave the station, take left and head down lista di Spagna (B2 on map) to get to any of the following:

Villa Rosa: Calle della Misericordia, 389, Venezia 30121. Telephone 71-65-69. It's the second little street on your left if you follow the above instructions. An undistinguished pink stucco building. Some of the rooms on the top floor have balconies. A very quiet spot. Not terribly cheap, but breakfast is included. A couple more *pensioni* are down the street.

Locanda Rosi: Calle della Procuratie (a one-way street off lista di Spagna), Venezia 30121. Telephone 71-51-64. The entrance to this street is through an attractive Gothic archway. Some of the rooms overlook a little garden that's also complacently surveyed by a statue of the Virgin. Not all that cheap.

Archie's House: Cannaregio, 1814B. Cross the ponte Guglie. It's at the intersection of rio Terra San Leonardo and rio Terra Cristo. The rooms are fairly expensive, but in the summer the dorm rooms are the cheapest thing going in this particular district. The decor consists of a fairly disorderly collection of information on local landmarks, plus mementos of Archie's own experiences in foreign parts. All this and clean sheets besides. The doors close at midnight; it's also closed between 1 and 4 P.M.

Allogi al Gallo: Santa Croce, 197G (calle Amai). Telephone 367-61. Take the ponte Scalzi across the Grand Canal. Right next to the chiesa dei Tolentini. Nothing special, but the interior has just been remodeled, and the rooms are very clean.

Locanda Stefania: Santa Croce, 181A. Not far from the preceding, on the fondamenta Tolentini, right behind the Papadopoli gardens. A nice old building next to a church, with rooms overlooking the canal.

• *Upscale*

Since, as Evelyn Waugh reminds us, "we possess nothing certain except the past," you might want to invest a few extra bucks in your future memories of Venice; we've also considered the possibility that you might be interested in something a little more intimate than a dorm room at Archie's.

Casa Frollo: Di Flora Soldan, Venezia 30124. Telephone 70-82-99. On Giudecca, opposite the Zattere *vaporetto* landing. Our honeymoon special is still a bit less expensive than the other entries in this category. A former convent with balconies. A garden in the courtyard and antique furniture in the public rooms. Rooms have the best possible view of the Doge's Palace. Imperishable memories are guaranteed.

Pensione Accademia: Dorsoduro, 1058, Venezia 30123. Telephone 378-46. Cross the ponte Accademia and turn right. A superb seventeenth-century villa located right at the confluence of 2 canals. Our absolute best bet in Venice, and one we much prefer to the Danieli or the Gritti hotels, assuming that we could afford the latter. Has its own little garden, overlooking the Grand Canal, with little tables suitable for the consumption of an apéritif or 2 before dinner. By no means cheap but still less expensive than a clone hotel like Sofitel or the Hilton. Reserve a few months in advance.

Pensione da Cici: Salut, 222, Venezia 30123. Telephone 354-04. Between the Collezione Guggenheim and the Salute (D6 on map). Not quite as elegant as the foregoing and a bit more expensive. Recently renovated. Overlooks a very peaceful little canal and has a delightful interior courtyard with a garden and more little tables.

Pensione la Calcina: Zattere, 780, Venezia 30123 (B6 on map). Telephone 70-64-66. On the fondamenta Zattere. Great view of Giudecca, across the canal. The great Victorian connoisseur John "Stones of Venice" Ruskin lived here during the previous century, which is no small recommendation in itself. Breakfast is included.

Hotel Marconi: Fondamenta del Vin. Telephone 220-68. Next to the Rialto, right over the Savoldi restaurant. Rooms overlook the Grand Canal. Try to get one on the second floor, with balcony. Antique panelling in the entrance hall is scrupulously maintained. By Venetian standards, a fairly noisy neighborhood.

• *Campgrounds*

Mestre is readily accessible by train but is perhaps a bit too close to the oil refineries as well. (Venice has partially recouped her former status as a city that holds the gorgeous East in thrall by becoming an important center of the spot-charter business and a popular destination with oil tankers.) The other campgrounds are in Littorale del Cavallino, on the Adriatic coast between Punta Sabbioni and Lido di Iesolo, which is pretty far.

... *in and around Mestre*

Alba d'Oro, Tessera, and *Camping Laguna:* On via Orlando. And *Camping Jolly:* By the *autostrada* exit in Marghera. The latter is a bit too close to the airport. Has a swimming pool. To get out there, catch a No. 15 bus about 200 yards to the right of the train station.

Camping Venezia: Right down the road from the preceding but less expensive. The No. 5 bus for Venice leaves every half hour. *Camping San Marco* is a little bit closer to the bus stop and costs about the same.

Camping Marco Polo: In Tessera, out toward Mestre, is right next to the airport. A pleasant, shady campground with a grocery store. Hot showers. A bus for Venice leaves every hour from the stop nearby.

. . . in and around Littorale del Cavallino

Ca'Pasquali, Ca'Savio, and *Union* and many, many more: On via Fausta. One of the best is *Miramare,* in Punta Sabbioni, only about 5 minutes from the *vaporetto* landing. Take either bus No. 14 or 15 from Venice; the latter is a bit faster but more expensive. The minimum stay is 3 days. At this campground you'll have all the amenities at your fingertips: stores, a church, hairdresser, and a hospital.

Note that the last *vaporetto* chugs away from piazza San Marco at 11 P.M. After that you'll have to take the bus for Lido di Iesolo; ask the driver where you should get off. You'll also note that the price differential between a campground and a hotel in town is somewhat reduced during the off-season, and even during the high-season most of what you save by camping out rather than springing for a hotel room will promptly be frittered away on the *vaporetto*.

Where to Eat, Where to Drink

A first-rate *torta de fromaggio* is available in the marketplace near the Rialto in the morning. For breakfast we also recommend that you station yourself at one of the outdoor tables of the *bar-gelateria* on campo San Barnaba, near the Accademia (B6 on map). The place is no great shakes in itself, but it's on one of our favorite piazzas, right by a canal, across from a lovely church—the perfect place to intercept the first bright rays of the morning sun while toying with your breakfast *cioccolato*.

Mensa DLF: About 60 yards down the embankment from the train station, to the right. A charmless cafeteria that serves a very inexpensive lunch. Open from 11:30 to 2:30. No dinner.

Locanda Montin: Fondamento di Borgo, 1147 (see above for particulars). Our favorite *pensione* in Venice, it is also the home of a splendid restaurant. The setting is very pleasant (beneath a flowery trellis in the courtyard), and the food is spectacular. We heartily recommend the *malfatti* and, for dessert, *tartufo nero,* a true Venetian celebrity. Useful phrase: *Mamma mia!* (to be uttered while kissing the fingertips, then thrusting them outward and upward with an operatic flourish). A bit expensive; cheapos will have to content themselves with pasta washed down with a glass or 2 of local wine. Closed on Tuesday night and all day Wednesday.

Da Bruno: Calle Lunga Santa Barnaba, 2754, near the Accademia and the delightful campo Santa Barnaba. Staple seafood and house wine are served in enormous carafes. *Menù turistico* is available for the impoverished. Gets crowded after 8 P.M. Closed on Sunday.

Trattoria ai Cugnai: Piscina del Forner, 857. A great little place between the Accademia and the Guggenheim. Broiled fish a specialty. The proprietor puts tables out in the garden at the first hint of sunshine. Closed on Monday.

Trattoria al Wagon: Sottoportego del Maggazen, 5597, on rio di

SS Apostoli (D3 on map), opposite the campo. Tables are set up under an arcade on the banks of the canal. Specialties include baked lasagna and grilled prawns. It is customary for disgruntled diners at less distinguished establishments than this one to manifest their displeasure by tipping the contents of their plates directly into the canal.

Trattoria Nuova: Lista di Spagna, 189, next to the station. A little place with 2 outdoor tables (weather permitting) and a nice menu. Specialties include first-rate fried seafood and veal Milanese.

Da Ignazio: Calle dei Saoneri, 2749, near the Frari (B4 on map). A *trattoria* with good food, great service, and a nice atmosphere with tables in an inside courtyard underneath a lovely arbor. Closed on Saturday.

• *Upscale*

Trattoria della Conchiglia: Fondamenta San Lorenzo (F4 on map). A charming, moderately expensive *trattoria* on the banks of a canal, opposite a splendid palazzo. Try to grab one of the two outdoor tables. Great Venetian specialties: fried shrimp and *calamari.* Closed on Wednesday.

Poste Vecie: Pescherie, 1608, near the Rialto, behind the fish market at the end of its own private bridge. Impressive menu. Eels are a specialty in season. Closed on Tuesday.

• *Watering Holes*

There are lots of unpretentious *osterie* (inns) that serve wine and little munchies. A fine opportunity to try some of those weird-tasting Italian apéritifs made from artichokes and such: *Cynar, Ramazzotti, Rosso Antico,* plus the more familiar *Martini* and *Cinzano,* of ashtray and umbrella fame.

Osteria al Mascaron: Calle Lunga Santa Maria Formosa, 5225 (E4 on map). There's no name on the front. An ancient and encrusted facade. Young and/or intellectual clientele. Excellent local wines, plus sausages and cold snacks when the proprietor is feeling especially amenable. Great atmosphere of an evening. Closed on Sunday.

Osteria al Million: Corte prima del Million. Not so easy to get to and therefore not much frequented by tourists. Well worth the trouble. Start by heading down the little covered passageway behind the chiesa San Giovanni Crisostomo (D3 on map); 3 minutes north of the Rialto. A choice selection of wines; the casks are right behind the bar. Big tables with checkered tablecloths. Cold snacks are available plus highly authentic Venetian ambience along toward the cocktail hour.

Harry's Bar: Calle Vallaresso, 1323, west of piazza San Marco. Celebrated for its inauthentic Anglo-American expatriate clientele. Not so much a shrine as it once was but still celebrated as the place where Hemingway invented the Montgomery (15 parts gin to 1 part Martini & Rossi). The adjoining restaurant is totally unaffordable, but the bar is still worth checking out, especially if you can find a contessa, a sheik, or a shipping magnate to stand a couple of rounds. Closed on Monday.

Bar Teatro: San Fontin, 1917. Near the Fenice theater (C5 on map), 5 minutes from San Marco. A nondescript bar that serves meals, has a nice terrace with an arbor, but doesn't amount to much until after 10 P.M., when it catches the after-theater crowd. Closed on Monday.

The Sights

Piazza San Marco: One of the world's best known and most frequently photographed public spaces, a place whose very pigeons are famous. Consists of an elongated, asymmetrical rectangle with the Basilica di San Marco at one end, flanked by long, 2-story colonnades (featuring all 3 classical orders), with the façade on the fourth side provided courtesy of Napoleon. The clock tower *(Torre dell'Orologio)* is an elegant Renaissance structure famous for its *Mori* (Moors), the 2 bronze stalwarts that strike the hour. There's a splendid view from the top, which you get to by ascending a very narrow staircase behind a black door, under the porch, and next to the jewelry store. The tower is open from 9 to 12 and from 3 to 5. Closes at noon on holidays. The piazza is also the home of 2 famous cafés, the *Florian* (check out the sumptuous decor of the interior rooms) and the *Quadri.* The Quadri is the less expensive of the 2, but even here a humble capuccino costs only slightly less than a year at Harvard Biz School.

Basilica di San Marco: Built to house the relics of the patron saint (surreptitiously removed by the Venetians from their original resting place in Alexandria). The 5 doorways in the main façade are surrounded by mosaics and surmounted by Byzantine domes covered with sheets of lead; the terrace on the upper level of the façade was built to enable the Doge or the patriarch to officiate at important civic and religious ceremonies. The bronze *Horses of St. Mark* near the center of the façade are copies, the originals (also obtained illicitly, as you may recall) are inside. (They were carried off a second time by Napoleon in 1797 to adorn the Arc de Triomphe du Carrousel in Paris and returned to the Venetians in 1815.)

The interior provides even more of a treat for lovers of Byzantine splendor, with its rich marble facings and approximately a thousand acres of mosaics, these being applied to a gold background in the orthodox manner prescribed by the monks of Mount Athos. Behind the altar is the *Pala d'Oro,* a golden screen encrusted with precious gems and decorated with scenes from the New Testament in high relief. Guided tours, conducted by young volunteers at no charge, start out just to the left of the entrance. San Marco is also noted for its incredible acoustics, but if you go to a concert here, make sure to dress extra warmly.

The Campanile: On piazza San Marco. Belltower of St. Mark's, 303 feet tall. An exact reconstruction of the original, which collapsed at 10 o'clock in the morning on July 30, 1902, showering the piazza with debris. (The only victim of this disaster was the sexton's cat, since Venetians of other species are not noted as early risers). There's an elevator to the top (paid admission) and a spectacular view of the city and adjacent islands. Open from 10 to 8:30.

Palazzo Ducale (Doge's Palace): The graceful colonnade running along the first story somewhat relieves the impression of overwhelming civic might and authority conveyed by the rest of this Venetian Gothic blockbuster. The interior is open from 8:30 to 6. Paid admission once you get past the courtyard; 50 percent student discount. Doges' apartments were adorned with works by all the worthwhile Venetian masters (Tintoretto, Tiepolo, Titian, Veronese), many of whom are only visible under optimal conditions since available light is minimal.

You'll also come upon a series of narrow passages leading across the *Bridge of Sighs* to the cells (the "leads" above and the "wells" below) of the Prigioni Nuove, reserved for those suspected of crimes against the state—including the young Casanova who had been denounced for sorcery and irreverence, perhaps by a jealous husband. There are 4 guided tours a day—at 9:30, 10, 11, and 12—which permit a leisurely inspection of all the above, plus a number of secret passages only recently discovered. But in our view, taking the extreme murkiness of the interior into account, the best part of the palace is the exterior colonnade; in particular, don't miss the 2 red marble columns, near the main entrance, where the bodies of executed traitors were displayed to the populace.

The Grand Canal: Then as now, this is the city's main commercial artery as well as her most elegant residential street, incorporating a remarkable variety of architectural styles and influences. Take the No. 1 or 2 *vaporetto* (both very cheap) down "the most beautiful street I believe there to be in the entire world" (according to Philippe de Commynes, a fifteenth-century French historian, and in his day most of the really gorgeous palazzi hadn't been built yet).

The high arch of the *Ponte di Rialto,* largest and most famous of Venice's many bridges, was designed to accommodate a war galley in full sail. Several of its predecessors had already tumbled into the canal, but the present structure, you may rest assured, is perfectly sound, though like the Ponte Vecchio in Florence it is bowed down by a top-heavy encrustation of stalls and little shops. Other landmarks include the Winter Casino *(Palazzo Vendarmin),* where Wagner died in 1883, and, most famous of all, the Venetian Gothic dazzler known as the House of Gold, *Ca'd'Oro* is especially noted for the delicate lace-curtain effect conveyed by the stone tracery of its double loggia.

Santa Maria della Salute: At the mouth of the Grand Canal, facing piazza San Marco (see map). Commemorates Venice's "salvation" from one of her numerous plagues and consists of 2 solid octagonal masses supporting an enormous dome, the whole supported in turn by over 1.5 million pilings. It was recently restored with funds provided by the French.

Collezione Peggy Guggenheim: Housed in the unfinished palazzo (whose incompleteness is most apparent from the Grand Canal) that also housed the late Peggy Guggenheim herself (celebrated Muse of Modern Art and the sometime Mrs. Max Ernst) in later life. Includes works by twentieth-century masters such as Magritte (notably his haunting *Empire of Light*), Miro, Kandinsky, Léger, Chagall, as well as a solid silver bedstead designed by Calder (which is even more impressive than the $25,000 model that Mr. Ernst put together for Nelson Rockefeller). Also note the equestrian statue by Marino Marini in the courtyard by the Grand Canal, which was equipped, according to Rubinstein's memoirs, with a detachable penis that was removed in anticipation of visiting clerics. Peggy Guggenheim died in 1979 and is buried at the bottom of the garden (amid all her little pet dogs). Open every day from 12 to 6 with free admission and on Saturday from 12 to 9, when there is a 50 percent student discount. Closed on Tuesday (and from October to March).

Galleria dell'Accademia: A former church that houses the city's most comprehensive collection of paintings of the Venetian School, from the fourteenth to the eighteenth century. Open only from 9 until

2 (and until 1 on Sunday and holidays). Closed on Monday. (Note that, as in the Doge's Palace, the lighting is all-natural and frequently murky.) The gem of the collection is undoubtedly *The Tempest* by Giorgione (gallery V), a strange, brooding work in which a group of isolated and enigmatic figures are disposed against an ominous classical backdrop. Gallery X contains, in addition to Titian's *Pietà,* Veronese's raffish masterpiece *Supper in the House of Levi* (originally called *The Last Supper,* until the Inquisition took exception to the presence of the dog, Germans, dwarfs, the man with the nosebleed, and other supernumerary figures in the background. A crypto-Satanist message was suspected). In gallery XX, *The Healing of a Man Possessed* by Carpaccio is of interest for the vivid renderings of the figures and period costumes (1494) and especially for the architectural details of the drawbridge across the canal (predecessor of the Rialto) and the fire-suppressant chimneys, shaped like the muzzle of a blunderbuss. *Reliquary Procession on the Piazza San Marco* provides a detailed view of St. Mark's and environs during the same period.

The neighborhood right behind the Accademia, tucked in between rio di Santa Barnaba and rio di San Trovaso, is our favorite part of the city, one of those Venetian backwaters (literally) where everything moves at a normal, everyday pace, where a commotion in the piazza might be caused by people hurrying off to work (or hurrying off to the neighborhood *osteria* after work) and not necessarily by the sudden eruption of a clump of tourists shuffling along at the heels of their guide. The only boatyard in Venice that still turns out gondolas is located on the San Trovaso canal, behind the Accademia; the neighborhood produce market is installed on a series of barges tied up along the Santa Barnaba canal.

Campanile di San Giorgio Maggiore: Much quieter than San Marco, with a more interesting view from the belltower. The ecclesiastical ban on bare shoulders, plunging necklines, and so forth, is strictly enforced. Closed from 12:30 to 2 and after 7 P.M. There's a Gregorian mass on Sunday, chanted by Benedictine monks. (For the schedule of masses, see the EPT Office.) Catch a No. 5 *vaporetto* at the San Marco-Zaccaria landing.

San Giacomo dell'Orio: A very beautiful church that dates back to the ninth and tenth centuries; it was rebuilt during the thirteenth. There's a remarkable wooden ceiling with extra-small coffers, plus first-rate paintings and statuary. The little bars that line the *campo* are at their liveliest around 7 P.M.

Other Sights to See

The list of first-string attractions is exhausted pretty quickly, but there are still plenty of little architectural and anthropological curiosities that make walking around almost anywhere in the city a tremendous pleasure. First of all, in Venice things may molder and decay, but they're rarely thrown out or replaced unless absolutely necessary —the lion's-mouth receptacles into which anonymous denunciations could be inserted in the days of the Council of Ten are still to be seen at various places around town. You'll also note that Venetian chimneys are still much as they were in Carpaccio's day. There's an enormous quantity of free-floating statuary, plus time-encrusted medallions, historic inscriptions, and so forth, perched on the wall of houses, staring down into canals, or tucked away in various holes and corners—the sort of thing you could easily walk right past a couple of times unless you had been tipped off. Jan Morris's book, *The World of Venice,* is very helpful in this respect. Modern, amateur efforts to spruce up the old place are often no less intriguing, such as the brightly painted collection of dozens of model windmills in a window overlooking the canal right behind the Scuola di San Rocco.

Colissi il Fornaio: Calle San Luca, 4579, near campo San Luca. Perhaps the world's most attractive bakery. Marvelous decor plus attractive breadstuffs.

The central post office is the former *Fondaco dei Tedeschi,* the German merchants' guildhall, and well worth a brief visit on that account. It has a very impressive interior with a courtyard and overhead skylight surrounded by a 3-story loggia; the doorway on the other side of the courtyard affords an unexpected and quite remarkable view of the Grand Canal and the Rialto.

The most attractive bridges are *storti* ("twisted"), that is, set at an oblique angle across the canal; in some places there are whole strings of bridges, one right after the other. There is said to be one place where 5 of them actually intersect in some unimaginable way. *Sottoportegi,* the covered arcades that run along the edge of a canal, are also worth watching for.

Venice, like London, is basically a collection of small villages. This is nowhere more apparent than in the *San Pietro* district, a good destination for a walk. Note the numerous Carpaccio characters sunning themselves on benches.

If you feel like going swimming (and checking out the famous *Lido,* which played a starring role in *Death in Venice,* plus a cameo in *Brideshead Revisited,* but which doesn't really amount to much), take a *vaporetto* No. 1, 2, or 4 from San Marco or piazzale Roma. The public beach is down past the end of viale Santa Elisabetta.

The younger Venetians like to hang out of an evening in the *campo San Bartolomeo* near the Rialto. We'd also advise you to revisit a few of the places you've been during the day, in order to find them wonderfully transformed. Venice is a particularly nice place to walk around in at night, though you do have to be a little careful about the canals.

Finally, try to get tickets for at least one performance (a concert or an opera) at the *Fenice* theater.

Shopping

Masks: Barbaria delle Tole, 6657. Telephone 231-10. A young craftsperson's collective that turns out splendid replicas of the masks worn by the commedia dell'arte characters; they use the traditional technique, building up the mask in papier-mâché over a plaster mold.

Musical Instruments (Riuteria): Cannaregio Maddalena, 2149. Telephone 366-58. Visit the studio of an instrument maker currently said to be in possession of the "secret of Stradivarius."

Posters: At Foto Renard, calle Larga, 2940, near the Frari. Nice ones, plus the proprietor knows an enormous amount about the city and can tell you about some interesting, little-known places to visit. (He goes on vacation in August, however, like everybody else.)

Venetian Glass: See Murano, below.

Ceramics: Rigattieri, on the street that runs between campo San Stefano and campo San Angelo. Tureens, animals, fruit baskets, and so forth, in polychrome porcelain. They're from Bassano, the former Venetian colony on the mainland, and they're really superb and relatively inexpensive.

The Islands

There are lots of them out in the lagoon and lots of retired pirates willing to take you on a half-day blitzkrieg tour of the 3 main ones for an exorbitant sum. It's far better to catch the No. 5 *vaporetto* at the San Zaccaria landing (250 yards east of San Marco). A very nice trip out to Murano takes you through the Arsenal, where you can see the ceremonial barges that are used as VIP reviewing stands during regattas and festivals. If you have the time, stop off at the cemetery island of *San Michele,* one of the most romantic and certainly one of the quietest places around these parts.

• *Murano*

Famous for its glassware since the thirteenth century. Anticipated the TV networks by several centuries by steadily debasing the product in accordance with what they imagined to be the public taste. Nowadays, the island (the least interesting of the 3 main ones, in fact) is underpopulated, and a great many of the glassworks have shut down. The *Museo d'Arte Vetraria,* installed in a handsome palazzo, is still worth visiting; they have a nice collection of fifteenth- to eighteenth-century pieces, including a beautiful blue goblet engraved with scenes of Rococco gallantry. Open from 10 to 4; closed on Wednesday.

Linea Muzzucato: Get off at the first stop on the island. An enormous factory outlet with the hideous contemporary stuff on the first floor. There are more attractive museum replicas upstairs.

Foscarini: Next door. Same basic deal, catering to a slightly more "advanced" taste.

• *Burano*

1 boat per hour from Murano, or take the No. 5 *vaporetto* from San Marco to the fondamenta Nuova and change for a No. 12 to Burano. Was once as strenuously engaged in lacemaking as was its sister island in glassblowing and celebrated for the fineness of its work (the Republic once presented Louis XIV with a lace collarette made of individual strands of human hair). By the beginning of this century the industry (in the person of the single elderly lady who still remembered how to make the stuff) had almost become extinct; several girl apprentices were hastily recruited, and lacemaking continues to flourish on Burano. It's also notable for its motley collection of houses, multi-family dwellings in which each tenant affirms his individuality by painting *his or her* floor a different color than the others. A very striking effect.

Burano's very appealing atmosphere, especially attractive to painters, is a bit reminiscent of Hydra and the other Ionian islands. Today the islanders are mostly concerned with fishing, so the place is largely deserted during the day (not too many tourists either) but gets livelier at night. Stroll around in the shadows of San Martino, with its campanile heeled over at a much more drastic angle than

Pisa's. More to the point, *Da Romano* is one of the best-known sea-food places in Italy, maybe even the best. This is a compulsory stop-over, though not exactly cheap. There's also a *trattoria, Al Graspo de Ua,* on piazza Galuppi that serves up a nice, affordable seafood dinner (dessert and coffee included) if you'd like to spend a few days on the island, there are a number of householders with spare rooms available (*aloggi* is the technical term), especially on calle Gianella.

• *Torcello*

Also accessible by the No. 12 *vaporetto.* A strange, even mysterious island that fades off at the edges into the reedy waters of the lagoon. Heavily populated during the Middle Ages, it was the seat of a bishopric until the eighteenth century (the cathedral gives some idea of Torcello's former importance). The population was largely wiped out by malaria, however, or persuaded to move elsewhere, and apart from a handful of houses that are still inhabited, Torcello exists today as a kind of Renaissance ghost town, the beauty of its stately public buildings enhanced by the loneliness and isolation of their surroundings. *Cipriani,* the only restaurant on Torcello, is far too expensive for the likes of us. Its previous clients include Hemingway, Giscard d'Estaing, and Queen Elizabeth). There's a little *pensione* across the street, however, that's perfect for misanthropes and contemplatives.

The *Feste*

The *Carnival* is held in mid-February. Recently restored to life after a long lapse, these days it is more of a popular family holiday than the steamy aristocratic revel it was a couple of hundred years ago. Still very well attended, making this the only time during the off-season that it's difficult to get a room. The cold, the fog, and the mist contribute to the spirit of masquerade and mystery.

La Festa del Redentore: Third Sunday in July (and the night before). One of the Western world's most spectacular religious festivals; 2 bridges of boats link San Marco, the Salute, and Giudecca. Venice's deliverance from the plague of 1576 is celebrated with music, illuminations, fireworks, and processions. Everything in the city is brilliantly lit up, from the gondolas to the domes of San Marco. It's best to lay claim to a table at an outdoor café or a restaurant along the Grand Canal during the afternoon; bridges and other convenient vantage points get a bit too crowded later on.

La Regata Storica: First Sunday in September. As much of the pomp and pageantry of the Republic as is currently feasible is re-created for the gala procession of boats down the Grand Canal that precedes the gondola races.

La Festa della Madonna della Salute: November 21. The city's deliverance from the plague of 1630 is commemorated by a procession across a temporary bridge between the Salute and campo Santa Maria Zobenigo.

Brenta Canal

The original shuttle service between Venice and Padua carried merchant princes, noblemen, and their retainers—accompanied by artists, actors, and adventurers, courtesans and even literary gentlemen such as Byron and Casanova—out to their villas along the canal. The little excursion boat that makes the run nowadays is managed by the CIT; it leaves the ponte Giardinetti near San Marco at 9:20 A.M. on Tuesday, Thursday, and Saturday between April 15 and September 30 and arrives in Padua at 5 P.M. the same day. There, the boat disgorges its passengers, who make the return trip by bus. The boat stays over in Padua and picks up a fresh cargo of tourists the next morning. The trip is fairly expensive; lunch is included in the fare. For info contact the CIT office in Venice, piazza San Marco, 4850; telephone 854-80, or in Padua, via Matteotti, 12; telephone (049) 288-62. The canal takes you through a soft and peaceful landscape, enlivened with locks and swing bridges; there are 3 brief stopovers to enable you to get a closer look at *Villa Pisani, Villa Widman,* and *Villa Foscari,* better known as *La Malcontenta.*

Villa Pisani, in the town of Stra, is the most opulent of them all and seems more like a royal palace than a mere country house. Distinguished visitors in the past have included Napoleon, Gustav III of Sweden, numerous grand dukes (both Austrian and Russian) and, most notably, Hitler and Mussolini, who held their first Axis summit meeting here. In the park, climb up to the roof of the stables and try to pick out the maze described by D'Annunzio, the Italian D. H. Lawrence.

La Malcontenta: Built by Palladio in 1571. Got its nickname from a woman's portrait in one of the frescoes, alleged to be that of the chronically unfaithful wife of the villa's original owner; she was kept out here in a state of dishonorable captivity by her husband, according to a local legend.

The same trip (total 26 miles) can also be made somewhat more cheaply by car. From Venice, head for Mestre, then Oriago (where *La Malcontenta* is located). The road runs along the canal through Mira, Dolo, and finally Stra (Villa Pisani), and it's only another 8 miles or so to Padua.

TRIESTE

A gritty seaport town where Joyce spent a few years teaching English. It still has some worthwhile monuments and other points of interest, including the handsome *palazzi* surrounding piazza dell'Unità d'Italia, the cathedral of San Giusto, the *castello,* the aquarium, and the oceanographic museum. Plenty of Triestines turn out for the evening *passeggiata* on mole Pescheria and piazza Venezia.

The *hostel* at viale Miramare 331 is rumored to have closed down permanently this year. If not, take a No. 6 Barcola bus, then change for a No. 36. If so, try the *Hotel Brioni,* via della Gimnastica, 2. In the city center, about 1 kilometer from the train station. Clean, unpretentious, and fairly inexpensive.

FRIULI

The inland region around Udine, between Venice and Trieste, was severely affected by the earthquake of 1976; since then its people, who have a proud tradition of autonomy and even their own language, Friulian, have devoted themselves courageously to the task of rebuilding their homes and villages. *Udine*—which recently distinguished itself by putting in the top bid for the Brazilian soccer superstar Zico—has an important fine arts museum and a rich architectural heritage (for example, piazza dela Libertà and the Tiepolos in the archbishop's palace).

The nearby village of San Daniele del Friuli is famous for *prosciutto di San Daniele,* a delectable smoked ham, the best in Italy, which should be consumed in the thinnest possible slices. The region also produces some excellent white wines, which are just starting to win a reputation for themselves in North America; probably the best and certainly the best known of these is Pinot Grigio.

CENTRAL ITALY

PARMA

A lovely city of ochre-colored walls, known for its ancient monuments, especially the spires and domes that confer upon it a remarkably handsome silhouette.

EPT Office: Piazza del Duomo. City maps are available.

Where to Sleep

Ostello per la Gioventù: Via Passo Buole, 7 (Citadella). Telephone (0521) 333-48. Take a No. 9 bus from the station. Entirely remodeled. Lots of rooms with 4 beds each; quiet and comfortable.

Campground: South of town. Clean. Good value for the money.

The Sights

The *Duomo* and the *baptistery,* the strange-looking hexagonal tower. Piazza del Duomo is also one of the most beautiful in Italy, especially at night.

Palazzo della Pilotta: Dates from the seventeenth century and named for the racquet-and-ball game *pelote,* a variant of court tennis that was played here in the old days.

Piazza Garibaldi: The deluxe sundial tells the time everywhere in the world.

BOLOGNA

A very attractive, very relaxed old city (during the summer, at any rate, when the university is on vacation). Bologna's political and architectural color schemes approach the reddish end of the spectrum. Abundant medieval arcades—they call them porticoes—protect you from sun, rain, and traffic. A pleasant luxury in the first 2 cases; sheer necessity in the third since there aren't many sidewalks in Bologna.

Where to Sleep, Where to Eat

Pensione Marconi: Via Marconi, 22. Quite inexpensive.

Pensione Fiorita: Via San Felice, 6. Very comfortable rooms at an affordable price. A cordial welcome is assured, and great local wine-tasting discoveries await in the *enoteca* across the street.

Camping Piccolo Paradiso: About 7 miles out of town, 2 kilometers from the Sasso-Marconi exit on the beltway around Bologna. The name is a bit of a brag, perhaps, but not entirely inappropriate. Not too expensive either.

Snack Lazzarini: Via Elevature, 1, next to piazza Maggiore. Cheap eats and copious portions.

Birraria Bologna: Piazza Malpighi, 1, about 5 minutes from the city center. Telephone 233-423. The same.

Self-service Bass 8: Via Ugo Bassi. Cafeteria. A youthful hangout.

University dining hall (Mensa Universitaria): A shame and a scandal (that is, one of the most expensive of its kind in Italy). There are plenty of places in town where you can get a great pizza for the same price and without having to stand in line.

The Sights

Piazza Maggiore: One of Italy's finest, what with the Basilica di San Petronio, the palazzo del Podestà, the palazzo Comunale, and Giambologna's Neptune fountain (in the piazza right next door).

The *university* has some nice post-Renaissance frescoes, plus satirical student wall paintings of more recent date. Pretty cute.

Due Torri: Piazza di Porta Ravegnana. Built by rival families during the eleventh century, perhaps overhastily since the top of one of them has long since fallen off and the other one leans quite a bit. There's a great view of the city and the surrounding countryside from the leaning one, the *torre degli Asinelli.*

Hitching Out of Bologna

If you're headed south or northeast, take bus No. 21, 22, or 42 to Casaleochio. Ask the driver to tell you when to get off; the highway is about 1 kilometer past that.

Toward Ravenna: Take a No. 15 bus. Get off right by the highway.

RAVENNA

A wonderful city, fresh and quiet, though it may seem a bit lackluster at first. In fact, we'd rank it right up there with Venice and Florence (and the outskirts of Naples) as one of the most beautiful places in Italy. Need we say more?

EPT Office: Piazza San Francesco.

Where to Sleep, Where to Eat

Ostello per la Gioventù Dante: Via A. Nicolodi, 12 (Trieste district). Telephone 420-405. Catch the No. 1 bus opposite the train station. A brand-new building. 120 beds. Breakfast and bed linen are included.

Camping "La Pineta": On the beach between Casal Borsetti and Marina di Ravenna. One of the nicest in Northern Italy. The proprietor is very cordial. Younger clientele. The bar stays open until 1 A.M. Only one house rule: The beach is designated a Quiet Zone between 2 and 4 P.M., and absolute respect for the sanctity of the siesta is enjoined: no cassette players or ghetto blasters, no orgasmic shrieks or mopeds revving up. . . .

Camping Rivaverde: In Marina di Ravenna, about 3 miles out of town. Catch a bus near the train station. On the beach. Clean, with all the amenities—hot showers, groceries, restaurant, bar, laundry room, and game room.

Pizzeria Jolly: Via Cavour, 82. Not far from San Vitale. Reasonably priced. The pizzas are first-rate. The proprietress herself presides, à la Leona Helmsley, at the oven door.

The Sights

Mosaics: Plenty of them. After the fall of Rome the Byzantine comeback attempt in Italy was based in what was called "the exarchate of Ravenna"; the political angle didn't quite work out, but the city's artistic legacy from those distant days is truly astounding. Many of the mosaics are quite high up and hard to see; load up on 100-lire pieces to make the lights work. It's also highly gratifying to have a pair of binoculars or a camera with a telephoto lens.

Basilica di San Vitale and the *Mausoleum of Galla Placidia:* The basilica dates from the sixth century; the campanile was rebuilt during the seventeenth. The mosaic decorations of the apse and the choir are spectacular, likewise the mausoleum, where the mosaics are somewhat more reminiscent of the Pompeian naturalistic style than your basic wide-eyed Byzantine. Spectacular organ recitals during the month of August.

Baptistery of the Duomo: The mosaics are remarkable for their realism.

Church of San Francesco: Well worth visiting in its own right; then follow the adjoining Braccioforte arcade to *Dante's Tomb,* which doesn't begin to do him justice.

Sant'Appolinare Nuovo: Elegant cylindrical campanile and more splendid mosaics, this time highly stylized and majestic.

Sant'Appolinare in Classe: About 3 miles south of Ravenna. Contains seventh- and eighth-century sarcophagi, plus more mosaics, somewhat like those in the other Sant'Appolinare, only more so—notably, *The Transfiguration.*

RIMINI

A well known, highly underdeveloped resort town also noted as Fellini's hometown (as seen in *Amarcord*). We'd advise you to check out the *Tempio Malatesta,* a fifteenth-century neoclassical blockbuster, then beat it out of Rimini. There's also an interesting little museum called *Italia in Ninatora* (Italy in Miniature), which is just that.

Ostello per la Gioventù Ost-Urland: Via Flaminia, 300, Rimini-Miramare 47045. Telephone 332-16. Take bus No. 9, 10, or 11. 100 beds.

Pensione Stefania: Intersection of via Destra del Porto and via Coletti, about 500 yards from the train station. Rather quiet and comfortable.

SAN MARINO

A little village on a hill that has hung onto its picturesque medieval fortifications and rejoices in the title of the world's oldest and smallest independent republic. It is also one of its most expensive. Budget travelers are advised not to let the sun set on them in San Marino. As you leave the republic in the direction of Ancona, you'll come after 1 kilometer to a parking lot with public sanitary facilities in good working order.

Camping della Murata: Via del Serrone, at a little spot (not a town) called Murata on the south flank of Monte Titano. Cheap and perfectly clean.

A Little History

The republic was founded in the fourth century by a Christian stonemason named *Marinus,* who had originally settled in Rimini to work on the fortifications around the port. The anti-Christian persecutions of Diocletian persuaded him to take refuge on nearby *Monte Titano,* whose summit can be seen from Rimini, where he could ply his trade and practice his religion undisturbed. His reputation for piety attracted a whole flock of disciples and imitators; the local landowner, a princess whose children he had cured of an illness, presented him with title to the entire mountain.

The republic thus inadvertently founded by St. Marinus snoozed through the next 1,500 years or so in blessed obscurity, untroubled by barbarians, Borgias, Bonaparte, or any of the other problems that beset the rest of the peninsula. In fact, Napoleon, as one republican to another, offered to present San Marino with an additional chunk of papal territory; the citizens of the republic wisely refused. Garibaldi sought refuge here in 1849; San Marino, though neutral, was bombed during World War II and still somehow managed to find room for 100,00 refugees from elsewhere in Italy.

Principal Products

Duty-free liquor and postage stamps, the latter very stylish indeed. San Marino is basically a ripoff and a bit too cute for its own good, but it's still worth checking out. You might think that prices would get a bit more reasonable as you descend from the trumped-up medieval village to the lower town, where the people actually live. Not so.

URBINO

Raphael's birthplace, now a town of some 17,000 permanent residents and 8,000 students. Excellent language programs in the summer for those desirous of learning Italian in a thoroughly agreeable setting. (What might seem like a deliberate government policy of putting big bustling universities in picturesque little towns is actually the result of the decline in the growth of most of Italy's big cities in about the sixteenth century. Anyway, suffice it to say things are a lot livelier in Urbino when the university is in session.

Much of the charm of the old city is provided by its sloping, often narrow streets, nestled within its ramparts and providing numerous unexpected and attractive vistas. Note that the entire region is bordered by the Adriatic on one side, and the line between Perugia and Arezzo on the other is called the Marches. Lots of mountains. Not so much traffic on the highways. Hitchhikers will have to learn exemplary patience.

Tourist Office (Azienda di Turismo): Piazza Duca Federico. Open from 9 to 2.

Where to Sleep, Where to Eat

During the summer, lots of *affita camere* (furnished rooms for students) should be available. If you happen to tap into the great landladies' grapevine at any point, they'll have you fixed up in a jiffy, assuming you're planning to stay for 2 or 3 days or are willing to practice a modest deception.

Hotel Panoramic: Via Nazionale, 192, down from the old city. Telephone 26-00.

Camping la Pineta: A mile or so out toward Fossombrone from the center of town. A great view of Urbino. Well run and not overly expensive.

Mensa Universitaria: Via Budassi, 4. Telephone 29-15. Not always open during vacations, but Urbino is a pretty, tiny town with just a few places to eat and drink; it's not so hard to pick out the good ones. We're going to trust you on this one.

The Sights

Palazzo Ducale: Urbino's greatest architectural treasure houses the amazing National Gallery of the Marches. A few Raphaels plus Piero della Francesca's *Flagellation of Christ,* which appears at first glance to be the work of an especially skillful Surrealist painter of the 20s. (When you study European history in school, you tend to get the idea that it was very wrong of the Italians of the Renaissance not to organize themselves into a well-knit centralized state as almost everybody else did. Maybe so, but there do seem to be certain compensations, such as the presence of a first-class art museum in a delightful nonmetropolis such as Urbino.)

Oratorio di San Giovanni Battista: Frescoes of the life of St. John the Baptist incorporate secular as well as sacred motifs but without the note of redeeming vulgarity that you find in works by the masters of Venice and Bologna. There's another oratory nearby; not much to look at, but you can pause to say a prayer or two.

In sum, the entire old city (with the possible exception of Raphael's boyhood home) is rather interesting and, as noted, a great place to wander around in.

GUBBIO

A medieval town that is somewhat smaller and, in our opinion, more attractive than Urbino, but not by much. There's no art museum, however. Note that the old houses always have 2 doors, one for the living, the other for the dead. The latter, exclusively for carrying out coffins, is kept bricked up when not in use. Try to make a few new friends in Gubbio; the people (that is, the sort who hang out in bars and cafés and don't mind talking to uneducated foreigners) will be delighted to fill you in on the local legends, most notably the famous one about St. Francis and the wolf, and take you around to some of the lesser-known points of interest. We promise you'll have to try hard not to love it.

Where to Eat

Rosticceria Gianna: Via Baldassani, 26. A family-type place that may be a wee bit overpriced.

Trattoria La Balestra: Via della Repubblica. Good regional cuisine, basically seafood and suckling pig. How bad can it be? The tables are in a nice garden looking out on the red-brick side chapels of the Church of San Giovanni.

Feste

There are 2 good ones that take place during the month of May:

Festa di San Ubaldo: May 15. Its highlight is the *Corsa dei Ceri,* a handicapper's classic in which 3 teams of 8 men race between the piazza and the basilica, each team carrying a 150-pound waxwork of a local saint.

Palio della Balestra: Last Sunday in May. The *balestra* is the "arabalest," a high-tension medieval crossbow, and this is a contest between the arabalestiers of Gubbio and nearby Sansepolcro. Participants and spectators don medieval costume for the occasion.

There's also an *antiques market* on via Valdassani on the second Sunday of every month.

PERUGIA

A very lovely city: For the past 20 years it has been the seat of the university for foreigners, located in the Palazzo Gallenga on piazza Fortebraccio, which gives it an especially youth-oriented, cosmopolitan character. The university organizes lots of free concerts, plus jazz festivals in July and August. The corso Vannucci is where everyone turns out at night. A nice place to stop and maybe take a little rest from your vacation.

Where to Sleep and Where to Eat

Ostello per la Gioventù: Via Bontempi, 13. From piazza IV Novembre, head to the right, toward a smaller piazza with a well. The hostel is on the little street at the other end of the piazza, about 120 yards to the right. You can get bus No. 11 or 12 from the station. Telephone (075) 228-80. Hot showers are included. Kitchen privileges and TV. Strict hours—open only between 7:30 and 9 A.M., and between 4 and 11 P.M. The hostel in Foligno (see below, Assisi) is also a possibility.

Camping Il Rocolo: Strada della Trinità. Telephone (075) 798-550. Take a No. 36 bus out of Perugia; the bus stop is about 300 yards from the campground. Swimming pool.

Camping Paradis d'Eté: Via del Mercato, Trinità-Fontana, about 3 miles out of town.

La Botte: Good food. Inexpensive. Cafeteria-style (pay now, eat later).

Rosticceria Peppino: Via Dangetta, 9. First-rate pasta *de la maison.*

Ristorante Priori: Via Vermiglioli, near via dei Priori. They've raised their prices, but they're still pretty good.

Mensa la Deliciosa: Via Deliciosa, 3. The price is incredibly low for an enormous plate of spaghetti *plus* an entree.

The Sights

National Gallery of Umbria: Located in the magnificent thirteenth-century Palazzo dei Priori. Many, many works by painters of the Umbrian School, thirteenth to eighteenth centuries. In particular, watch for the Madonnas by Fra Angelico and Piero della Francesca (in the gallery devoted to fifteenth-century Tuscan painters). Perugino, of course, is the hometown favorite.

La Fontane di Maggiore: A Gothic fountain, one of the most beautiful in all of Italy.

As noted, the evening *passeggiata* takes place along corso Vannucci—also a very good street to explore while the sun is shining. Gives birth to several delightful sidestreets ascending in stairsteps or lined with arcades. The Carducci gardens is an excellent place from which to view an amber-tinted Umbrian sunset.

Hypogeum of the Volumni: On the road that crosses the Ponte San Giovanni, about 4 miles out of town. One of the most beautiful of the many Etruscan rock tombs that have been discovered around these parts. Open from 9 to 1. Closed on Monday.

ASSISI

A marvelous little town with some great churches and, above it all, a medieval castle called *La Rocca.* Plenty of tourists, to be sure, but these folks are *pilgrims,* not the ordinary kind you get in Venice or Florence.

Tourist Office: Piazza del Commune.

Where to Sleep

Travelers in a state of holy poverty will have a hard time finding an ordinary hotel room in Assisi. There are several monasteries and convents in the neighborhood that may be able to put you up; the *Colettine Sisters,* for example, at Borgo San Pietro, 3, have rooms with single beds, and breakfast is included for a very reasonable price. Telephone 81-23-45.

Ostello: Piazza San Giacomo, in Foligno (not far from Assisi). Telephone (0742) 525-82. Take a No. 1 bus.

Camping Fontemaggio: 1 kilometer above the town of Assisi. There's an excellent restaurant nearby where the food is cooked over a wood fire. The landscape is straight out of a medieval book of hours.

The Sights

In spite of everything, a medieval and almost mystical spirit still pervades the narrow streets of Assisi. Start by walking around a bit to put yourself in touch with same.

Basilica di San Francesco: Dates from the thirteenth century and contains a splendid fresco cycle by Giotto, Simone Martini, and several of Giotto's pupils, plus *Madonna with Saint Francis and Angels* by Cimabue, who was Giotto's teacher.

Eremo delle Carceri: About 2.5 miles above the town. This hermitage, once frequented by St. Francis, clings to the mountainside and is surrounded by quiet forest trails. Makes for a first-rate excursion and, if you like, you can have a Franciscan for a guide.

ORVIETO

An obligatory stopover before you move on to Rome. Orvieto perches grandly atop a massive chunk of volcanic lava, all puffed up with pride over its 2 municipal treasures—a fine cathedral and a fantastic local *vino bianco.*

The Sights

Palazzo Soliano: An imposing medieval pile with very nice windows and an exterior staircase. Houses the *Museo dell'Opera del Duomo* (paintings by Simone Martini, Perugino, and others).

Duomo: As noted, a prime specimen of Italian Gothic architecture, with a heavily Romanesque aftertaste. Built c. 1290. Contains a number of frescoes, some interesting altarpieces (one in particular that seems to be striving for a kind of holograph effect), a solid silver reliquary studded with gems, and a Renaissance pulpit.

Palazzo del Populo: Another handsome palazzo with an exterior staircase. Also built in a style that combines Gothic design elements with a number of holdovers from the Romanesque.

Il Pozzo de San Patricio: "St. Patrick's Well." An architectural nonesuch that dates from the sixteenth century. The shaft is almost 200 feet deep and over 40 feet wide. Light is provided by 72 large windows, and 2 intertwined spiral staircases lead down to the water level.

TARQUINIA

About 60 miles from Rome and not far from the coast. Another plump little city on a hilltop with its Renaissance palazzi and its medieval streets. Most notable as the chief city of the ancient Etruscans. There's a very fine museum in town devoted to Etruscan art and archeology and, just a mile or so outside of town, an Etruscan necropolis, featuring quite a number of rock tombs decorated with lively frescoes. The *tombe Etrusche* are supposed to be open for inspection between 9 A.M. and 7 P.M. Get your tickets at the museum.

ROME

The incomparable charm of 1,500 years of urban decay. There's nothing more rewarding than a long, pointless stroll past all those buildings of ocher-colored stone, mysterious little plazas, cf. *Fellini Roma* half-hidden palazzi and, of course, the ruins of 3 (going on 4) different epochs in world history. Rome has gone beyond disorder to achieve true randomness, and the intermingling of all possible archi-

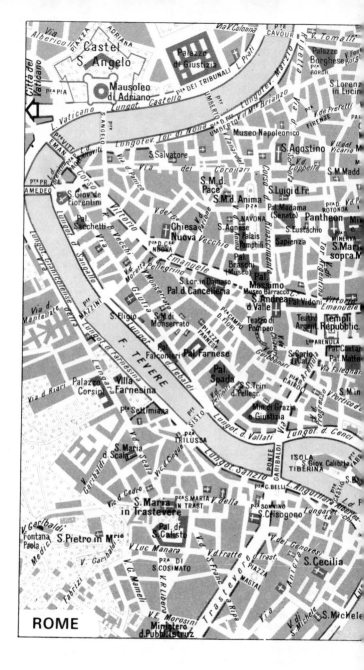

ROME

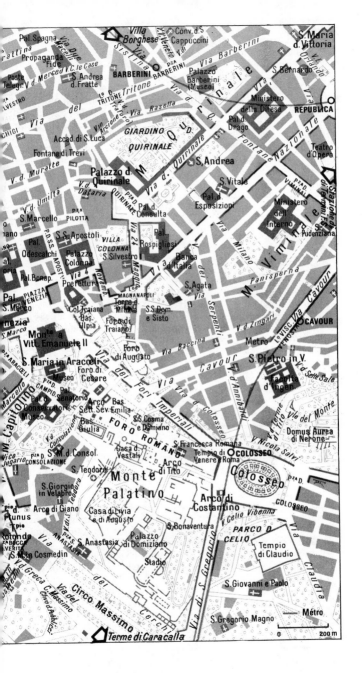

tectural styles, from Roman Republican to Mussolini Modern and beyond, as turned out to be a great success. The people of Rome, all but perhaps the very richest and the very poorest, have chosen as well to live in similar ill-assorted harmony.

In spite of all the care (and neglect) that has gone into the realization of the set decor, the Romans themselves are still the undoubted stars of this production. They can easily be recognized in profile and by their approach to life that is frequently undisciplined and never overly anxious. It's worth noting that Rome is closer to Istanbul than Paris and has already turned her face toward the East. We should confess to a certain bias here since we intend to settle down permanently in Rome, perhaps as soon as we've seen this little volume safely through the presses. We understand that all roads lead there in any case.

Many thanks to our friend and colleague Catherine Domain, author of the inestimable *Rome en Jeans,* for helping us out with this section.

Useful Addresses

EPT Office: Via Parigi, 5, and in the Termini station. Open from 8:30 to 2 and from 3 to 8:30. Free city maps.

U.S. Embassy: Via Veneto, 119A. Telephone 46-74.

Canadian Embassy: Via G. B. de Rossi, 27. Telephone 855-341.

Central Post Office: Piazza San Silvestro. *Fermo posta* facilities.

American Express: Piazza di Spagna, 38.

Bank of America: Largo Tritone, 161. Telephone (06) 67-181. Cash bailout for VISA cardholders.

English-language Bookstores: Economy Book Center, piazza di Spagna, is cheaper. *American Bookshop,* via della Vite, 57, is better. Foreign newspapers are available at the newsstands in the city center.

Tutto la Città 85: A 220-page book of maps plus info on public transportation, museum schedules, and so forth. Absolutely indispensable.

When in Rome: English-language bulletin with listings of current films, plays, cultural events, and other items. There's a similar magazine called *Settimana* (in French and Italian), but this one is actually more complete.

Currency Exchange: At Termini station, Fiumicino (also known as Leonardo da Vinci) Airport, and most banks. Travel agencies take too much of a rakeoff. Change money only at the big tourist hotels in case of necessity (on a Saturday, for example).

Car Rental: Tropea, via San Basilio, 63, corner of via Veneto. Telephone (06) 46-11-89. Best rates that we know of. Also has offices in 7 other Italian cities.

Albergo Diurno: In Termini station. A truly wonderful place equipped with full-service bathrooms (including showers and spotless bidets), for just a few lire. Open until 10:30 P.M. There's also a drugstore that stays open until midnight, a tourist information booth (by track 20), international telephone office, a barbershop, and a baggage check (closes at 8:30 P.M.). You'll also note as you leave the station that there's a signboard to your right (labelled ATAC) with complete bus information plus a city map with a very convenient index of city streets. Finally, you can catch an ACOTRAL bus out to *Fiumicino Airport,* to your left as you leave the station.

Laundromat, Drycleaning: Lavaservice, via Montebello, 11. In the *pensioni* district by Termini station.

Swimming Pool: Foro Italico. Take bus No. 32 or 90. Open sporadically from June to September.

Where to Sleep

If you get into town in the afternoon or evening, you've already blown your chances of finding a really cheap place to stay. It would be best to lay over the first night in one of the *pensioni* near Termini station, get up early the next morning, and head out to the youth hostel which, along with the campgrounds, is the cheapest thing going (if you don't count the cost in human suffering, for which see below). If you don't already have an international hostel card, you can buy one on the spot for a reasonable sum. Note that crashing in and around Termini station is not recommended; it often results in sudden luggage loss or slashing of backpacks with razors and subsequent removal of contents.

• Hostels (and the Like)

Ostello per la Gioventù (youth hostel): Viale Olimpiadi, 61. Telephone 396-47-09. A gigantic, reasonably modern building in the northwest corner of town, way out on the other side of the Tiber. Take the A subway line all the way to Ottaviano, then a No. 32 bus. The stop is Foro Italico. The registration process is lengthy and none too pleasant. Show up around 11:30 to get your registration ticket. Registrations are confirmed at around 2 (by calling out the lucky ticket numbers). The staff is rather fussy and disinclined to give a sucker an even break; for example, breakfast is included, but you have to pay extra for jam and butter (plate and spoon furnished gratis). Maximum stay of 3 days. There is a useful map in the lobby indicating the numbers of the buses you should take to get to various points of interest.

Albergo del Populo: Via Apuli, 41. Tel. 49-05-58. Head to the right from the station and then walk parallel to the tracks for about 15 minutes. This residence for men is run by the Salvation Army, but it is not the least bit shabby. A well-maintained modern building with a cafeteria. Single rooms at rates equivalent to a *pensione.* (Women pay a bit less for dorm rooms at No. 39).

Casa dello Studente: In the university complex, via Cesare de Lollis, 20, between the station and the Church of San Lorenzo. Rooms with 1 or 2 beds. Available only during July and August. Often full. Take a No. 66 bus from the station.

YMCA: Piazza Independenza, 23. No less expensive than a room in a good hotel. Perhaps intended for those willing to pay a premium for being able to partake of the high moral tone of this establishment.

• Pensioni

There are 3 streets near the station chock full of them: *via Principe Amadeo* (has the most), *via Palestro,* and *via Montebello.*

—via Principe Amadeo: Head left as you leave the station. As far as cost and cleanliness are concerned, the following are about on a par: *pensioni Orlando, Guilio, Milo,* and *Tito* at No. 76, *Giorgina* and

Acropoli at No. 67 (the latter is full of Soviet Jewish émigrés), plus *Tony* at No. 79 and *Delfina* at No. 82.

—*via Palestro:* Take via Solferino to your right as you leave the station, then count off until you reach the fifth street on the left.

Pensione Lauretta: At No. 43. A deluxe *pensione* with plenty of rooms (3 or 4 beds apiece). The proprietress is German and a great one for tidying up. She'll also make up your bed as soon as you check in (proof positive that you're sleeping on clean sheets). Also at No. 43 you have the luxury of an English-speaking management (on the fifth floor) at *Locanda Marini.* The last-named is the friendlier of the 2, plus you get your own key so there's no problem about coming in late.

Cervia: At No. 55. Telephone 49-10-57. Clean but a little more expensive.

Corallo: At No. 44. Recommended for those who are working on a tan. All the rooms have access to a great big balcony.

Dora: At No. 34. Telephone 48-28-21. More expensive, as is *Mimi Cardinali,* at No. 13. Telephone 48-67-38. The latter is quite clean, is full of cryptic little placards in Russian, and has a nice view of the British embassy. *Lella,* at No. 9, second floor, is a little off-color without being positively dirty.

—*via Montebello:* Crosses via Palestro. *Pensioni* are not so numerous but a bit cheaper than on the other 2 streets. At No. 114, *Locanda Cina* and *Locanda Manita.* The latter even offers a student discount. Clean rooms. Run by a very nice family. The former is okay as well.

—*elsewhere in the same neighborhood:*

Dino: Via Cernaia, 47. Tel. 475-90-93. A 5-minute walk from Termini station. Take via Volturno, across from the station, which runs into via Cernaia. Family atmosphere; especially hospitable to students and footloose foreigners. Rooms are inexpensive and otherwise in good order. You get your own key.

Otello: Via Marghera, 13. Take a right as you leave the train station. Continue until you come to a very large café, then head down the street across from the café for about 50 yards or so. The proprietress will subject you to a searching personal examination before she agrees to rent you a room (shower included). Once you're in, it's strictly first-class treatment and a front-door key besides.

Pensione Monterosa: Via Alfredo Cappellini, 46. Telephone 732-332. Run by a very nice couple (she's Italian, he's American). 5 very clean rooms. Quite cheap.

—*piazza della Repubblica:* For those who are willing to up the ante a bit, we heartily recommend the 3 small hotels at piazza della Repubblica, 47. Large rooms, most of them overlooking a quintessential Roman piazza (with a fountain in the middle, filled with cafés that work up to a very nice atmosphere by the end of the day). Our favorite is *Pensione Eureka,* on the fourth floor, if only for the ceiling frescoes in the outer hall. Telephone 475-58-06. Not really what you'd call cheap, however. *Pensione-Albergo Terminus,* downstairs, is perhaps the least appealing of the 3 but still quite acceptable. That leaves *Pensione Esedra* somewhere in between. A little expensive but not unreasonably so.

—*via Chiavari: Near Campo dei Fiori,* one of the nicest parts of the city:

Albergo Piccolo: At No. 32. Quite small, as advertised, and on a quiet street. Near a corner much frequented by street musicians in the evening.

Albergo Pomezi: At No. 12. A little more expensive than the preceding. Okay but nothing special.

Albergo Smeraldo: At the corner of Vicolo del Chiaderoli. Reasonably priced and squeaky clean, thanks to the ceaseless vigilance of Mamma Clara. In a nice old building with a modern eyesore of a doorway.

—*near the Vatican:*

Pensione Alimandi: Via Tunisi, 8. Telephone 679-93-43. Right opposite the entrance to the Vatican Museum. Very nice place. Reasonably priced.

• Convents (and the Like)

The usual advantages (cleanliness and tranquility) and disadvantages (sexual segregation and curfews). Also a bit more expensive than a *pensione,* as a rule. The following are all affordable and conveniently near the Vatican:

Suore Oblate dell'Assunzione: Via Andrea Doria, 42. Telephone 38-53-37. For both sexes. Take a No. 64 bus from the station to St. Peter's or the A subway line to Ottaviano. The Sisters are not terribly forthcoming, but the premises are very clean indeed. Curfew is at 10:30 P.M.

Suore Elisabetta: Via dell'Olmata, 9. Comfortable and quite affordable.

Suore Sacra Famiglia: Viale Vaticano, 92. Telephone 319-572.

Suore dell'Adorata: Borgo Santo Spirito, 41.

158 via Urbana: Right next to the Termini station, on the street across from the church of Santa Maria Maggiore. An inexpensive *pensione* run by a religious order.

• Campgrounds

Happy Camping: Via Prato della Corte, 1915. Telephone 642-24-01. Take the A subway line from Termini station to piazzale Flaminio, then change for the Prima Porta station, where a bus from Happy Camping should be somewhere in evidence. Recently opened, good location, comfortable, and offers all the amenities: supermarket, laundry facilities, bar, pool, free hot water, and great bathrooms. You'll get a 10 percent discount on presentation of a copy of this book. This is only supposed to work with the French edition, but you can still give it a try.

Camping Flaminio: Via Flaminia Nuova, north of the city, out toward Terni. Telephone 327-90-06. Closest campground to the center of Rome; you can still count on about 45 minutes one way. Proceed as above; take bus No. 203 (the only one that runs at night), 204, or 205 from piazzale Flaminia to the campground. Groceries, restaurant, and pool. Not terribly expensive.

Camping Tiber: In Prima Porta, same general area as the preceding. Take the subway to Prima Porta (changing at piazzale Flaminia) or take bus No. 202 or 204. Relevant train and bus schedules plus city maps are provided gratis. Well equipped. Right next to a dance hall.

Camping Seven Hills: Via Cassia, 1216. Take the A subway line all the way to Ottaviano, then a No. 32 bus (likewise to the end of the line), then a No. 201, then take the shuttle bus (or walk 2 kilometers) to the campground. Very pleasant but not cheap, and the bus trip alone takes an hour. Also, lockup is promptly at 11 P.M. (with 2 snarling junkyard dogs to make it stick).

Camping Lido di Ostia: By car: Get off at the Lido di Roma exit, about 1 kilometeṛ further in the direction of Ostia. By public trans: Subway to the Cristoforo Colombo station, then a No. 7 (striped) bus.

Camping Nomentano: Via Nomentana (Km 8 on the Raccordo Annulare). Telephone 61-00-296. Catch a No. 36 bus in front of Termini station and then change for a No. 337 at piazza Sempione. The stop is Camping Nomentano. Nice shady spot. Showers included. Groceries and snack bar. Open all year round.

• Upscale

Scalinata di Spagna: Piazza Trinità dei Monti, 17. Telephone 679-30-06. At the top of the Spanish Steps. Ideal for newlyweds or for the wildly impulsive and extravagant. Only 14 rooms, but with luck you'll get one that overlooks the entire city. There's another splendid view from the terrace where breakfast is served. Best to reserve well in advance—the place is getting quite popular with your fellow *Americani.*

Albergo Portoghesi: Via dei Portoghesi. Telephone 645-51-33. Heading toward the Tiber from the via del Corso (opposite the Spanish Steps). On a very peaceful little street with rooms overlooking a lovely terrace with a garden. For lovers and neo-Romantics.

Albergo Sole al Pantheon: Piazza della Rotonda, 63. Telephone 679-33-29. Favored by Jean-Paul Sartre and Simone de Beauvoir, another hard-working couple who really needed to step out from time to time (like the character in one of his plays who saw crabs crawling around on the ceiling of his bedroom). You'll find nothing like that here. The hotel faces a lively little piazza, especially on summer nights, right across from the Pantheon, with an outdoor café that's a wonderful place for breakfast on a bright, sunny morning. Free parking.

Pavia: Via Gaeta, 83. Telephone 475-90-90. To your right as you leave Termini station. A converted private villa that is approached by a walkway shaded by an arbor. The interior has recently been remodeled.

Where to Eat, Where to Drink

Pizzeria da Boffeto: Via del Governo Vecchio, 114. About 50 yards from piazza Navona, heading toward the Vatican. The undistinguished exterior conceals one of Rome's most celebrated *pizzerie.* The pizzas are arguably the best in town; the large-sized ones are truly enormous. A less elaborate treat is called *bruschetti*—garlic toast with tomatoes. Relaxed, pleasant atmosphere. Agreeably hideous decor. Not too expensive. Only open for dinner. Closed on Sunday and during the entire month of August.

Settimio: Via del Pellegrino, 117, on the other side of corso Vittorio Emanuele from piazza Navona. Home-style cuisine (created with raw materials from Grandpa Settimana's farm). The few tables are often occupied by regulars (Alberto Moravia among them).

Pizzeria: Campo dei Fiori. A couple of interesting specialties (lasagna with salmon, pasta with nuts and basil) and a voluptuous mild cheese. Decidedly worth investigating.

Trattoria della Moretta: Vicolo della Moretta, 6, near Campo dei Fiori. A small place with a few outdoor tables. Inexpensive and very nice. The proprietor is justly proud of the house wine, which comes from his own vineyards. Closed on Sunday.

L'Eau Vive: Via Monterone, 85A, a little street near the Pantheon. Exotic specialties prepared by the group of nuns who run the place (many of them from Asia and Africa) with a backstop of reliable French cuisine. Not your everyday pizza parlor. Open from 12:30 to 2:30 and from 8 to 9:30. It's best to make reservations for dinner. Closed on Sunday and all of August.

Ristorante Polese and *Trattoria da Luigi:* Piazza Cesarini Sforza, not far from Campo Fiori. Both have terraces on a shady little piazza, are frequented by artists and literati, and serve hearty Roman specialties. On the expensive side but cheaper than the places on piazza Navona.

Ostello alla Concordia: Via della Croce, 81, right near the Spanish Steps. Telephone 679-11-78. Noted for its interior garden courtyard, where tables are set up the moment weather permits. Back inside, the walls are decorated with drawings and framed engravings. A fairly classy joint in a fairly classy neighborhood, specializing in well-prepared Roman specialties. Closed on Sunday.

Il Grottino: Via Benjamino Franklin, 9. In a fairly remote location but should suit those who are heading out to the Prima Porta flea market on a Sunday morning. (It's right across the river.) An affable place, abounding in neighborhood characters. The cuisine is basic, hearty, and wholesome. No daily specials, but you'll be able to think of something.

Trattoria Rudy: Via Montebello, 114A. Near the Termini station (over by the Ministry of Finance). Good, nourishing food at highly competitive prices (one of the cheapest places in Rome).

Al Tettarello: Via dei Cappocci, 4. Telephone 474-21-80. Conveniently located on a slanty little street between the Colosseum and Santa Maria Maggiore. Inexpensive and very friendly. The proprietor tends to be very generous with the house wine.

Trattoria da Enzo: Vicolo Scavolino, 72–73, right near the Trevi Fountain. Very pleasant and hospitable. Serves Roman specialties at moderate prices. Sufficiently obscure that, with luck, there won't be a tourist in the place.

• *Trastevere (Across the River)*

Mario's: Via del Moro, 53. For those who yearn for the company of their fellow North Americans. Good, reasonably priced Roman specialties. Well-stocked menu, though no *menù* in the Italian sense of a daily special. Closed on Sunday.

Augusto: Piazza Cola da Rienzi, 15, near Mario's. There's no name outside. The only authentic old neighborhood place in Trastevere. Patronized by students, workers, and what Philip Marlowe would call "the local wiseguys." Augusto himself is a bit abrasive, but his wife is very nice, and fortunately she's the one that looks after the cooking.

Taverna la Trasteverina: Via di Ponte Sisto, 80. Barnyard decor that's meant to suggest wholesome rural surroundings. Popular with the same kind of scruffy urban characters you'd expect to find at Augusto's. Fairly limited menu.

Mozzicone: Piazza del Catone, near the Vatican. In the heart of the old *borghi,* near via Concilazione. Great food, though a bit more expensive than the preceding. Extensive terrace.

• *Canteens*
Workers' canteens are also open to the general public and serve good, nourishing meals at affordable prices. A convenient example:

Mensa del Dopolavoro Ferrovario: Piazza de Cinquecento, 88. In the big building to the right as you leave Termini station. Railworkers' canteen. Very clean. Good food. Open from noon to 8:30.

• *Upscale*
La Rampa: Piazza Mignatelli, 18, to the right as you face piazza di Spagna. The interior appears to be an ornate stage set so that you half-expect the waiters and busboys to bust out with one of the noisier operatic choruses at any moment. The food is good, however, and the excellent house wine helps to induce these peculiar expectations. In the summer they put some tables out on the piazza, which is a very nice one.

Romolo: Via di Porta Settimana, 8. Best as a one-time-only extravagance for newlyweds and other celebrants. It's well out of our ordinary price range, but in all other respects it's about our favorite restaurant in Rome. Its tables are set up in a little garden shaded by a vine arbor at the foot of a venerable stone wall. Nothing is left to chance (the menus, for example, were designed by Miró). Popular with the wealthier sorts of Americans (who must have read about it in some damned book or other). Closed during August.

Beltramme: Via della Croce, 3/9, not far from piazza di Spagna. Tiny, elderly establishment popular with journalists and persons of discernment. It's best to get there before 12:30 for lunch or 7:30 for dinner if you want to avoid the crush.

Il Giardino: Via Zucchelli, 29, right by piazza Barberini, as you come down from via del Tritone. A pleasant garden restaurant with a superb selection of traditional Roman specialties. The perfect compromise between quality, which is unsurpassed, and price, which is not all that bad, considering. We suggest you start out on the *assagini della casa,* a copious assortment of hors d'oeuvre, each more delicious than the last. Closed on Monday.

Grotta Azzurra: Via Monza, 17, where it intersects via Terni. Telephone 77-48-15 and 75-79-260. A very good seafood place equipped with the standard fishnet decor. Fairly remote from the city center and fairly expensive. Hors d'oeuvre and wine in unlimited quantities. Of the 3 available pasta-with-seafood combos, we recommend the tonnarelli with salmon. Closed on Monday.

• *Gelato (and the Like)*
Giolitti: Uffici del Vacario, 40, not far from via del Corso, between piazza Navona and piazza Colonna. The best ice cream place in Rome, or at any rate, less expensive than *Tre Scalini,* the only other possible claimant to the title. Packed by 7 P.M. In the afternoon it's full of frisky old gentlemen and their old ladies plying one another with pastries.

Pascucci: Via di Torre Argentina, 20. Doesn't look like much, but they make the best *frullati* (milkshakes) in Rome. The consensus is that the best flavors are peach, *zabaglione,* crème fraîche, and marron glacé. No rocky road.

Gelateria della Palma: Via della Maddelena, 23, right near the

Pantheon. Marble floors, bogus palm trees, and 50 delicious flavors (give or take). They have recently opened a branch in New York City.

Tre Scalini: Piazza Navona. Also rates low on atmosphere, but you can't leave Rome without experimenting with the *tartuffo,* famous glazed pastry encrusted with big chunks of chocolate.

• Watering Holes

Caffè Greco: Via dei Condotti, 85, near piazza di Spagna. Founded in 1760, and the decor seems basically unchanged. Patronized by artists, writers, and most illustrious visitors to Rome, including Goethe, Gogol, Stendhal, Berlioz, Baudelaire, and Wagner. It's scarcely more expensive than any other café, but we'd recommend that you simply station yourself at a table with an espresso and a pastry *alla pollenta* and check out the scene.

Cul-de-Sac: Piazza Pasquino, 73, next to piazza Navona, heading toward the Tiber. A great selection of wines, cheeses, and charcuterie. Patronized by visiting glitterati and the local hip establishment. Open from 8 to midnight. Closed on Sunday. The adjacent piazza contains the famous statue of *Pasquino,* whose base served as the Renaissance version of the Wall of Posters, to which Romans affixed satirical poems and sketches (so-called pasquinades) primarily concerned with the naughty behavior of the higher clergy.

Pace: Via della Pace, 5, in back of piazza Navona and not far from the preceding. The exterior is covered with ivy. The interior decor, though far from moldering, is essentially that of the last century. A good place to stop in for a drink before getting down to a serious reconnaissance of some of the excellent little streets in this area.

Enoteca il Piccolo: Via del Governo Vecchio, 74–75. Very good wine, good music, and a good place to meet people. Antique decor. A very tiny place; it's best to get here early.

Outdoor Markets, Shopping

Open every morning (except Sunday), on Wednesday afternoon, and on the afternoon before a holiday. (They're not entirely open on Saturday afternoon, but they're sort of left ajar.) Eminent social historian Christine Domain was perhaps the first to observe that the Romans have to have so many markets because they have so few grocery stores (practically none, in fact). There are also very few florists or delicatessens, let alone Oriental vegetable stands with kiwi fruit and a day-old salad bar, so the Romans, poor devils, have no choice but to head for the market. Budget travelers, compulsive bargain hunters (or cheap charlies), and action photographers would do well to do as the Romans do.

This is where you, as a visitor, can get your fullest experience of actual Roman life. The atmosphere varies tremendously from one market (even from one day) to the next and, on an only slightly more prosaic note, it's also a very good place to have a cheap lunch. (A useful term: *Concetramenti* means an open-air minimarket, usually just a few vendors selling old clothes and knickknacks, old doorknobs, and the like.) Here are some of our favorites:

Piazza Vittorio Emanuele II: Not far from Termini station. Vegetables, fabulous cheeses, sausages, poultry, and fish. With luck you may run into the snail seller, anxiously watching over his tiny flock. This is one of the largest and funkiest of Roman markets.

Via Montebello: Also near the station. Fruits and vegetables.

Campo dei Fiori: Originally the flower market, it now has a little of everything.

Porta Portese: Flea market, only on Sunday morning. Take a No. 57 bus from Termini station. An impressive assortment, including some new clothes. One corner of the market is reserved for Soviet Jewish refugees, a great many of whom live out here in Ostia, selling things they've brought out of Russia with them or just the usual flea-market items. Don't forget to have lunch at *Il Grottino,* across the river.

Porta San Giovanni: San Giovanni subway stop or take a No. 85 bus from piazza Venezia. This flea market specializes in leather goods, men's jackets with very wide shoulders, some new clothes and shoes (some of the latter imported from the U.S., oddly enough).

There are some wonderful secondhand stores (especially women's clothes) over in Trastevere and along via del Governo Vecchio. Great stuff, and reasonable.

Those more seriously interested in new clothes themselves than the process of acquiring them are directed to via Corso and via Nazionale (very chichi and expensive "important" accessories and the like), via Appia Antica (for that fashionably strumpetty look), and, for the bargain-conscious shopper, the little stores around Termini station. Shoestores are to be found along via Veneto; shoes are very stylish though reasonably expensive but less so perhaps than in the U.S. Finally, you might care to contemplate the impulse purchase of an alb, a cope, or a surplice from one of the ecclesiastical outfitters on via dei Cestari.

La Festa de Noantri (Our Festival)

Takes place during the second half of July and the beginning of August. A gala street fair during which communal activity in Trastevere, plus its residents' highly developed tendencies toward salesmanship and musicianship, are at their peak. Goes on all day and well into the night. There are singers and musicians thumping out traditional and popular favorites (in Rome these are often one and the same) from portable stages in the piazzas, with dub mix provided by the amateur aria singers on the sidewalks, amateur marksmen in the shooting galleries, and the cheerful din of the crowd. Meanwhile, retail commerce runs riot in the street, all local products from cotton candy to wicker sofas plus Africans peddling their masks and art students their nudes and neo-Expressionist shockers.

Getting Around

• **Addresses:** Merely knowing the street and the street number of, say, a restaurant is often insufficient, and it's generally helpful to have the name of an adjacent street or piazza as well, since (a) buildings on a single street are not always numbered consecutively, so that No. 40 is often to be found between No. 28 and No. 13, (b) even the shortest, straightest, most unassuming of streets may be arbitrarily divided into several different segments (each of them bearing a different name), and (c) in spite of numerous bends and puckers and right-angled turns, the same street may cling perversely to its original name. No matter what, the *stradario della città* (street index) in the *pagine gialle* (yellow pages of the telephone book) will always be able to help you out.

• **Buses:** Not too comfortable (especially at 6 P.M.) but very practical. Bus routes on the maps are none too legible, but the buses themselves are cheap and turn up punctually and frequently. Tickets can be bought at newsstands and from ticket machines. There's also a 3-day *Roma Pass* for tourists and (as of 1984) a deluxe version that includes free admission to all city museums (available at the ticket booth in the Termini/piazza de Cinquecento subway station). A monthly pass *(Tessera)* costs the same as 60 bus tickets (which is also, coincidentally enough, the amount of the fine you pay if you're caught riding the bus without a ticket); ask for them at the tobacco shop.

Bus and subway maps are a very sound investment and are especially useful for getting around the suburbs; both are available at the ATAC information booth, piazza de Cinquecento. English-speaking personnel are in attendance. Updated transit information is posted at the kiosks at the end of every bus line and is also available by calling 46-95. Finally, note that bus lines designated by an asterisk have limited service after midnight (about every half hour) and backpacks do not ride for free; they have to buy tickets (full fare) just like everybody else. A list of selected bus routes follows:

No. 64: the Vatican, piazza Venezia, Termini

No. 118: from the Colosseum to the Catacombs

No. 93: from the Termini to the Baths of Caracalla

No. 75: from the Termini to Gianicolo

No. 910: Termini to the Villa Borghese

No. 32: from the youth hostel to the Vatican.

You can traverse vast distances for a very small sum; 2 lines are especially noteworthy in this respect: *No. 64* (Termini–St. Peter's) and *No. 85* (piazza Silvestro–San Giovanni in Laterano). Trains *No. 29* and *No. 30* make interesting citywide sweeps as well.

• **Subways:** A very convenient way of getting out to Ostia Antica, Lido di Roma, and San Paolo Fuori le Mura, the Esposizione Universale, and so forth. There are now 2 subway lines. The original, now called line B, stops at Stazione Termini–Cavour–Colosseo–Circo Massimo–Piramide Cestia–Basilica di San Paolo–Magliana–Esposizione (west)–Esposizione (east)–Laurentina. The newer and more extensive line A stops at the same stops (through San Paolo), then Lido Centro–Lido Stella Polare–Lido Castel Fusano–Lido Cristoforo Colombo. And there you have it.

• **Scooters:** A very pleasant and totally authentic way of getting around the city. To rent one, you need a valid driver's license and, generally, a deposit, unless you're paying by credit card. It's a bit expensive, but don't forget that there's room enough for 2. Here are 2 rental agencies:

Scooter Rental: Via Cavour, 302. Telephone 67-80-206.

Scooter For Rent: Via della Purificazione, 66. Telephone 46-54-85.

• **Cars:** Driving around in a rented car might make sense in some of the more sparsely settled parts of Italy but definitely not in Rome. Traffic moves either too fast or not at all, and the slower it moves, the more noise it makes. Permanent hazards include torn-up pavement, burnt-out traffic lights, and other drivers. It's interesting that the stress of ordinary driving, the constant yelling and gesticulating and leaning on the horn, is so unbearable that when an accident occurs, it seems to come as a great relief to the Roman driver—on whom the sight of a red light or a pedestrian crosswalk normally has the same effect as a one-way street on an American teenager, who considers it a contradiction in terms. Finally, Rome has a highly specialized criminal element, some of whom specialize in tires and trim, some in radios and interiors, others in trunks and their contents; when they're all through, somebody else steals the car.

• **Taxis:** Pick one that has a meter and then, at journey's end, unless you're a party of 4 or more with lots of luggage and it's after 7 P.M. on a holiday, we'd still advise you to bargain rather than pay the grossly inflated fare that shows up on the meter. There's not much point in calling a cab (on the telephone, that is); turn instead to the city bus map in the yellow pages. It's bound to be much quicker that way.

The Sights

You may feel stupid looking up the Colosseum or the Circus Maximus in the Rome phone book, but we'd advise you to do so all the same. The invaluable *annuario* lists all the principal monuments, museums, and so forth (along with the numbers of the buses that stop nearby), their telephone numbers, and opening hours. We'd also suggest you call the one in order to verify that the other is still current since, as mentioned earlier, Italian museum schedules, like Italian currency, seem to be highly unstable. You'll feel even stupider if you miss out on the Museo Borghese because you get there after 2 o'clock (closing time). Note that most museums and national monuments (excluding those of the Vatican) are closed on Monday and *free* on Sunday morning.

• Ancient Rome

Forum and *Palatine Hill:* A quasi-sacred site containing a sizable fraction of the surviving temples, palaces, and public monuments of republican and imperial Rome. The admission is fairly steep; it's a must-see, of course, but the radically cheap and the ahistorical may prefer just to look through the bars. Closed on Tuesday. Some visitors may have problems with the haphazard way that things have been excavated or restored, but this just seems like a quibble; taking it all together, the Romans seem to be the ideal custodians of their great architectural heritage, striking the perfect balance between culpable negligence (the Egyptians) and well-intentioned vandalism (the Parisians).

Colosseum: From Termini, take the subway to Colosseo station. The outer shell is ornamented with 3 tiers of columns (starting with Doric at the bottom, Ionic in the middle, and Corinthian at the top). Its original seating capacity was 50,000, and the spectators' seats were shaded by a gigantic silken awning. Specialized in gladiatorial combats, of course (but no Christian martyrs or other nonprofessionals), and sometimes the arena was flooded to become the scene of highly realistic naval battles, during which the normal house practice of sudden-death overtime was generally invoked. While we're on the subject, perhaps it's worth noting that when Caesar turned thumbs *down,* that actually meant the vanquished gladiator was off the hook; it was only when Caesar jerked his thumb toward his chest, in the manner of the late Edward G. Robinson, that the loser was cut from the squad. Open from 9 to 5 (except Sunday).

From the Colosseum, head down via dei Fori Imperiali. On the left, take note of the large-scale wall maps indicating the impressive extent of the Roman Empire at its apogee.

Catacombs of San Callisto: Take a No. 118 bus from the Colosseum; the bus takes you right along via Appia Antica (Appian Way), which nowadays is just a street like any other. The catacombs are an intricate system of tunnels and grottoes, excavated by the early Christians as a burial place (grudgingly tolerated by the Roman authorities as such), a clandestine place of worship, and a refuge from persecution. These particular catacombs are perhaps the most famous since a number of the early popes were originally buried here. Closed on Wednesday, making this a bad time to visit the other catacombs, which get pretty crowded.

Interested parties will also want to check out the frescoes in the *catacombs of Priscilla.* Closed on Monday.

Catacombs of San Sebastiano: Via Appia Antica, 132. Not bad, but the guided tour is compulsory. Closed on Thursday.

Baths of Caracalla: Get back on the No. 118 bus at the Catacombs of San Callisto, or take a No. 93 from Termini. In their day these baths could accommodate some 1,600 bathers, with maybe a little pushing and shoving. The main impression its ruins convey today is one of absolutely overwhelming size; pretty astounding all the same. Open from 9 to 4; from 9 to 1 on Monday. Makes an especially impressive backdrop for the operas that are performed here during the summer. Great stuff. For info contact *Teatro della Opera,* piazza Beniamino Gigli, 1. Telephone 46-17-55.

Pantheon: Piazza della Rotonda. Dedicated as a temple to "all the gods," one of Rome's most remarkable and best preserved ancient monuments. Its most striking feature is the gigantic eggshell dome, pierced by a tiny skylight at the top. The atmosphere of the interior seems fittingly pantheistic and a bit spooky to boot. Another point of interest: Since the roof of the colonnaded vestibule is still intact, it allows us to visualize what a number of its ancient prototypes, notably the Parthenon, must have looked like when they were in their prime. Closed on Monday.

• Monuments

Il Vittoriale: An extremely ugly memorial to King Vittorio Emanuele II, known by a variety of derisive nicknames. Bears a remarkable resemblance to an old-fashioned standup manual typewriter, c. 1930 vintage (probably an Olivetti). The balcony from which Il Duce used to harangue the adoring mobs is attached to the Pallazzo Venezia, in the piazza in front of the memorial.

Campidoglio: Capitoline Hill, right behind the great big typewriter. (A spectacular piazza designed by Michelangelo, who also designed or overhauled a couple of the adjacent buildings). The piazza's trapezoidal shape enhances the effect of perspective and makes this elegant expanse seem even more expansive than it is. The entrance to the piazza is flanked by 2 very fine statues.

Palazzo Farnese: Piazza Farnese. One of Rome's most attractive palazzi, currently occupied by the French embassy. (The French government pays a rental of 1 lira per year, in spite of the fact that there's no such thing as just 1 lira.) The interior not open to the public since they're still a little nervous about terrorists.

Castel Sant'Angelo: On the Tiber, near the Vatican. Originally "Hadrian's Mole," a mausoleum built (A.D. 139) for the emperor Hadrian and his successors (so-called because Hadrian had amused the clean-shaven Romans by growing a beard to cover up an unsightly mole on his cheek). Later a papal fortress. It now contains a military museum featuring artifacts of the Stone Age to the Renaissance. Open from 9 to 1. Closed on Monday.

• *Churches*

Herewith a very subjective list of favorites just to get you started:

Santa Maria in Trastevere: Piazza Santa Maria. Said to be the oldest church in Rome (though not in its present form) and still one of the prettiest. Situated on a very handsome piazza.

Santa Maria in Cosmedin: Piazza Bocca della Verità, also in Trastevere. Noted for its campanile and the "Mouth of Truth" underneath the porch, a great circular slab of marble (actually a kind of classical manhole cover) carved in the shape of a grotesque, open-mouthed face, which is said to clamp down on the fingers of any liar so imprudent as to poke them in there. Across the street, a couple of Roman temples, including an interesting round one and the admirably well preserved *Temple of Fortunus.*

San Luigi dei Francesi: On the piazza of the same name. Noted for its 3 Caravaggios (in the fifth side chapel from the entrance on the left-hand side of the nave). Caravaggio, recently called "the first of the moderns" by Frank Stella, was a brawler and a murderer who lived for a time on the immoral earnings of his girlfriends. He was also the forerunner of today's photorealist school, in that he invented a system (involving a studio with black walls and a set of movable shutters) that enabled him to trace an image of his model directly on the canvas. Today his works emerge from the darkness when you plunk down a 100-lira piece for the overhead lights.

Santa Maria Maggiore: Piazza Santa Maria Maggiore, near Termini. Remarkable mosaics in the nave.

San Pietro in Vincoli: Near the preceding, at the end of via Cavour. Famed as the abode of Michelangelo's *Moses,* a father figure of such commanding strength and presence that he brought about the suicide of one of Michelangelo's contemporaries, who had rashly attempted his own Moses in piazza San Bernardo. It was later psychoanalyzed by Freud.

Il Gesù: Piazza Sant'Ignazio. Tremendous frescoes, the embodiment of seventeenth-century Jesuit militancy; the trompe-l'oeil effect of the frescoes in the vault is especially amazing.

• *Human Interest*

Capuchin Crypt: Beneath Santa Maria della Concezione, via Vittorio Veneto, 27. The earthly remains of some 4,000 departed brothers, tastefully distributed among 5 subterranean chapels. Intended to teach us that life is but a walking shadow. It now has something of the same atmosphere as a haunted-mansion amusement park. Not unimpressive, all the same. Open from 9 to 12 and from 3 to 7 (6 in the winter). Free admission, but you can still leave a little something in the offering box.

Via Vittorio Veneto itself is Rome's most famous street, a combination of upper Fifth Avenue and Sunset Strip (to put it crudely). However, most of the *dolce vita* that Marcello Mastroianni found here in the late 50s has long since been quarried out; in addition, at around the time of the Aldo Moro killing and the heyday of the Red

Brigades, the curtain times of the theaters in Rome were pushed forward so people could get home a little earlier, a not unreasonable desire in an era when even the humblest of functionaries and the most junior of executives were routinely becoming the targets of kidnappers and kneecappers. Though it's still very pleasant to stroll through the piazzas in the moonlight (perhaps in search of Marcello and/or Giulietta Masina), you'll find that at night many of them, excluding the ones that have been colonized by tourists, now display no more signs of animation than the Capuchin Crypt.

• *The* Piazze

Drop around a few hours earlier, say around 5 P.M., and you'll find about as much animation as you'd care to see in the more popular piazze; in good weather, the tables of the outdoor cafés are preempted with typically good-natured Roman ruthlessness. Jokes and greetings are shouted from table to table, people settle back to watch the traffic, and tourists go by and enjoy the pleasures of *dolce far niente,* far less strenuous and ultimately more rewarding than *la dolce vita.*

To the tourist, nose in guidebook, back bent beneath a weight of a cabinet minister's ransom in photographic equipment, except for certain architectural peculiarities, all these piazzas may seem basically the same. Not so. All of them have their regulars, distributed according to a subtle demographic code (based on age, political opinions, and basic social orientation) among the various *piazze.* A basic breakdown follows:

Campo dei Fiori: A big favorite with backpackers and other youthful foreigners, plus indigenous Roman weirdos. Sometimes has a nostalgic sort of summer-camp atmosphere (sitting around a bonfire while somebody strums a guitar). Also frequented (especially after 10 P.M.) by loose-joint peddlers, narcs, junkies, and highly proficient motorized bag-snatchers (mounted on Vespas).

Piazza Navona: Leftish in orientation politically and somewhat less marginal socially than Campo dei Fiori. One of Rome's prettiest *piazze,* in fact, with lots of outdoor cafés filled with young couples out for their evening *passeggiata.* The story is that the Church of *Sant'Agnese* is built on the site of a famous brothel where the fourth-century virgin martyr St. Agnes had her miraculous escape. After she rashly defied her parents by refusing to marry the nice young man they had picked for her, she was exposed (quite literally) at auction in the brothel. Suddenly, miraculously, her hair began to grow until it completely concealed her nudity, and all bids were off. That time she got away with it, but she was martyred later on during the infamous persecutions of Diocletian.

The piazza itself occupies the site and still preserves the outlines of a Roman arena, and it contains no fewer than 3 Bernini fountains, of which the middle one, the *Fountain of the Four Rivers,* is the most spectacular. The figures represent the 4 great rivers known to seventeenth-century geographers: the Danube, the Ganges, the Plata, and the Nile (whose face is veiled because its source had still not been discovered). You'll note that all 4 rivers have their arms raised in a pantomime of horror and loathing, which appears to be directed toward the façade of Sant'Agnese. The latter was designed by Bernini's chief competitor, Borromini. Borromini had his revenge by adding a statue of St. Agnes to the pinnacle of the church's façade; the statue's face is pointedly averted, seemingly more in sorrow than in anger, from the sight of Bernini's colossal fountain.

Fontana di Trevi: An eighteenth-century extravaganza made famous by Perry Como, Connie Frances, and other interpreters of that 50s jukebox favorite, "Three Coins in the Fountain." This is the world's most ingenious spare-change racket; the coins are harvested by neighborhood kids after dark. So-called because it was located at the confluence of 3 different streets, though irresponsible persons may tell you stories about another pious virgin by the name of Trevi who was saved from defilement by licentious Roman soldiers when a spring suddenly, miraculously gushed out of the ground at this very spot. (True or not, the plot was later lifted by Ingmar Bergman for one of his early films.)

Piazza Santa Maria in Trastevere: Leftish, but not really very political. Frequented by well-heeled weirdos, fashionable dabblers, and Americans (who have driven the rents in the neighborhood sky-high). Still a pretty nice piazza, though. For the church, see above.

Piazza della Rotonda: In front of the Pantheon. Site of numerous demonstrations. Frequented by students and left- and ultraleft ideologues.

Piazza di Spagna and the Spanish Steps: Very beautiful, very touristy. Lots of young folks, a surprising number of them sitting on the steps having their portraits drawn in charcoal. Much of the Romans' reputation as persistent and incorrigible hasslers of foreign women (especially blond ones) was garnered on this very spot.

Piazza del Popolo, piazza delle Muse, piazza Bologna: All hangouts of the extreme right, frequented by intense young men in pointed shoes, tight black jeans, leather jackets or black raincoats (black shirts, however, not being much in evidence), and Ray-Ban wraparounds (as worn by the creepy blond assassin in the film *Diva*). They speak in the warmest possible terms of Benito Mussolini and occasionally greet one another with the straight-armed, open-palmed "Roman" salute (so that some people have referred to them as Neo-Fascists).

• *Museums*

Museo Borghese: Villa Borghese (park). The basis of the collection was assembled by Pope Paul V and his nephew, Cardinal Scipione Borghese, during the seventeenth century. A later Borghese married Pauline Bonaparte, Napoleon's sister, and was obliged to sell off a great many paintings to help pay for his brother-in-law's campaigns. Some of the Borgheses preferred classical, others contemporary (that is, Baroque and Rococo), so that there's plenty of both in the current collection. Highlights include Bernini's *David* (gallery 2) and his sci-fi *Apollo and Daphne* (gallery 3), depicting the initial moments of Daphne's metamorphosis into a tree, plus a number of Caravaggio's incredible ventures into the field of warts-and-all realism (gallery 14). Open only from 9 to 2. Note: As of November 1985 the museum has been closed for renovations. Check with the Ente Provinciale per il Turismo (EPT), telephone 47-50-078 before going.

Galleria Nazionale d'Arte Moderna: Via delle Belle Arti, 131, across the park from the Borghese. Nineteenth- and twentieth-century Italian painters and a number of distinguished foreigners (Klimt, Degas, Malevich, Henry Moore, Jackson Pollock). Lots of outrageous stuff by nineteenth-century admirers of Bougereau and the flossier academic painters. Lots of good (if not great) stuff by the Futurists and other modern artists not very well known outside Italy.

Galleria Nazionale d'Arte Antica: Palazzo Corsini, via della Lungara, 10. All the greats, from the twelfth to the sixteenth centuries: Simone Martini, Fra Angelico, Raphael, Titian, Caravaggio. Be sure to visit their other fine location in the Palazzo Barberini, via delle Quattro Fontane.

Musei Capitolini: Piazza del Campidoglio. Extensive collection of antiquities and Renaissance masters housed in 2 adjoining palazzi. Highlights include the famous bronze Etruscan she-wolf (fifth century BC) that has become the emblem of Rome (with figures of the infant Romulus and Remus dubbed in during the Renaissance), the *Dying Gaul,* a number of other famous statues from antiquity, and the dove mosaics from Hadrian's Villa. Open from 9 to 2. Closed on Monday.

Musical Instrument Collection: Piazza Santa Croce, 19A. An interesting assemblage of over 800 historic instruments. Closed on Monday.

• Parks and Villas

Peaceful green oases that furnish a convenient refuge from Roman traffic and the rigors of the traveling life. We especially recommend the *Villa Pamphili,* in the western part of the Trastevere, which is practically deserted. It is filled with luxuriant vegetation and a couple of crumbling little palazzi that take on a remarkable series of colors at sunset, from russet brown to golden ochre.

Movies

Not to be missed. Continuous showings of top-quality films, Italian and foreign, classic to avant-garde, on giant screens (20 × 30m) set up in the ruined Basilica di Massenzio, right next to the Colosseum. Starts at 8:30 P.M. and lasts until 4 A.M. For schedules, watch for the heading "Massenzioland" in the movie listings of the papers. It's an amazing spectacle, attended religiously by Rome's substantial community of would-be actors and directors and the public at large as well; we know some people who would give their left foot to see the uncut wide-screen original version of Abel Gance's *Napoleon* in these majestic surroundings.

The gigantic moviemaking complex *Cinecittà,* created by Mussolini and immortalized by Fellini, is right outside town but unfortunately off-limits to the general public, unless you want to engage in the time-honored Roman scroungers' occupation of trying to get work as an extra.

From the standpoint of the consumer, first-run films are quite expensive (third- or fourth-run perennials cost only a fraction as much) and are almost invariably shown with a dubbed Italian soundtrack. There are plenty of air-conditioned theaters, but since tickets are sold on the basis of the number of customers instead of the number of seats available, you may end up standing or sitting in the aisles. Check the listings in *Paese Sera* or *Settimana Romana.*

Pasquinio, vicolo del Piede, 19, in Trastevere, is about the only theater in town that shows foreign films with their original, undubbed soundtracks intact. It also has a sliding roof in lieu of air-conditioning. Well worth your patronage on both accounts. The prices are considerably reduced for non-first-run films.

For a total cinematic experience, we recommend checking out a popular Italian film (preferably something with a high anxiety level and lots of tragic relief, on the order of *Ben-Hur*) in a fleabag neighborhood theater. You may find miniature soccer riots in the ticket line, lots of snuffling and honking during the sad parts which can be highly infectious, and the wrath of Michelangelo's *Moses* unleashed and multiplied several hundredfold when the projector breaks down.

For a somewhat more rigorous approach, you can join the heavy-duty fans at *Filmstudio 1,* via Orti d'Albert. Telephone 654-04-64. Basic film-society repertory followed by discussion, analysis, and hanging out.

For the more politically oriented, try *Uscita,* via dei Banchi Vecchi, 45. Telephone 652-277.

VATICAN CITY

St. Peter's, Cradle of Lutheranism

Around 1515, the papacy, with the old basilica of St. Peter's falling down around its ears, decided to build a much bigger and better one. To finance the project, they also decided on a massive sale of indulgences, offering the purchaser or a departed relative time off from Purgatory in return for a cash payment; in the latter case, the indulgence seller would ring a little bell to signify that the loved one's soul had just ascended into Heaven. A young theology instructor at the University of Wittenberg, Martin Luther, objected very strongly to this practice and to a great many others. Luther was excommunicated from the Catholic Church and went off to become a Lutheran. The new basilica was not completed, what with one thing and another, for another 100 years. Take a look around inside and see if you think it was worth it, bearing in mind that the ecclesiastical dress code is strictly enforced at the door: No shorts for men *or* women, and no sleeveless dresses or skirts above the knee.

The Sights

The present boundaries of the Vatican city-state were fixed by the Lateran Treaty of 1929. The Vatican is administered by its own governor; it coins its own money and issues its own stamps. It has its own press and radio station (with occasional broadcasts in Latin), its own railroad station, its own court and electrical systems and, most conspicuously, its own armed forces, the Swiss Guards, who still wear the elegant blue-and-orange-slashed doublets designed by Michelangelo along with their shiny steel helmets and breastplates.

Piazza San Pietro: At noon on Sunday, the Pope blesses the crowds in the piazza and says a few words. Between the obelisk and each of the fountains, you'll find a disk on the pavement that marks the spot where the 3 rows of columns at the edge of the piazza appear to resolve into one. (Bernini again.)

St. Peter's: Not a cathedral, which makes it the world's largest basilica, with more than twice the square footage of Notre Dame.

Michelangelo was only 25 when he finished his incredible *Pietà,* which you'll see on your right once you get past the bouncers at the door; it is now shielded by a sheet of bullet-proof glass from future lunatic attacks. Inside you'll find the apostolic throne and pulpit, the elaborate *baldacchino* (altar canopy) designed by Bernini, and a statue of St. Peter that adorned the older basilica, his one foot considerably eroded by the lips of adoring pilgrims, and an extra-heavy-duty bronze halo above his head. Right by St. Peter is the entrance to the *crypt,* which is interesting and contains the tomb of St. Peter himself and a number of early popes. The basilica is open from 7 A.M. to 7 P.M. (5:30 in the winter).

The *treasury* (open from 9 to 4) is best for fans of gold-embroidered vestments, gem-encrusted liturgical vessels, and the like. There is one especially nice piece, said to be *Charlemagne's dalmatic.* Back in the nave of the basilica you'll notice a circular slab of porphyry set into the floor to mark the spot where Charlemagne was crowned Emperor of the Romans by Pope Leo III on New Year's Eve of the year 800.

Take the elevator up to the *cupola* (also the work of Michelangelo) for an impressively vertiginous view of the interior of the basilica and the entire city besides. When you get back down, ask about the free guided tour (to the right, under the portico), which sets out once every day.

Vatican Museum: An awesome assemblage of 11 museums, 5 different galleries, 1,400 rooms in all (including the Sistine Chapel, Raphael's *School of Athens,* and numerous other frescoes and painting by the greatest masters of the Renaissance). Some may object that the great treasures of the Vatican were acquired by making poor folks pay an exorbitant price for their small spiritual comforts; on the other hand, few if any were acquired by pillage and conquest, as is notoriously the case with the Louvre and the British Museum, or by making poor folks pay an exorbitant price for their small material comforts, as with most of the great collections of North America. The thing we mostly object to is that admission to the Vatican collections costs more than any other museum in Rome (50 percent discount for students, however). The museum is open from 9 to 4 (until 1 in the winter). Closed on the first 3 Sundays in every month; free admission on the 4th. Closed on religious holidays. Flash photography is permitted in the galleries.

The problem is that if you start out with the mummies and sarcophagi in the Egyptian Museum and work your way doggedly through the other collections, you'll arrive at the end of the line, the public galleries of the *Vatican Library,* hollow-eyed, weak-kneed and haggard—hardly in a fit state to appreciate the world's most astounding collection of illuminated Gospels and manuscripts. Our advice is to avoid gallery burnout by seeing the Vatican collections on 2 different days (at least). Also, since there aren't many cheap places to eat in the papal state, we'd advise you to pack a lunch.

The Outskirts of Rome

• *Ostia*

A bustling seaport in imperial times, left stranded 6 miles from the present coastline by the silting up of its harbor (plus something else

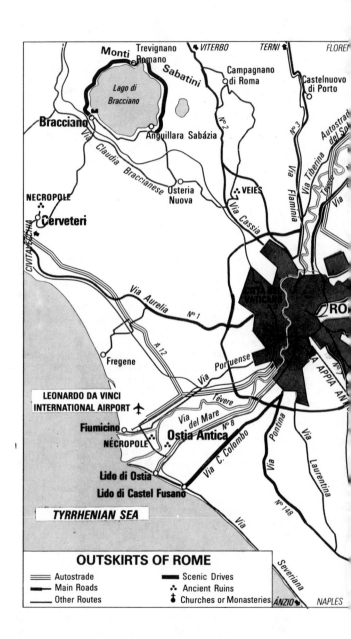

OUTSKIRTS OF ROME

Autostrade
Main Roads
Other Routes
Scenic Drives
Ancient Ruins
Churches or Monasteries

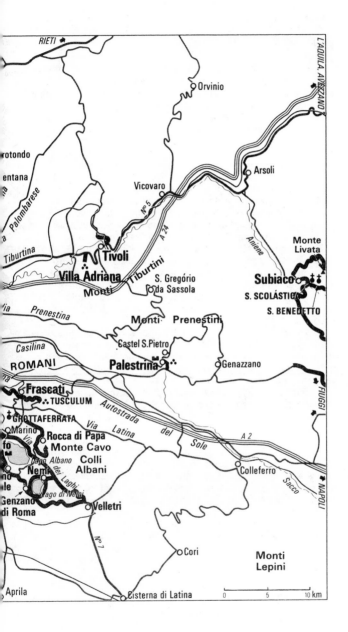

to do with the polar icecaps that we're not exactly prepared to go into right now). Its extensive ruins are interesting, ideal for historically-minded persons of the if-these-mute-stones-could-only-speak persuasion. Take the subway from Termini to Ostia Antica. Don't go on a weekend, when the human backwash from the nearby beaches at Lido di Roma is considerable.

• *Tivoli*

Catch an ACOTRAL bus on via Gaeta, near piazza della Repubblica. The fare is very reasonable, so it doesn't make much sense to hitch. Tivoli market is held every Wednesday morning. It's easiest to start with the Villa d'Este, then take bus No. 2 or 4 to Hadrian's Villa (which is closed on Monday).

Villa d'Este: The villa itself, a Benedictine abbey redone to suit the tastes of a wealthy Renaissance cardinal, doesn't have much going for it except a number of flaked and peeling frescoes. The real attraction is the fountains and artificial geysers, 500 of them in all, strewn all over the parks and alleyways of the estate. The most spectacular is the Organ Fountain, the spot chosen by the Abbé Liszt for his belated ordination as a Catholic priest. The fountains have also inspired musical works by Ravel and Respighi, and even a grudging testimonial from that crotchetiest and most reluctant of tourists, Michel de Montaigne. The admission cost is a bit steep.

For lunch we suggest you try the *Sibilla* restaurant, above the nearby Villa Gregoriana. Its terrace surrounds a superb Roman rotunda, and it directly overlooks a waterfall, of which there are several in the adjacent park. The place specializes in cannelloni and isn't all that expensive, considering. The setting is unforgettable. Check out the guest book's testimonials from visiting monarchs and other satisfied customers.

Hadrian's Villa (Villa Adriana): Hadrian was a notably restless emperor who presided over the empire at its greatest territorial extent. He traveled extensively in Greece, Egypt, and Asia Minor, and retired to this villa after his main squeeze, a beautiful youth called Antinous, was drowned while swimming in the Nile. The architecture is predictably eclectic and includes several replicas of famous monuments of antiquity, notably the *Canapo,* a sacred pool surrounded by a colonnade interspersed with statuary and dedicated to Canopis, the Egyptian god of healing. Its waters were thought to have curative properties, and follow-up care was provided by temple harlots (an ancient Roman's idea of holistic medicine). The perfect proportions of the colonnade surrounding the *Villa d'Isola* contrast very nicely with the slightly scruffy country landscape that surrounds it; the baths *(thermae)* are, as usual, mostly remarkable for their bulk plus the audacious engineering of the vaults that supported the roof. A beautiful spot, an absolute must-see.

Castelli Romani: A couple of little hilltop towns about 20 miles southeast of Rome (see map), each with a famous vista from the top and vineyards along the slopes below. It's an easy hitch (in conjunction with bus No. 515, 551, 561, or 612), but not nearly as interesting as either of the excursions listed above.

Hitching Out of Rome

Toward Florence: Take bus No. 201, 202, 203, or 204 out to via Flaminia Nuova. Get off at the intersection and start hitching on the lengthy access road to the *autostrada* or walk a few kilometers further on to the highway entrance.

Toward Naples: Take a bus out to Tiburtino, then a No. 209, which lets you off at the southbound Raccordo Annulare (ring road), not far from the on-ramp for the *Autostrada del Sole.*

BOMARZO

About 60 miles north of Rome, between Orte and Viterbo (accessible by train and bus). This village is renowned for its *Park of the Monsters,* a bizarre sculpture garden created from the living rock of a nearby estate at the behest of the late sixteenth-century Count Orsini (about whom we know nothing other than what can be deduced from the bizarre sculptural phantasmagoria that is his legacy—sort of a "Scenes We'd Like to See" version of Bernini). As you stroll through the valley of Bomarzo, you'll come across all sorts of outsize sculptural oddities: nymphs and dragons (presumably life size), odd composite animals, an enormous tortoise, a giant lifting up another giant by the legs, an elephant crushing a Roman soldier in his trunk, a Pegasus emerging like Venus from a fountain, a trio of triple-tailed sirens, and (the one that always makes it into the coffee-table books) the mouth of a grotto transformed into a yawning, all-devouring hellmouth.

Some of the figures are erotic, some are comical, most are merely puzzling and strange. Scholars are still uncertain about precisely what Count Orsini thought he was up to—whether he was trying to make some sort of private metaphysical statement (perhaps a Borges-like attempt to express the infinite mystery of the universe in terms of his own twisted personal mythology) or simply felt a natural artistic urge to give form and completion to the fantastic creatures he saw struggling to liberate themselves from the weathered volcanic rocks that littered his estate (something like the Surrealist compositions traced by Max Ernst from the random textures of lavatory tiles). At any rate, it all makes an interesting excursion for lovers of Surrealism, Mannerism, and all-around weirdness.

TUSCANY AND THE RIVIERA

SIENA

Siena excels in the production of chianti, mushrooms, and *panforte nero* (a famous pastry containing nuts, honey, and almonds) but owes its current prosperity to an import rather than an export (namely, tourists). Nevertheless, the *panforte* and the mushrooms are very much in evidence, and the chianti-tasting goes down at the Enoteca in the cellars of the *Medici Castle* outside town. The city itself is very, very beautiful; it has its own colors (burnt sienna and raw sienna among them) and its own atmosphere—a very soft and pleasant one, in keeping with the gentle slopes and curves of the 3 hills on which the city was built. Everything seems to converge on *piazza del Campo,* shaped like a seashell or a beckoning open hand —a harmonious effect that was achieved not by luck or instinct but by statute (a whole series of strict city-planning regulations, first adopted in the thirteenth century).

Like Florence, Siena was a city of merchants and bankers, many engaged in the high-risk, high-return occupation of providing financial backing for the Renaissance popes. The warm pinkish brick of their town houses and churches is uniformly appealing, and it's probably going a little too far to suggest that there's something of the taste of a cultured, intelligent banker to be found in the richness, the cautiousness, and the complacency of the Sienese school of painting. Modern Siena, no longer a banking center, is expensive (as much as Venice), but it's still one of our favorites.

The Palio

One of the world's most famous horse races, which gives the people of Siena a very good excuse to re-create some of the pageantry of yesteryear, more important, to give free reign to their individual and collective personalities. The city is divided into 3 *terzi* by its 3 main streets and further subdivided into 17 different neighborhoods, or *contrade.* Each *contrada* has its own church, its own piazza, its own colors, and its heraldic animal mascot from which it takes its name—there's the She-Wolf, of course, as well as the Dolphin, the Screech Owl, the Goose, and so forth. Of the 17 *contrade,* 10 are selected by lot to prepare an entrant for the Palio, which takes place twice a year (on July 2 and August 16) and is preceded in each case by a massive display of *contrada* colors and of virtuoso Renaissance-style baton twirling on the part of the heralds.

The race around the piazza lasts for only about a minute and a half. The jockeys *(fantini)* ride bareback, and the ordinary rules of the turf are not very scrupulously observed. Fistfights among the fans break out frequently enough to suggest that this is not just another Renaissance costume spectacular put on for the benefit of tourists, who are very much in evidence all the same. It's best to get to the piazza pretty early. The evening's victory revels are not confined to the winning *contrada* by any means, and the neighborhood *feste* of the other 16 *contrade* are providentially and pretty much evenly distributed throughout the rest of the year.

Useful Addresses

Tourist Office: Piazza del Campo, 55. Telephone 28-05-51. Open from 9 to 12:30 and from 3:30 to 7:15, but they're no help finding a hotel room (see below, Where to Sleep).

Baggage Check: In the train station. To get to the center of town, take bus No. 9 or 10 to piazza Matteoti. Buy a ticket in the station.

Bus Station: Piazza San Domenico.

Post Office: Piazza Matteotti. Open Monday to Friday from 8:15 to 7:30 and on Saturday from 8:15 to 1.

Emergency Medical Assistance: Via Pian d'Olive, 13. Open every day from 8 to 8.

Where to Sleep

In the summer there's a serious shortage of empty beds. Make inquiries at the *Guide Turistico Autorizzate,* across from the Basilica San Domenico (C2 on map), between the hours of 9 and 1, 4 and 7:30 (but just 9:30 to 12:30 on Sunday). They may be able to fix you up with something.

Ostello per la Gioventu: Via Fiorentina, 17. Telephone (05-77) 522-12. More than a mile north of the city center. Take a No. 15 bus from the station (a No. 3 on Sunday). If you're coming by bus from Florence, get off right after the Esso station. Run by the city, but an international hostel card is still required. A well-run, well-equipped hostel in a modern building, one of the nicest in the country. Doubles or triples (with sink). Cafeteria on premises. Closed between 9 A.M. and 5:30 P.M. Doors close at 11:30 P.M.

• *Pensioni near the Piazza del Campo*

If you end up making the rounds, the following itinerary may save you some time:

Locanda Garibaldi: Via Giovanni Dupré, 18. Telephone 284-204. A restaurant on the ground floor. Nothing special, apart from its great location, due south of the piazza. It's the cheapest place in town, and not too bad in other respects.

Albergo Nuovo Donzelle: Via Donzelle, 3. Telephone 288-088. On a narrow street, near the northeastern edge of the piazza. Showers are included. Well maintained. A little more expensive than the Garibaldi.

Tre Donzelle: Right next door. Same basic deal. A little more expensive. No funny business is implicit in the name (The 3 Wenches).

Albergo Centrale: Via Calzoleria, 24. Telephone 280-379. Attractive doorway, in a street right near the preceding 2. Same basic price range. Very clean.

La Perla: Via delle Terme, 25. Telephone 471-44. Right by the piazza (northwest). More expensive than the others. The entry hall is newly redone. Most of the rooms overlook a pretty piazza (Indipendenza).

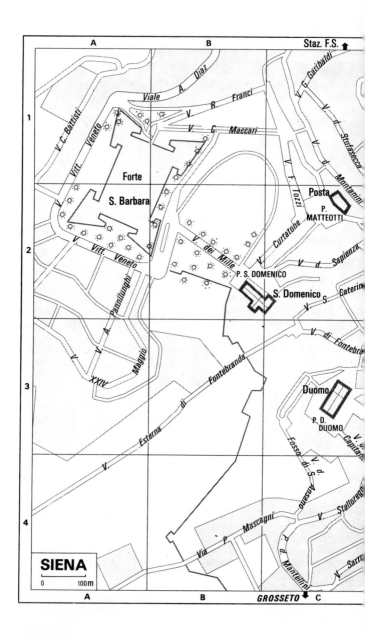

SIENA

0   100 m

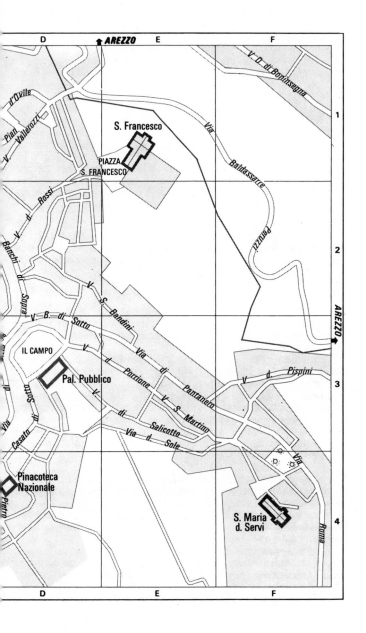

• *Upscale*

Albergo Chiusarelli: Via Curtatone, 11 (C2 on map). Telephone 28-05-62. Right by piazza San Domenico. An enormous 19th-century villa with florid visage, columns, and hardworking caryatids, and a garden inside. Not as expensive as it looks.

Casa del Pellegrino: Via Camporegio, 31, right by San Domenico. Telephone 441-77. An old-time pilgrims' inn; married couples are allowed, but not the other kind. Run by a very charming group of nuns. Most of the rooms have balconies with a splendid view of the old city. Less expensive than the Chiusarelli.

Albergo la Toscana: Via Cecco Angioleri, 12. Telephone 460-97. By the north end of the piazza del Campo. An old medieval building whose interior is not as picturesque as the facade but very nice all the same.

Palazzo Revizza: Pian dei Mantellini (C4 on map). Telephone 28-04-62. A seventeenth-century town house that has belonged to the same family for the past 200 years. Unassuming exterior; the dark panelling of the entry hall makes it seem more like a private house than a hotel. Antique furniture may be found in some of the rooms. Piano. Half-pension (breakfast and lunch included).

• *Campground*

Camping Colleverde: Strada Scaciapensieri, 37. Telephone 280-044. About 2 miles north of the city center. Take a No. 8 bus from piazza Matteotti. Delightful setting. Facilities in good order. Slight extra charge for the use of the swimming pool.

Where to Eat, Where to Drink

Cuisine is basic Tuscan (somewhat more refined than that of Florence). Uses lots of herbs, and mushrooms are all the rage—hence, *pizza ai funghi*. Spaghetti is often coated with oil and served with little peppers called *peperencini,* which are pretty hot. You should have no problem whatsoever with *tortellini all panna* (tortellini with cream). Oven-fresh *panforte (al forno)* at the bakery, apart from tasting better, costs about a third less than in a pastry place. The market square *(piazza del Mercato)* is right down from the piazzo del Campo. A good place to go food shopping in the morning.

Mensa Universitaria: Via Sant'Agata, 1, not far from the Church of Sant'Agata. A vast, efficient, air-conditioned cafeteria. Open to all with a valid student ID, from 12 to 2 and from 7 to 9:30. Closed on Saturday P.M. and all day Sunday.

Most of the restaurants on piazza del Campo are ludicrously expensive, with the following 2 exceptions, which should enable you to dine at least in the vicinity of the quality folks:

Rosticceria la Mossa: Piazza del Campo, 29. The cheapest of the lot. Not enough level ground for outdoor tables, but the food is decent and quite affordable. Closed on Tuesday.

Pizzeria Speranza: The nearby restaurant of the same name is much more expensive. Here you can actually eat a pizza on the piazza. Inexpensive, but watch out for the *coperto* (cover charge). Closed on Tuesday.

The next 3 are at least pretty close to the piazza, the others less so:

Osteria le Logge: Via del Porrione, 33 (near the southeastern corner). Posh decor but reasonably priced. In the main dining room there's a real gentleman's library in which the books have all been replaced with bottles. Good Tuscan cuisine. Several daily specials.

Quatro Cantoni: Piazza Postierla, 5. Between piazza del Campo and the Duomo. Makes no attempt at atmosphere but still provides tasty and not unreasonably priced Tuscan specialties: *Bistecca alla fiorentina* (nice thick steak—cheapos and ascetics will want to ask for a *piccola*) and spaghetti al gorgonzola. Closed on Wednesday.

Rosticceria: Via Calzoleria, 12 (near the northeastern corner of the piazza). Noted for a local pâté that's very good with chianti. You'll also observe that they have a number of chickens roasting on spits.

Da Dino: Via Casotto di Sopra, 71, not far from the Pinacoteca (D4). The *Da* has recently fallen off the sign. Good *menù turistico.* Closed on Friday.

Papei Cucina Casilinga: Piazza del Mercato, 5. We're very fond of this little restaurant, run by a group of women and not much frequented by tourists. Just a few tables inside. When the weather is good they set up a few more outside under great big parasols right across from the imposing Palazzo Pubblico.

Enoteca Italia: As noted, in the bowels of the Fortezza Medicea, outside town. Well-stocked cellars with wines from all over the country (the *locale,* of course, is chianti, so there's no problem there at all) and a nice terrace to drink them on. Note that carry-out bottles of the local product are cheaper in the grocery stores in town. Open from 3 P.M. to midnight.

Bar Costarella: Via di Città, 33. Has a balcony, equipped with a bench, overlooking piazza del Campo. Otherwise, nothing special.

Gelateria Fonte Gaïa: Piazza del Campo, 21. Here you get the piazza plus ice cream, available in many delicious flavors.

The Sights

Piazza del Campo: The historic, geographic, and social center of Siena. Its unique seashell design, gently sloping down toward the Palazzo Pubblico, makes it one of the most intriguing public spaces in Italy. The 9 light-colored bands in the pavement represent the 9 noble lords who ran the city in medieval days. In the evening, after the tourists have all stumped off to bed (there's not a whole lot else to do after dinner), it's nice to take a walk through the neighboring streets, then to come back to the piazza for a nightcap before stumping off yourself. Always a great moment.

Palazzo Pubblico: With its gently concave façade to match the curve of the piazza, the palazzo is surely the most elegant Gothic building in Tuscany. The *Torre del Mangia,* "Glutton's Tower," named for a medieval town character, just to the left of the palazzo, rises to a height of 316 feet. The interior of the palazzo, which includes the Museo Civico, contains some remarkable frescoes by Lorenzetti, Simone Martini, and other Sienese masters (providing numerous views of the city as it was during the late Middle Ages). Open from 9 to 6:30 in the summer and from 9 to 1 on Sunday, holidays, and off-season.

Duomo: Built on the highest of Siena's 3 hills, faced with alternating bands of light- and dark-colored marble, and over 2 centuries in the making (as evidenced by the contrast between the Romanesque portals down below and the Gothic tracery up above). The interior pavement is one of the greatest art treasures of Siena—37 separate panels of incised or inlaid marble, representing biblical scenes for the most part and comprising more than 10,000 square feet overall. The octagonal white-marble pulpit, supported by its 10 slender columns, is an impressive proto-Renaissance effort by Nicolo Pisano. Perhaps the most amazing thing about the cathedral is that the present structure, but no means unimpressive in itself, is merely the transept (the short end) of the original cruciform design; the enormous space that was cleared for the construction of the nave (reluctantly cancelled on account of the Black Death) may still be seen outside the Museo dell'Opera.

You might be interested to know that the patron saint of Siena is *San Bernardino,* a preacher so eloquent that he routinely moved entire audiences to tears, and caused ancestral enemies to embrace and gamblers (in those days regarded as the most hardened of sinners) to throw away their cards. He was the obvious choice when Pope John XXIII was asked to come up with a patron saint for the advertising business.

Tolomei bank building: Piazza dei Salimbeni. A family concern that's been around for quite some time. It was featured in one of Maurice Druon's historical potboilers, *Les Rois Maudits.* The bank's been refitted with a handsome new interior without doing an injury to the original façade (we should all be so lucky).

Pinacoteca Nazionale: Via San Pietro, 31. Housed in the Palazzo Buonsignori, one of Siena's most beautiful Gothic buildings. Contains over 600 works by Sienese artists, distinguished by a remarkable degree of continuity (some would even say monotony) of theme and execution. Be sure not to miss Duccio, the Lorenzetti brothers, and Simone Martini's *Virgin and Child.* (According to legend, she weeps bitter salt tears twice a year because she's the only one in Siena who can't make it to the Palio.) Open from 8:30 to 1:45 (1 on Sunday and holidays). Closed on Monday. Free admission on the first and third Saturdays and the second and fourth Sundays of every month.

Museo dell'Opera: Next to the Duomo. A collection of paintings and sculptures originally displayed in the cathedral, notably Duccio's famous *Maestà* altarpiece, remarkably well preserved (though a few of its panels are in other collections). Open from 9 to 7:15 in the summer, but just until 1:45 in the off-season.

Palazzo Chigi-Seracini: Home of a famous music school, the Accademia Chigiana. The palazzo dates from the thirteenth century. Every summer the Academy sponsors a series of free concerts in the courtyard, featuring students, faculty, and first-rate guest artists, young audiences, and a casual atmosphere. There are plenty of other open-air concerts in and around town during the summer—an excellent excuse to get out and taste the delights of the Tuscan countryside.

SAN GIMIGNANO

From Siena or Florence, take a bus to Poggibonsi, then change for an immediate connection to San Gimignano. Without a doubt the most beautiful village in Tuscany (and at its most seductive in the fall). Nestled picturesquely on a hilltop and surrounded by its 3-ply medieval ramparts. The spirit of paranoid ostentation that distinguished the ruling classes of Tuscany's communes during the early Middle Ages is still very much present in San Gimignano.

A dozen or so (out of an original total of 72) medieval towers are still standing; they provided a deterrent against surprise attack during clan feuds and a sublime source of irritation to lesser proprietors during peacetime. In Florence, the end of this period of feudal anarchy, the era of keeping-up-with-the-Medici, was symbolized by the appearance of the municipal fortress of the Palazzo Vecchio, with a tower that outbristled and overshadowed all the lesser fortifications of the noble families (which were subsequently dismantled). Take 3 or 4 hours to explore the streets, which have a habit of spitting you out abruptly at the edge of the hilltop. *La Rocca park,* up by the citadel, as well as any of the surviving towers, affords a splendid view of the village with adjoining vineyards and a very attractive Tuscan landscape.

Where to Sleep, Where to Eat

San Gimignano, as you might imagine, is a popular tourist stopover with just a few hotels and restaurants, nearly all of them too expensive for the likes of us. As you come into town, however, there are some family *pensioni* that advertise themselves with little placards reading *Camera/Zimmer.*

The nearest hostel is in *Tavernelle Val di Pesa.* About an hour away by SITA bus, change at Poggibonsi. Telephone (807) 70-09. Not many beds. It's best to call ahead.

Campground: In Santa Lucia, a few minutes from San Gimignano (by SITA bus). Attractive site. Nice view of the village. Clean and inexpensive.

La Mangiatoia: Via Mainardi, 8. An affordable restaurant in San Gemignano specializing in tripe and home-style ravioli with spinach.

AREZZO

Don't miss the *Church of San Francesco* with its astounding fresco cycle by Piero della Francesca. Also, the piazza *behind* the Duomo is worth exploring. Lots of little craftsmen's studios in the adjacent streets: cabinetmakers, picture restorers, and the like.

Hotel Africa: Via Adigrat, 1. Not too expensive. Near the train and bus stations. One of the buses takes you right out to the tollbooths on the Rome-Florence *autostrada.*

CORTONA

A thoroughly charming town between Arezzo and Perugia that has not been substantially altered since the Renaissance. Surrounded by some very beautiful countryside. A very tranquil spot in its own right (except during July and August) and a good place to settle down for a while and learn Italian. The *Koine* center favors a total-immersion approach that is intended to give you a thorough grounding (assuming that an immersion can give you a grounding) not only in the language but also the politics, economics, art, and literature of the region (in this case, Tuscany). Some of the classes are given in Cortona, others in Florence. For info: *Koine,* via de Pandolfini, 27, Firenze 50122. Telephone (055) 26-50-88.

Tourist Office: Piazza Signorelli, 1. Telephone 60-30-56.

The Sights

Etruscan Museum: Palazzo Casali. Artifacts from the dawn of Tuscan civilization, c. 800 BC, notably a big bruiser of a sixth-century ritual lamp that weighs about 60 kilograms/130 pounds.

Museu Diocesano: Near the Duomo. This former church now houses an interesting art collection, including works by local hero Luca Signorelli.

Head up *via Santa Margherita,* a stiff climb to be sure. When you get to piazzale del Sanctuario, you'll be rewarded wtih a magnificent panoramic view of the entire region.

Outskirts

Chiusi: A little town stuck to the side of a large splinter of rock, with an interesting Etruscan museum and Etruscan rock tombs 2 kilometers from town. Make inquiries at the museum.

Città del Pieve: 7 miles from Chiusi. A very nice little town, the birthplace of Perugino (in spite of what you might have been told in Perugia), and proud possessor of Italy's narrowest street, Baciadonne (etymology available on request).

Montepulciano: Another handsome hilltown with an impressive roster of Renaissance buildings, better known outside Tuscany for its august *vino nobile.* The *Tourist Office* is located in the Palazzo Comunale, a splendid sixteenth-century structure that may remind you of the Palazzo della Signoria in Florence. From the top of the tower you can see Siena, Cortona, and Lake Trasimeno. Head up via di Gracciano and make a leisurely reconnaissance of piazza Grande and the town's showier palazzi. Local edible specialties include *pia* (potato gnocchi) and a delicious cheese called *pecorino.*

Lake Trasimeno: Italy's fourth largest lake. Lovely shoreline, and there's a nice 15-minute boat ride out to Isola Maggiore. More intimate contact with the water is discouraged on account of algae and other organic pollutants. Site of a notable Roman military disaster, which is nice for those who always root for the Carthaginians.

FLORENCE

We're prepared to go out on a limb and say that Florence is the most beautiful city in Italy. Apart from its astounding heritage of Renaissance art treasures, it also has a very attractive personality, very lively and animated—so that the summertime hordes of tourists yammering away in German and Californian seem to fit right in—though perhaps a tiny bit self-conscious about having grown up to be, in strictly twentieth-century terms, second-rate provincial city (unlike Venice, which seems not to have noticed). In any case, Florence is also the place where you'll find the best traveling art exhibits and the best classical concerts in Italy. Perhaps the optimal time to explore the city is after dark when the tourists are covered up for the night and the Florentines are treating themselves to lavish meals in their *trattorie*. Everything is suddenly very calm, the streets are empty and inviting, and the air is warm and soft—and nothing remains of that faint hint of escaping sewer gas you may have been aware of during the day.

Getting Around

The city is highly compact and can be conveniently explored on foot; driving is out of the question, but the Florentine bus system is fast and efficient. Like Venice, Florence has its own peculiar street-numbering system but one that's much easier to adjust to: You'll note that street numbers are either red or black and are frequently nonconsecutive. The red numbers are reserved for businesses (notably restaurants) and the black (sometimes blue) ones for private houses (including hotels). In print, the street number is followed by a lowercase *r* (red); the *n* (black) is frequently omitted.

Useful Addresses

Tourist Office: In the Stazione Centrale (A1 on map); sometimes referred to as Sta. Maria Novella station. Open from 9 to 9 every day. Free city maps and hotel reservations service; takes at least half an hour to get through the line, maybe an hour in the summer. There's a less popular facility right outside the station (see below, Where to Sleep). Main EPT office at via Manzoni, 16 (over on the east side of town). Telephone 678-841.

Azienda Autonoma di Turismo: Via Tornabuoni, 15, upstairs (B3 on map). Telephone 216-544. Info on museum schedules (which are often eccentric) and cultural activities. They're no help in finding accommodations, however.

Currency Exchanges: At the Tourist Office inside the station. *Banca Nazionale delli Communicazioni,* also at the station. Open from 8:20 A.M. to 7 P.M. Closed on Sunday. There's a tiny little place at *via della Ninna, 9r* (off piazza della Signoria), that changes money on Sunday.

Banca d'America e d'Italia: Via Strozzi (B3 on map). Telephone 278-721.VISA cardholders take note.

American Express: Via degli Speziali, 7r (C3 on map), near piazza della Repubblica. Telephone 217-241. Closed on Saturday afternoon and all day Sunday.

American Bookstore: Paperback Exchange, via Fiesolana, 31r. Opportune trade-ins on used paperbacks.

24-hour Drugstore: At the station.

The invaluable *albergo diurno* at the station offers the usual amenities: bathrooms, showers, and haircutters. The *albergo* is closed on Thursday and Sunday afternoon.

Post Office: Via Pelleceria (B3 on map), near piazza della Repubblica. Closed on Sunday. The *fermo posta* office closes at 1 P.M. on Saturday as well.

Telephone Office: In the station. Open late. Less expensive direct-dialing facilities for some overseas calls.

Emergency First Aid: Misericordia, piazza del Duomo, 20. Telephone 272-22. Open 24 hours.

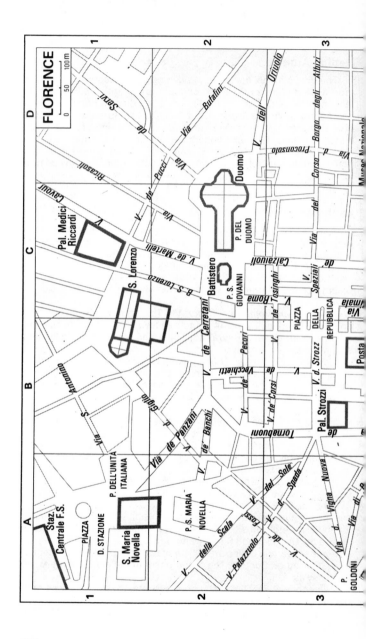

FLORENCE

0 50 100m

Staz. Centrale F.S.

PIAZZA D. STAZIONE

S. Maria Novella

P. DELL'UNITÀ ITALIANA

P.S. MARIA NOVELLA

V. della Scala

V. de' Fossi

V. Palazzuolo

P. GOLDONI

V. del Sole

V. d. Spada

V. d. Vigna Nuova

Via di

Via Sant'Antonino

Via de Panzani

V. de' Banchi

Tornabuoni

Pal. Strozzi

Posta

V. de Cerretani

B S. Lorenzo

S. Lorenzo

Pal. Medici Riccardi

V. de' Martelli

Via de' Pucci

Via Ricasoli

Via Cavour

Via de Ginori

V. de' Pecori

V. de' Vecchietti

V. de' Corsi

V. d. Strozzi

V. d. Tosinghi

PIAZZA DELLA REPUBBLICA

Battistero

P. S. GIOVANNI

P. DEL DUOMO

Duomo

Calzaiuoli

Via del

V. d. Speziali

Via degli Albizi

Borgo

Corso

Via d. Proconsolo

V. dell' Oruolo

Via Bufalini

Via de' Sanzi

Museo Nazionale

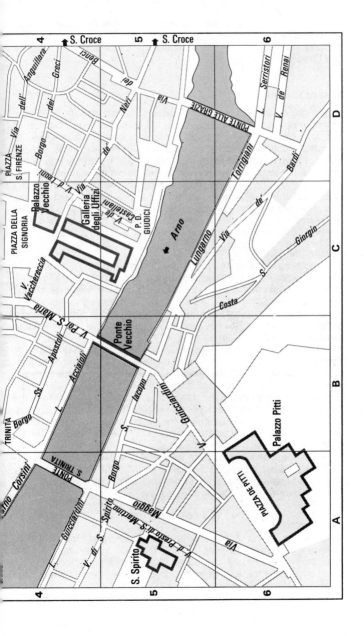

S. Croce

S. Croce

PIAZZA S. FIRENZE

Via Anguillara dell'

Via dei Greci

Borgo dei

Via de' Neri

Benci

PIAZZA DELLA SIGNORIA

Palazzo Vecchio

V. d. Leoni

Via

Galleria degli Uffizi

V. de' Castellani

P. D. GIUDICI

PONTE ALLE GRAZIE

L. Serristori

V. de' Renai

Via Torrigiani

Bardi

Arno

Lungarno

Via de'

S. Giorgio

V. Vacchereccia

Ponte Vecchio

Costa

TRINITÀ

V. Por S. Maria

Borgo Ss. Apostoli

L. Acciaioli

S. Iacopo

Via Guicciardini

Borgo

PONTE S. TRINITÀ

Lungarno Corsini

Lungarno Guicciardini

S. Spirito

V. di S.

V. d. Presto di S. Martino

Via di S. Spirito

Via Maggio

PIAZZA DE PITTI

Palazzo Pitti

Via

ITALY • 107

Student Travel Info: Centro Turistico Giovanile, via della Terme, 53r. Telephone 292-150. Discount train and airline tickets.

U.S. Consulate: Lungarno Vespucci, 38, near the station. Telephone 212-222.

SITA Buses: Via Caterina da Siena, 14r. Numerous departures for Siena and San Gimignano.

Lazzi Buses: Piazza della Stazione. Bound for Pisa, Viareggio, and Lucca.

Where to Sleep

It's not so easy to find a spot, especially in the summer. Single rooms are in very short supply, though luckily there are a number of *pensioni* that have single beds available, usually in some kind of dormitory context. If the Tourist Office in the station is already swamped when you get there, it's best to head out to the little *Informazione Turistica* kiosk to your left as you leave the station. If you're coming in on the highway, there's a handy registration office (no charge) at the AGIP station just to the north of town. In either case, you may find that the obvious financial benefits of staying in a religious hostel or *pensione* are more than offset by the midnight curfew —when prime viewing hours in Florence are just about to begin.

• *Near the Station*

If nothing turns up for you at the information kiosk, we suggest you check your backpack at the station and hit the bricks immediately—after maybe a beer or 2 to freshen up your language chops. Useful phrase: *Completo* (No vacancy). The following itinerary is arranged entirely with that eventuality in mind, and not in any special order of preference. Start by turning left as you leave the station and head down via Nazionale:

Pensionato Studentesco Suore Oblate delle Spirito Santo: No. 8n. Telephone 298-202. *Women only.* A bit more expensive than the *pensioni*, but showers and breakfast are included, plus the premises are very clean and heavily fortified. Open from June 15 to September 15.

Pensioni Bellavista, Ester, la Cascine, Maggiore: No. 6. Take the elevator to the top and work your way down. One *pensione* per floor. We admit to a certain fondness for rooms 10 and 12 (Bellavista), which have a great big balcony overlooking the city. La Cascine is a bit more expensive than the others.

Pensione Daniele: No. 22 (a fourth-floor walkup). Telephone 21-12-93. Cheapest around these parts, though often crowded. Noisy and could use a paint job. Don't be tempted by the overpriced *Soggiorno Nazionale* at the same address.

The next 4 are all on via Faenza, a cross-street off via Nazionale, to the left:

Locanda Giovanna, Nella, Pina, plus *Soggiorno d'Errico:* No. 69n. One per floor. The building doesn't look too appetizing from the outside, but the rooms aren't bad. Start at the top, if only to give yourself more time to admire the trompe-l'oeil decoration on the ceiling of the elevator cage.

Pensione Apollo/Tony's Inn: No. 77n. Telephone 21-79-75. It may be 2 names, but it's a single *pensione.* More expensive than most but squeaky clean. Rooms have private baths. Breakfast is included.

Pensione Marini, Armonia, Azzi: No. 6n. There are 6 *pensioni* in all, equivalent in quality and price. Located in a handsome old building that has just been restored.

Soggiorno Monica: No. 66n. Telephone 23-38-04. On the depressing side, especially the wallpaper, but inexpensive.

There are a few more *pensioni* on the piazza Indipendenza, all the way at the end of via Nazionale:

Pensione Indipendenza: Piazza Indipendenza, 8n. Telephone 49-66-30. Attractive ochre-colored façade with a number of rooms overlooking the piazza. Fairly expensive, but showers and breakfast are included.

Pensione Roxy: No. 6. Entry hall does not inspire confidence, but the price is right and the proprietress is very nice. The *Pensione Mary,* upstairs, is a lot more expensive and hardly worth it.

There are a couple of *pensioni* on and around piazza Santa Maria Novella (A2 on map), about 5 minutes from the station:

Pensione la Mia Casa: Piazza Santa Maria Novella, 23. Telephone 21-30-61. In a handsome old building right on the piazza. Its interior is not as well preserved.

Pensione Ottaviani: Piazza Ottaviani, 1. Telephone 29-62-23. Take via Fossi, across from the church of Santa Maria Novella. More expensive than la Mia Casa, but breakfast is included. Try not to get a room that faces the street (quite noisy).

• Near the Ponte Vecchio

Locanda Archibusieri: Vicolo Marzio, 1 (a tiny street that runs down to the river, between the Duomo and the Uffizi). Telephone 28-24-80. A great location. Some rooms have a view out over the Arno. No more expensive than most, unlike the Hotel Ermitage in the same building.

Soggiorno Castelli: Borgo Santi Apostoli, 25, near piazza Santa Trinità. Telephone 21-42-13. Clean and a nice location, but otherwise nothing special.

Pensione Davanzati: Via Porta Rossa, 15, a gloomy little street off piazza Santa Trinità. Cheap and not too elegant; more problem wallpaper.

• Southeast of the Duomo *(D3 on map)*

Locanda Orchidea: Borgo degli Albizi, 11. Telephone 29-66-46. In an old, old building where Dante's wife once lived (who wasn't Beatrice, by the way). Antique furnishings and timeless atmosphere. Some of the rooms overlook an interior courtyard with a fountain. No more expensive than many others.

Soggiorno Bavaria: Borgo degli Albizi, 26. Telephone 28-24-79. An old building surrounding an arcaded courtyard. Inexpensive. Youthful clientele.

Pensione Chiazza: Borgo Pinti, 5. Telephone 21-32-63. Quite clean, if you don't count the staircase. A very peaceful courtyard. Rates are competitive with the Orchidea and the Bavaria.

• Otrarno (other side of the river)

Ostello Santa Monaca: Via Sànta Monaca, 6, not far from the Church of Santa Maria del Carmine. Telephone 26-83-38. A private hostel in a great neighborhood (Santo Spirito). Inexpensive. Dorm rooms. Extra charge for linen unless you have a sleeping bag. A very nice place with a fairly exacting regime: Wakeup call at 8 A.M.; rooms vacated by 9:30; public rooms closed between 1 and 3 P.M.; curfew at midnight. Free showers, free currency exchange, and kitchen privileges, but no breakfast. Sign-up sheet is posted at 9:30; generally fills up by noon. If you can get your name onto it, you can be sure of a night's lodgings and come back to register any time after the hostel reopens at 4.

Pensionato Pio X-Artigianelli: Via dei Serragli, 106, not far from the Palazzo Pitti. Telephone 22-50-44. 16 rooms, 3 beds in each. Free showers. Spotlessly clean, and the brothers are very nice. No breakfast, though, and the doors close at 11:30 P.M.

Istituto Gould: Via dei Serragli, 49. Telephone 21-25-76. About 15 rooms, and a splendid interior courtyard. No curfew; you get your own key. Note that the registration desk is open only between 9:30 and noon, and again between 5 and 7 P.M.

• A Little Bit Out of It

The next 2 are accessible only by bus:

Ostello per la Gioventù (Villa Camerata): Viale Righi 2/4. Telephone 60-14-51. Take a No. 17B bus from the station and get off at Salviatino (about a 30-minute ride). A very pleasant though remote location shaded by pines and cypresses. International hostel card is obligatory.

Centro de Ospitalità Sette Santi: Viale dei Mille, 11. Take a No. 17 bus to Sette Santi church. Fairly far from the city center. Doubles, triples, and dorms. Inexpensive. Midnight curfew. Open only for the summer.

• Campgrounds

Camping Olivades: Viale Michelangelo, 80, usually just called the *parco municipale.* Take a No. 13 bus from the station. In the summer, it's best to get out there early. Try not to get a spot in the lower left quadrant, next to the outdoor disco. A panoramic view of the city.

Camping International: 50029 Bottai Tavarnuzze. Telephone 202-04-45. Take a No. 36 bus to the end of the line. Not as convenient as the foregoing, but there's a better chance of finding an empty spot in August. Hot showers (not included). It's best for the motorized and the stout of heart.

Camping di Fiesole: See below, Outskirts. The campground is well equipped and shaded by cypresses. Its facilities are all in good order, and there's a supermarket nearby. Trailers and bungalows are also available. The place gets crowded (and expensive) in the summer.

Mugello Verde International Camping: Via Masso Rondinaio, 2, in San Piero a Sieve. Telephone (055) 84-85-11, about 15 miles north of Florence. It's off exit 18 (Berberino de Mugello) on the Florence-Bologna superhighway, also on scenic route SS65. Frequent bus service from Florence. A recently opened campground in a very pleasant and instructive setting (wooded hills with Etruscan, Roman, and medieval ruins nearby) and all the amenities: bar, grocery, pool, and restaurant. Bungalows are also available.

• Upscale

Same principle as in Venice: Make phone reservations a month or 2 in advance and follow up immediately with a check or international money order (equivalent of 1 or 2 nights' lodging).

Pensione Consigli: Lungarno Amerigo Vespucci, 50, Firenze 50123 (to the left of A3 on map). Telephone 21-41-72. A renaissance palazzo on the banks of the Arna. Spacious rooms. Wonderful frescoes in the salon and the dining room, and a roof terrace with a view of the river and the city. Very reasonably priced, considering, and breakfast is included.

Pensione Rigatti: Lungarno Generale Diaz, 2. Telephone 21-30-22. Same basic format, exquisitely maintained, but note that not all the rooms overlook the river.

Pensione Bretagna: Lungarno Corsini, 6, Firenze 50123 (A4 on map). Telephone 26-36-18. Its doorway is uninviting, but a striking frescoed interior awaits, plus a grand salon with windows overlooking the Arno. Breakfast is included.

Pensione la Scaletta: Via Guicciardini, 13n, a street that starts at the Ponte Vecchio, across the river in Oltrarno. A lovely view of the Palazzo Pitti from the terrace. The atmosphere is hushed, the reverse of funky. Breakfast is included.

• *Truly delux*

Hotel Porta Rossa: Via Porta Rossa, 19. Telephone 28-75-51. About 3 minutes from piazza della Signoria. For fans of patrician decor—lustrous ancient paneling (waxed daily, it would seem, for the last several centuries) and a sumptuous stained-glass ceiling in the great hall.

Hotel Monna Lisa: Borgo Pinti, 27, Firenze 50121. Telephone 247-97-51. One of the nicest Renaissance palazzi we know of, tucked away in an unassuming little street to the east of the Duomo. Coffered ceiling with frescoes in the entry hall. Additional paintings and sculptures are inside. Most of the rooms overlook a little secret garden; all have private bath.

Where to Eat

A flourishing year-round tourist trade has also ensured the proliferation of dozens of "typical" tourist restaurants with bogus Tuscan cuisine, flickering candles on the tables, and bad paintings on the walls. Trillin's Law ("Bad cooking drives out good") is manifestly in operation here, and so for most of us Florence must remain primarily a feast for the eye. The places we've picked out all have the advantage of being inexpensive; some of them are pretty good too, but this is not going to be the place where you'll have your most memorable budget-gourmet experiences.

Cheapos will want to concentrate on *panini,* rolls stuffed with ham, mushrooms, and vegetables. More substantial local specialties include *trippa alla fiorentina* and the aforementioned *bistecca alla fiorentina,* which is basically top sirloin, broiled and served straight up without sauce, garnish, or condiments (except for a little salt and olive oil at the last possible moment). To avoid an unseemly wrangle over the check, note that the listed price on the menu is just for an *etto* (100 grams—roughly a quarter-pounder, in other words), but a healthy *bistecca* can easily weigh 300 grams. If you still feel driven to some sort of excess, we recommend the local wine, which is still chianti.

• *Extra Cheap*

The *supermarket* just to the right of and in the same building as the train station is useful for stocking up before you get back on the train! Good selection: thin-sliced Parma ham, good cheeses, and drinkables. Closed on Wednesday afternoon; otherwise open from 8 to 1 and from 5 to 8.

Mensa DLF: Via Luigi Alamani, 6, about 250 yards to the right of the station. A railworker's canteen that is open to the public. Has 3 or 4 daily specials with copious portions.

Mercato Centrale: Down via Nazionale from the station. Big, old, cast-iron job, intelligently restored. North Italian genius for point-of-sales display is apparent at almost every stall. Country ham, cheeses, wines, and sausages are on the ground floor; fruits and vegetables are upstairs.

Casa di San Francesco: Piazza Santissima Annunziata, 2 (on the left as you face the church). Tasty Franciscan fare. For lunch only. Closed on weekends and for the month of August.

Mensa Universitaria: Via San Gallo, 25n, north of the Duomo. An international student ID is required (may not even be sufficient). There's a vast dining hall on the second floor of one of the main university buildings. Closed on weekends and for the month of August.

• *Centrally Located*

Da Mario: Via Rosina, 2, next to the *mercato centrale.* Inexpensive full-disclosure *trattoria* (that is, kitchen and customers are in the same room). Oilcloth on the tables. Heavily patronized by proprietors of market stalls, and so forth. A great place. Closed on Sunday.

Trattoria Sostenza: Via del Porcellana, 25r, between the river and piazza Santa Maria Novella. A tiny, typical Florentine layout (long and narrow). The walls are decorated with postcards and some remarkable photos of the floods of '66. Good food. Closed on Sunday.

Pizzeria Nut: Borgo San Lorenzo, 39, between piazza San Lorenzo and the Duomo (C2 on map). Industrial decor but not chic. Thought by a number of Florentines to serve the best pizza in town, especially those with 4 different cheeses on top; and those with ham.

Chianti: Via Cimatori, 38r, north of piazza della Signoria. A tiny place (about as big as the inside of a Toyota) that serves the proprietor's hand-picked reserve of local wines plus your choice of Parma ham or succulent local pâté on bread. Stand-up Tuscan cuisine (to be consumed at the counter; no chairs).

Ristorante Pennello: Via dei Alighieri, 4r. Telephone 29-48-48. Very popular with local folks. Has a good selection, especially of fish. First-rate atmosphere. Moderate prices. Closed on Sunday night and all day Monday.

• *In Otrarno*

Trattoria Casalinga: Via Michelozzi, 9r, right off the piazza San Spirito. Our favorite restaurant and our favorite neighborhood in Florence. Always lively and often crowded; attracts a very discerning and nice clientele. The house chianti is excellent, and the decor is execrable. Affordable prices. Closed on Sunday and during August.

Quattro Leoni: Via dei Vellutini, 1r. Telephone 21-85-62, between piazza Santo Spirito and the Pitti palace, at the intersection of via Toscanello. Not far from the preceding, though a little hard to find. Same basic format, plus a view of a delightful little piazza that has a few outdoor tables when weather permits. Closed on Saturday and during August.

Trattoria-Rosticceria: Via Romana, 8r, intersection of via Maggio, near the Pitti palace. No special atmosphere, other than the delectable bouquet of that good stuff that's turning on the spit.

• *Upscale*

Osteria 1 Rosso: Borgo Ognissanti, 1r (A3 on map). Telephone 28-48-97, near piazza Goldoni and the river. Nice old-fashioned *trattoria* in a typical setting (down in the cellar). Reliable Tuscan specialties include *trippa,* scampi, scallopini, pasta, and *croztini*—croutons or toasted *polenta* (cornbread) with pâté.

Trattoria Angiolino: Via Santo Spirito, 36r (A5 on map), in Otrarno. The atmosphere is positively chic. Your fellow diners more likely to be prosperous Florentines than spendthrift tourists. The serious menu has a choice of 4 or 5 entrees, with prices fairly serious as well.

• *Gelato*

You may not agree that it's the best in Italy (hence, the world), but you can easily see how a person could arrive at that opinion.

Vivoli: Via dell'Isola delle Stinche, 7 (a little street between the Bargello and Santa Croce). Take the street opposite the church and a little to the right, then take your first available right. Patronized by the youth of all nations. Incredibly good ice cream.

Gelateria: On piazza Santo Spirito. Our favorite. It has a wide selection of flavors fully comparable in quality to the above but with lower prices. See below, Sights of Otrarno, for additional details.

Cultural Enrichment

If you feel as we do about ostentatious displays of learning, be it ever so wide-ranging and profound, you'll want to skip the next few paragraphs.

• *Michelangelo*

He started out as a gifted counterfeiter of ancient Roman reliefs but quickly broke with the classical canon of idealized bodily proportions and turned toward a more expressionist approach—to make the hands of a statue larger (as in the case of *David*), for example, to enhance the impression of adolescent gawkiness conveyed by the torso. The bodily proportions are subtly distorted to achieve a certain psychological or dramatic effect; the problem is, of course, that the statue has to end up looking like something. Michelangelo's disciples, the Mannerists, routinely took more extreme risks and some fairly serious pratfalls as a result, but in the case of Michelangelo we think you'll agree that, on the whole, he got away with it. From time to time doctors have been heard to object that none of his human figures are anatomically correct; take a look and see whether this bothers you or not (if it doesn't, you're an artist; if it does, you're a doctor.

• *The Medici*

Already frequented by Greek and Syrian traders in classical times, who sailed up the Arno to display their wares, Florence has always been a commercial city. The Medici made their fortunes in the silk trade, then switched over to banking and government. Initial family ventures into politics during the fourteenth century ended unhappily, in several cases fatally; but by the early fifteenth the Medicis were responsible for fully half of the GNP, and their mastery of the banking system made them the real rulers of Florence during the lifetime of *Cosimo the Elder* (1389–1464), though the city remained nominally a republic with various elected bodies and councils (in the manner of most modern authoritarian states).

Cosimo was a miserly tycoon who lived on porridge in a shabby old palazzo and built up an enormous stock of political credit by bailing out financially distressed foreign potentates (specializing, as have many modern lending institutions, in the less trustworthy rulers of emerging states, such as Edward IV of England, who never paid back a florin). The name of Florence became practically synonymous with money in both England and the Netherlands. Militarily powerless, surrounded by aggressive foreign rulers who owed him plenty of money, Cosimo was one of the first to understand the importance of maintaining the balance of power, in Florence, in Italy, and in Europe; less predictably, he was a bountiful patron of Renaissance art and learning. Brunelleschi was only one of many who specialized in turning hard-earned Medici ducats into Prato, Maremma, and Carrara marble.

His grandson, *Lorenzo the Magnificent,* hoped to establish Florence as the cultural and intellectual capital of Europe. Toward this end he paid out lavish stipends to artists and scholars in residence at his court and spent enormous sums on poetry competitions, public monuments, and popular festivities. (The Medici bank underwent a severe and finally terminal fiscal crisis during this period.) Lorenzo died in 1492. His son, Piero the Unfortunate, was driven out of Florence when the French invaded Italy. An illegitimate nephew, *Alessandro* (son of an African slave girl and Pope Clement VII), was restored to power by the Spanish a number of years later (so much for the balance of power), and as Florence went into decline, other Medicis went on to successful careers as popes, queens of France, and grand dukes of Tuscany. After the first duke, the dissolute Alessandro, was assassinated by his cousin Lorenzino, known as *Lorenzaccio,* the title reverted to the legitimate line, and the Medicis became very respectable, though no one ever showed much interest in reviving the family banking business.

The Sights

Piazza del Duomo (C2 on map): Has 3 main attractions: the *Duomo* and the *campanile,* faced with white, red, and green bands of marble (from Carrara, Maremma, and Prato, respectively), plus the *baptistery,* with the astounding bronze "Doors of Paradise" by Ghiberti.

The Campanile: 260 feet tall, its first couple of stories designed by Giotto, is a slightly garish masterpiece in the Florentine tricolor style, its soaring monumentality somewhat relieved by the bright colors and graceful fenestration (windows). You'll love the breathtaking panorama from the top (actually the topmost story but one), which is reached by ascending 400 stairs, no less breathtaking in their way. Open from 8:30 to 12 and from 2:30 to 6 (until noon on Sunday).

The Duomo: The construction of the dome was an engineering problem that had sent several different architects tumbling down to defeat before a sculptor and amateur architect, *Brunelleschi,* devised a very elegant solution: an inner and outer shell on an elliptical base with a framework of metal struts between them to distribute the stresses more uniformly. This worked out very nicely and even allowed Brunelleschi to build his dome without first erecting a scaffolding, which caused a tremendous sensation at the time (all the more so when the dome actually failed to collapse). A century later, Michelangelo was the first to point out that his design for the dome of St. Peter's was an enlarged but not necessarily improved version of Brunelleschi's. The *Pietà* that the 80-year-old Michelangelo had originally intended for his tomb and later abandoned is now in the Museo dell'Opera.

The Baptistery: During the Middle Ages unbaptized persons were not allowed in church, which is why the baptistery is frequently housed in a separate building (as in Parma and Pisa, for example). Ghiberti, a goldsmith turned sculptor, worked for 50 years on the carved and gilded reliefs that cover the main doors of the baptistery. The conception of many of the scenes, with great unruly mobs compressed into very tiny spaces, seems fairly medieval, but the execution, with a perfect command of perspective and recession of pictorial planes is full-fledged early Renaissance.

Galleria degli Uffizi: Piazzale degli Uffizi (C4 on map). The entrance is near piazza della Signoria. The story is that part of the Uffizi collection originally adorned the convenient private gallery that connected the Medicis' private apartments in the Palazzo Pitti (Otrarno) with the municipal offices *(uffizi)* in the Palazzo Vecchio across the river—entertainment, in other words, for the tired bureaucrat. The gallery is still there, for the most part—it passes right over the Ponte Vecchio—but after a century or so, when the press of city business began to relax a bit, the art was gradually moved over to the Uffizi. Today, it is certainly the most important of Florence's many museums, housing what is very probably the most beautiful collection in the world.

The paintings are arranged chronologically, beginning with the primitives in which the flat pictorial space may be divided into a series of episodes, like a Chinese scroll or a comic strip, in order to make the sacred text (the life of Christ or of a particular saint) more readily accessible to the illiterate medieval viewer. Very early on, the gold background, part of the heritage of Byzantium (galleries 2 and 3), gives way to a kind of antiseptic lunar landscape or, more interestingly, to crowded, meticulously detailed scenes of medieval urban life (well worth a closer look in the second case). The early Renaissance artist's increasing confidence in his abilities to create the illusion of depth and 3-dimensional solidity on a flat panel or canvas is already quite apparent in Uccello's *Battle of San Romano* (gallery 7).

The Botticelli paintings (galleries 10–14)—notably his 2 most famous works, *The Birth of Venus* and *The Primavera*—demonstrate, among other things, the incredible freshness and verve that an artist of the high Renaissance (an artist of genius at any rate) could bring to these 2 very characteristic genres, the scene from classical mythology and the pastoral allegory, which were to stale very quickly in the hands of lesser masters. In gallery 15, you'll find *Adoration of the Magi* by Leonardo da Vinci, an unfinished work that gives us some insight into the artist's methods, particularly the way the figures really *are* grouped, like a still-life with apples, pears, and bananas, as a series of interrelated forms in space.

In gallery 20, works by Dürer and other northerners recall the

Medicis' extensive commercial ties with Germany and the Netherlands as well as the even more pervasive influence of Italian artistic innovations in the countries beyond the Alps. In galleries 25 and 26, with the works of Raphael and Michelangelo, we come to the very height of the Renaissance. The figures seem more alive, less rigid; the women even venture an occasional timid smile. In spite of their obvious ecclesiastical associations, these folks seem to have much less to do with religion than the stiff hierarchical figures in galleries 3 and 5.

Finally, in gallery 28, you'll find Titian's *Venus of Urbino,* in which, unlike Botticelli's *Venus,* the painter's interest in re-creating an episode from classical mythology seems very much subordinate to his desire to provide us with an image of a beautiful naked woman. At this point an artist such as Titian, who—as a famous anecdote illustrates—had an emperor to pick up his paintbrushes for him, did not have to worry too much about incurring the displeasure of the Church. The Museum is open from Tuesday to Saturday from 9 to 7 and from 9 to 1 on Sunday and holidays. Free admission.

Piazza della Signoria (C4 on map): Where most important civic events took place—popular gatherings and attempted uprisings, public executions and elaborate public festivities orchestrated by the Medici and financed by the state. One side of the piazza is dominated by the majestic *Palazzo Vecchio;* on the other side is the *Loggia della Signoria* which contains a number of important sculptures, including Cellini's *Perseus.* Giambologna's *Neptune Fountain,* in the middle of the piazza, dates from the regime of Cosimo de Medici and marks an early reappearance of the undraped human form in a prominent public space. The yellow stone of the buildings around the piazza is especially attractive when brightly lit at night, which is also when latter-day festivities and impromptu public gatherings tend to take place.

Ponte Vecchio: This oldest and most famous of the city's bridges escaped (though just barely) the fury of the retreating Wehrmacht in 1944 and the rising floodwaters in 1966. The old buildings on both sides of the river, however, did not escape the first of these disasters; they have since been restored, though not with any great conviction. Both neighborhoods were heavily commercial in the old days, and the bridge itself, as was the custom, was also occupied by a warren of little shops with picturesque wooden backhouses projecting out over the waters of the Arno. The original tenants, butchers and tanners, were evicted by the Medici for throwing their unwanted hooves and entrails into the river; they were replaced by goldsmiths and jewelers, who had no such unsavory habits and thus continue to occupy the site.

Galleria dell'Accademia: via Ricasoli, 60, north of the Duomo (D1 on map). The new home of Michelangelo's *David* (his old spot on the piazza della Signoria is now occupied by a copy). As noted, the strange tension between the figure's boyish softness and virle self-confidence—very apt in a representation of David right before his encounter with Goliath—also marks an important transition in the history of art. You'll also find other important works by Michelangelo, notably the unfinished *Captives* with their raw, anguished faces, originally intended for the Medici tombs. Open from 9 to 2 (until 1 on Sunday and holidays). Free admission on the first and third Saturdays as well as the second and last Sundays in every month.

Santa Croce (to the right of C4 on map): A great church that is sometimes overlooked by overly efficient sightseers. Its treasures include the Bardi Chapel by Giotto and others, the famous Cimabue *Crucifixion* that was injured by the '66 flood (now in the adjoining Museo dell'Opera), and the tombs of Michelangelo, Machiavelli, Galileo, and Rossini. The Déjà-Vu Award has to go to the statue on your right as you come in; it inspired Bartholdi's design for the Statue of Liberty.

At the rear of the church, a leatherworkers' school is run by the Franciscan fathers. You'll see some interesting frescoes, and have a chance to watch genuine old-world apprentice craftsmen at work. The articles made by the students are offered for sale. Open from 9 to 12:30 and from 3 to 6:30 (6 on Sunday).

Fresco Museum, Cloister of San Marco: Piazza San Marco (next to the church). Contains most of the important works of *Fra Angelico,* perhaps the sunniest and most genial of Renaissance painters. The pilgrims' hospice, a long, narrow dormitory, has several of the more impressive frescoes, including the *Last Judgment;* lesser works adorn the main refectory (note the lectern, from which an improving book would be read aloud during meals). In the chapter room is the *Crucifixion,* enormous in size and allegorical in intent. Upstairs are the cells that were occupied by the brothers, including *Savanarola,* second floor back, each with its own fresco. Savanarola was a charismatic Dominican preacher who took over as unofficial autocrat of Florence after the Medici fled the city in 1494. His regime turned out to be a bit too much for the Florentines, who burned Savanarola at the stake in the piazza della Signoria a few years later; there are 2 interesting paintings of this event on the premises.

Imafechoroni: Borgo Pinti, 18r. An old-fashioned workshop that turns out spectacular masks. Spectators are encouraged. Open from 9 to 1 and from 2:30 to 7:30. Closed on Monday morning.

• *Lesser Attractions*

Capella dei Medici: Around the back of San Lorenzo (C1 on map). The massive granite sarcophagi of the later grand dukes in the main crypt strike the right note of funereal solemnity; floral tributes are still in evidence. Near the exit, a corridor leads off to the funeral chapel designed and partially executed by Michelangelo, with its famous family portraits (a Lorenzo *penseroso* and brother Giuliano, was was assassinated, still *furisoso*) plus the allegorical *Night and Day.*

The Bargello: Via del Proconsolo. An impressive palazzo that once housed the chief magistrate and the city prison. It now houses the national sculpture gallery, (including cabinetry, ceramics, and so forth).

Santa Maria Novella (A1 on map): Frescoes in the cloister by Uccello and in the choir loft by Ghirlandaio and pupils (including a number of figures by Michelangelo, Leonardo da Vinci, and other promising members of the younger generation). Check these out after you've been to the Uffizi, so you'll know who did what.

• *In Otrarno*

So-called, you may have noticed, because it's the *other* side of the *Arno.* More residential, less touristy, hence a place where the monuments of the past (except for the Palazzo Pitti) seem less monumental, more on a human scale: beat-up old palazzi with carved escutcheons over the doorways alternate with funky neighborhood *trattorie* (the kind that are always called "homely" in travel books), plus a number of interesting churches and piazzas at the end of dark little streets. (Don't miss the astounding frescoes by Masaccio in *Santa Maria del Carmine,* out near the hostel of Santa Monaca, possibly *the* big artistic breakthrough of the early Renaissance).

Piazza San Spirito (A5 on map): The steps of the church are a popular gathering place for the younger crowd at nightfall. You'll note that the façade is practically bare of decoration (especially by Florentine standards)—another grand design by Brunelleschi that none of his successors felt up to completing when he left it unfinished at his death. The owner of the homely *gelateria* right across the piazza has been sponsoring a Finish the Façade contest among the local artists for some time now; entries are displayed in a special little gallery inside (you may have to switch on the light to see them). Definitely not to be missed.

Palazzo Pitti (A6 on map): Built by Pitti; improved and expanded by the Medici. Has several impressive features—a 600-foot façade, a steeply sloping site, and an enormous piazza out front. The palace was the girlhood home of Marie de Médicis, wife of Henri IV of France, who did what she could to make sure that the Luxembourg palace in Paris turned out the same way. Now contains a couple of different museums, notably the *Galleria Palatina,* which has still more Medici treasures on display: works by Botticelli, Raphael, Tintoretto, Titian, and Ruben. Closes at 2 P.M. Free admission on the first and third Saturdays and the second and last Sundays.

Boboli Gardens: Behind the palace. Features an interesting artificial grotto, the *Buon Talenti,* with frescoes and statuary and an atmosphere of mysterious coziness much in favor during the sixteenth century *plus* the *piazzale dell'Izolato,* an elaborate water garden with an artificial island in its center (very much along the lines of Hadrian's Villa at Tivoli), the island dominated by a fountain adorned with crags and boulders plus a striking representation of the sea monster Oceanus.

A wonderful view of all of the above (especially at night) can be had from *piazza Michelangelo* and from the *Forte Beleve dere,* on top of the hill above the Boboli Gardens. To get there walk up via di Costa San Giorgio (second on your left after the Ponte Vecchio).

Night Life

Concerts and lots of action abound on piazza della Signoria, but we still favor piazza San Spirito. For those who prefer a more structured setting:

Caffè Voltaire: Via degli Alfani, 26r, to the east of the Duomo. A good mix of the younger crowd and the local yuppies.

Space Electronic [sic]: Via Palazzuolo, 37. Florence's biggest and best known disco features 2 floors, a laser show, video screens, and live music, Palladian decor (that is, in the manner of New York City's the Palladium). A giant fish tank is built into the bar and is said to contain piranhas. An excellent chance to familiarize yourself with the Italian Top 100.

Outskirts

You'll find excellent bus service to the hill towns, with their stately cypresses; magical, tranquil atmosphere; breathtaking panoramas; and numerous art treasures (often not much inferior to those of Florence itself). However, we'd suggest renting a moped, minibike or, if you're really panting to get at those Tuscan hills, a 10-speed bike at *Nogello's,* Borgognissanti, 96n, on the Duomo side of the Ponte Vespucci. Telephone (055) 28-29-16. There's no sign, but it's right next to a big garage. No license or deposit is necessary (just leave a piece of ID in lieu of deposit). Rentals are by the day or by the week. A suggested itinerary: Make a loop through Siena and San Gimignano, always sticking to the smallest roads you can find.

If a shorter excursion is called for, we'd suggest *Fiesole,* a hilltop town about 5 miles from Florence with an incredible view: vineyards and olive groves in the foreground and all the taller monuments of Florence laid out along the horizon. This was the pleasant rustic retreat where Boccaccio and his friends took refuge from the plague, as described in the *Decameron,* but note that this is also where a great many people come to escape the human tide that envelops the valley every summer. Catch a No. 7 bus on via de Cerretani; there's another bus from the station.

Hitching Out of Florence

Toward Siena: Take bus No. 36 or 37 out to Tavarnizze.

Toward Pisa, Livorno, and Genoa: Get on bus No. 29 or 30 at the Stazione. Ask to get off at *la fermata per la autostrada Firenze-Mare.* There aren't any tollbooths. It's best to stand right by the traffic light (in front of the No Hitchhiking sign).

All Destinations: Take a bus out to the intersection of the A1 and A11 highways, to the east of town. The stream of traffic between the 2 highways moves at a nice vulnerable pace, and the tollbooths are always backed up something dreadful.

PISA

Back in the Middle Ages, when the Pisans first discovered that their new campanile was seriously out of plumb, they became quite upset, so much so that further construction was halted for 90 years. No doubt they had a word or 2 to say to the architect, little knowing that when they were deprived of their profitable trade routes to the East, a substantial fraction of their descendants would have to earn their livelihoods by manufacturing and marketing little Leaning Tower of Pisa keychains and ashtrays.

Useful Addresses

EPT Office: Next to the above-mentioned campanile (C1 on map). Currency exchange, facilities for overseas phone calls, info on cultural activities, free city map (with hotels and prices clearly marked), but no reservations service. Open from 8 to 1 and from 3 to 7, just until 1 on Sunday. There's another currency exchange at the train station (off the map right below D4, where it says Staz. FS). Open from 9 to 12 and from 2 to 7.

Airport: About 2 miles (3k) from the center of town. Catch a No. 5 bus in front of the station.

Where to Sleep

With no hostel and a superabundance of tourists in town during the summer months, there are still a number of avenues worth exploring. You might begin by taking a left as you leave the station:

Albergo Rosetto: Via Pietro Mascagni, 3. Closer to the station than the 2 places listed below and somewhat nicer; on the other hand, it's no Pitti Palace. Some rooms have a balcony.

Albergo Milano: Via Pietro Mascagni, 14. Same basic deal, same prices, but the owner is none too friendly and perhaps overconfident in asserting any claim to fluency in a language other than his own.

Albergo la Torre: Via C. Battisti, 17. Telephone 252-20. Clean and unpretentious. No more expensive than the other 2. Located on a fairly noisy street (first on your left after the Albergo Milano).

• Near the Leaning Tower
Cheaper than the last batch. About 15 minutes away by foot, or take a No. 1 bus from the station. Once again, the following are grouped according to what we hope will prove a convenient itinerary and not in any order of preference:

Locanda Galileo: Via Santa Maria, 12, not far from the river (C2 on map). Telephone 246-49. One of the cheaper places, with a depressing entry hall and a weird assortment of furniture inside.

Pensione Helvetia: Via Dongaetano, 31. Watch for a right turn off via Santa Maria. Single and double rooms. A very peaceful establishment a stone's throw from the tower.

Locanda Santa Maria: Via Santa Maria, 175. Telephone 246-49. Has a very handsome doorway but not many rooms. Right next to the tower.

Albergo Gronchi: Piazza Archivescovado, 1. Telephone 236-26. Past the tower, before you get to the EPT. Pretty nice building. Good price-quality ratio.

Albergo di Stefano: Via Santa Apollonia, 35. Telephone 263-59. Located on a quiet little street. Well-maintained and inexpensive. There's a café on the ground floor.

Locanda Giglio: Via San Lorenzo, 23 (E2 on map). Telephone 233-04. Near piazza Martiri della Libertà, one of the most pleasant spots in all of Pisa. Inexpensive. Splendid frescoes adorn the elevator cage; even more splendid ones are on the ceiling of the *locanda,* though the effect is partly spoiled by the presence of the room partitions.

Pensione Giardino: Via Commeo, 1. Telephone 247-41. About 5 minutes west of the tower, heading toward the baptistery. A fairly attractive yellow building with a great big cafeteria downstairs.

• Upscale
Hotel Victoria: Lungarno Pacinotti (D3 on map), next to the Ponte di Mezzo. Telephone 233-81. A big, old-fashioned hotel with attractively gloomy wooden paneling in the entry hall, of a kind you hardly see these days (except in places such as this). Not as expensive as it looks. Rooms are with or without bath.

Hotel Arno: Piazza della Repubblica, 6. Telephone 222-43. Stylish ochre-colored façade and a recently remodeled interior; adjoins a peaceful piazza. Well maintained and centrally located (right by the tower and 3 minutes from the Arno). Rooms with showers.

Hotel Roma: Via Bonnano Pisano, 111. Telephone 226-98. Modern, clean, and efficient. 5 minutes from the tower. Some rooms have balconies with a view of same. Rooms with or without bath.

• *Campgrounds*

Campeggio Torre Pendente: Via delle Cascine, 86 (off to the left of A1 on map). Telephone 501-512. Conveniently situated (only about 1 kilometer west of the tower) and well kept. Catch a No. 4 bus from the station. There's a supermarket nearby (250 yards).

Marina di Pisa: Via Litoreana. Telephone 352-11. On the water, almost 10 miles from Pisa. Packed in the summer. Drive right along the river (*with* the current) or take an ACIT bus. There are more campgrounds further south as well, in Tirrenia and Calambrona.

Camping Viarregio: In Viarregio, about 9 miles north of Pisa. For the motorized. Cheap.

Where to Eat

Try to avoid places frequented by the great migratory herds along via Santa Maria, where the service is likely to be slow and the tab excessive.

Pizzeria da Giulia: Via Domenico Cavalca, 11, near the Ponte di Mezza (on the tower side of the river). A tiny place that serves inexpensive specials. Giulia is very nice but definitely has a way about her. Smokers are obliged to sit at a little outdoor table, which shouldn't pose too much of a problem.

La Mescita: Via Domenico Cavalca, 2, near the marketplace and right next door to Giulia's. More expensive. Handsome vaulted ceiling with a fan. A couple of daily entrees, both meat and fish. Nice place.

Trattoria: Via l'Arencio, 46. Walk down via Santa Maria from the tower and count off 4 streets on the left (about 550 yards). A no-name establishment with pizza, great lasagna, and draft beer *(alla spina)*. Vaulted ceiling but an unexciting decor.

Da Toppa: Via Nunziatina, 27. Walk down corso d'Italia from the station. It's off to the left, not far from the river. Straight-ahead family-style cuisine, and you can eat out in a little courtyard if the regular dining room is full.

The Sights

The Campanile (C1 on map): Take the No. 1 bus from the station; get your ticket to the left as you leave the station. You may have pictured it standing all by itself in the midst of a vast, featureless plain, but it actually forms part of a very attractive architectural ensemble—along with the Duomo, the Battistero, and the Camposanto (medieval cemetery; a must-see)—set out on a luxuriant green lawn. The building of the tower began in 1174, and work had already been completed on the first 3 stories of this stylish Romanesque structure before it was noticed that the subsoil had begun to subside in a very alarming way. (This was when the 90-year stoppage occurred.)

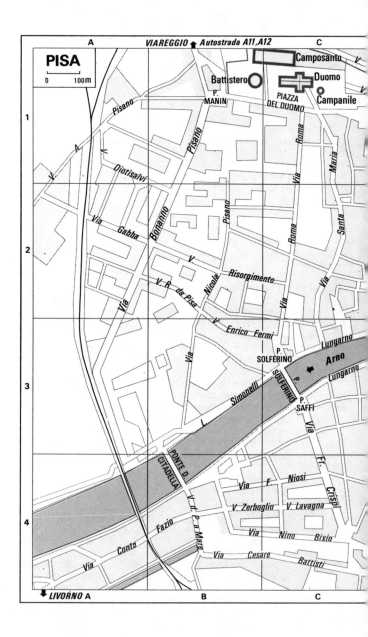

PISA

0   100m

VIAREGGIO ↑ Autostrada A11,A12

Camposanto

Battistero

Duomo

P. MANIN

PIAZZA DEL DUOMO

Campanile

Pisano

Diotisalvi

Pisano

Via

Roma

Via

Maria

Gabba

Bonanno

Pisano

Via

Roma

Santa

Via R. da Pisa

Nicola

Risorgimento

Via

Via

Enrico Fermi

Lungarno

P. SOLFERINO

Arno

SOLFERINO

Via

Lungarno

Simonelli

P. SAFFI

Via

PONTE D. CITADELLA

L

Via

F.

Niosi

Fr. Crisoi

V. P. a Mare

V. Zerboglio

V. Lavagna

Fazio

Via

Nino

Bixio

Conte

Via

Cesare

Battisti

LIVORNO A

A

B

C

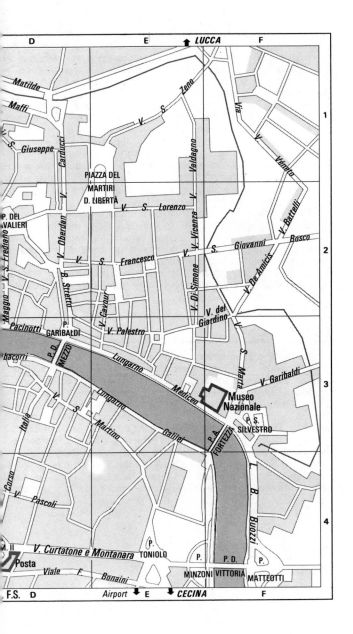

Afterwards you'll observe that the builders tried to compensate for this crippling declivity in various clever ways—at first by reducing the height and circumference of the upper stories (thus the overall mass of the tower), and then by shifting the central axis of the top story, the belfry, which points off in a different direction altogether. Nowadays there's little that can be done to conceal the fact that one side of its base has sunk down 10 feet lower than the other and continues to do so at a rate of almost a millimeter every year. Learned opinions differ as to how much longer the tower is actually good for, but the odds in favor of its making it safely through its first millennium now seem reasonably high.

As for that business about Galileo and the weights, historians now believe that it might actually have been somebody on the other side (a follower of Aristotle) who dropped the 2 unequal weights off the tower and that everyone who witnessed this experiment went away perfectly convinced that the heavier weight *had* been the first to hit the ground and that old Aristotle was right, sure enough. It was only later on, when Galileo had become a world-famous scientist and by far the most famous Pisan who ever lived, that the punchline got turned around a little bit. Interesting if true.

The Duomo (C1 on map): Also begun during the twelfth century. A splendid interior decor and pulpit by various members of the Pisano family. Beautiful bronze doors over by the tower and Galileo's famous swinging lamp. Ecclesiastical dress code is enforced (no shorts, short skirts, or bare shoulders).

The Market: piazza Vetto Vaglio, not far from the Ponte di Mezzo (tower side of the river). Held only in the morning in a very cute little piazza surrounded by an arcade.

LUCCA

Its sixteenth- and seventeenth-century *ramparts,* planted with shade trees, provide a not too strenuous excursion of a mile or so. You'll find a number of interesting sights, starting with the *Duomo* and its campanile on the elegant *piazza San Michele,* which occupies the site of the original Roman forum. Also on the piazza spare a glance for the *Palazzo Pretorio* (1492), with its portico and handsome windows, and the Church of *San Michele* in Foro (1143, with a thirteenth-century facade). Particularly worth exploring are 3 streets lined with palazzi and impressive medieval mansions: *Cesare Bathiti, Fillungo* and *Guinigi.* The *Museo Nazionale,* in the Villa Guinigi, is mostly devoted to flashy furniture. We respectfully suggest that the paintings in the Duomo and the *Pinacoteca* are more worthy of your attention.

EPT Office: Via Vittorio Veneto, 40. Telephone 469-15.

MARINA DI CARRARA

Take a D bus to Marina di Carrara from the train station in the nearby town of Massa. Service is not all that frequent (in keeping with the demand, as you'll discover).

Ostello Apuano: Viale delle Pinete, 89. Telephone (05-85) 202-88. The street parallels the shore. This hostel is in a beautiful old villa that has now greatly gone to seed. Kitchen privileges. Nice view of the water from the large, overgrown garden. A beach is nearby, but you have to pay!

LERICI

About 6 miles south of La Spezia. A seaside resort on a beautiful little inlet called the Bay of Poets. A lovely spot, though unfortunately not frequented only by poets, especially in the summer. There was a very nice hostel in the local *castello,* but it was closed down as a result of a referendum organized by the Christian Democrats in February '82. With Socialism on the march again in Italy these days, it is worth checking to see if they have opened it up again.

Where to Sleep, Where to Eat

Camping Maraluga: A mile or 2 from town (uphill all the way). Your best bet is to head straight for the campground when you reach the turnoff above the town instead of continuing into the center of town. The old quarter of Lerici, with its narrow streets, looks very intriguing from above.

Cucina Emiliana: Piazza Garibaldi, 26. Telephone 967-300. Very good fish, plus seafood salad and pasta, Emilian-style. Not cheap.

Outskirts

Whether by boat or along the highway, it's a nice trip down to *Piascerino,* 2 miles to the southeast. Has a nice rocky cove with a beach. You may want to continue on to *Tellaro,* a few more kilometers down the coast, a medieval-looking village on top of a rocky promontory overlooking the sea.

PORTOVENERE

Just a few miles to the southeast of La Spezia. Accessible by boat (regular service) or the P bus. This delightful fishing village occupies a little cleft in the rocks at the edge of a tiny harbor. Its houses are tall, narrow, and painted in bright colors. Massive old buildings, a precarious setting, gardens, and a fortress above all contribute to a very convincing and attractive medieval ensemble. Hasn't yet gone the way of its high-tone cousin, Portofino, but it isn't likely to remain in its present semi-pristine condition much longer.

CINQUE TERRE

Five picturesquely sited villages—*Riomaggiore, Manarola, Corniglia, Vernazza,* and *Monterosso*—strung along some 30 miles of footpath, starting with the famous *via dell'Amore,* between La Spezia and Levanto. All 5 are accessible by car or rail, but walking is optimal. *Vernazza* is perhaps the best known, but you'll find that none of them is entirely unappreciated. *Corniglia* is the only one with a real beach. This is also a noted wine-producing region, home of the exquisite *bianco sciacchetra,* and you'll see the terraced vineyards tumbling down with lemminglike abandon right to the very edge of the sea.

PORTOFINO

This natural harbor is now the home, as someone once said about Chicago, "of every kind of dubiousness." It still makes a very nice stopover. Regular boat service from Santa Margherita (every half hour); no train station. Take a walk up to the castello; the headland overlooking the harbor is a natural park crisscrossed with hiking trails. There's a great view from the top—you can watch the fishing boats sailing out at dusk.

The most interesting of the trails, *San Fruttoso,* takes you down by the water, with the possibility (if the water is clear) of catching a glimpse of the submerged statue of Christ on the bottom, more than 50 feet down. About a 3-hour excursion.

GENOA

Venice's ancient rival for the mastery of the seas can be approached now only from the landward side by negotiating a seemingly endless suburban sprawl that just goes on and on for kilometers and kilometers. Sleek galleys charged with cargoes of spices and silks no longer tie up along Genoa's scuzzy waterfront (site of Columbus's boyhood home). The historically minded and those who require very little visual stimulus should try to imagine things as they once were.

Where to Sleep

Ostello del Mare: Via Cinque Maggio, 79, Frazione Quarto dei Mille. Telephone 387-370. Bus No. 15 or 31 from Brignole station (bus tickets remain valid for 90 minutes). An international hostel card required. Has 180 beds.

Camping Villa Doria: In Pegli. Take the No. 18 bus to Sampierdarena, then change for a No. 3 bus. No. 34 bus from the ferry terminal. A very nice place and quite peaceful.

Where to Eat

Mensa Universitaria: 3 different locations: via del Campo, corso Gastoldi, and via Asiago.

The local specialty is *farinata,* a little cake made with chickpea flour. It is widely available in the restaurants along piazza Tommaseo, piazza Carimento (which also has lots of seafood places), and via Donghi. After Columbus, Genoa's most famous contribution to the modern world is *pesto,* a delicious sauce heavily impregnated with basil; it is very good in *trofi* [a kind of pasta] *al pesto.*

The Sights

Old fortifications on the hills surrounding the city can be reached by the funicular railway that starts out from *largo della Zucca* (and accepts bus tickets).

Staglieno Cemetery: Near Brignole station. No. 34 bus from piazza Principe. Tombs of Genoa's merchant princes. A nice stylistic mix of Gothic morbidity with the most extravagant ostentation, both somewhat reminiscent of Venice. Highly recommended if you go in for this sort of thing at all. Open from 8 to 5 every day.

Hitching (or Driving) Out of Genoa

To get to all points there are interminable lines of cars at the tollbooths right outside Genoa. It should be rather easy to connect with one headed for the *French Riviera* (by way of Savona, Imperia, and Ventimiglia), *Turin* (by way of Alessandria), or *Rome* (by way of La Spezia and Livorno).

If you are driving and/or in no particular hurry, you'll see much more interesting countryside if you turn off in the direction of Tende (across the French border) just before you get to Ventimiglia. There's a very cute border crossing at *Piene* with French customs officers; if you have some time to hide, it's best to cross while they're still digesting their lunch. Next comes Breil and then Sospel by way of the col [pass] de Brouis, and then Menton (by way of the col de Castillon) or Nice (by way of the col de Braus), where you would have been sometime earlier if you'd gone across the normal way.

One final motoring tip: If you're heading inland toward *Piacenza* (in Emilia, roughly between Parma and Milan), be advised that the twists and turns of the *nazionale,* though picturesque, take quite a lot out of both car and driver. The long way around, the *autostrada* (which links up with the one to Turin), is recommended.

THE SOUTHWEST

An exuberant, explosive city with a bad reputation and a great deal of charm if you stop and take the time to figure things out. The best approach at first is just to plunge right in (with your eyes wide open, as always) to the everyday reality of the place. Rarely have so many, in Europe at any rate, had so little to do in the way of gainful employment, and so forth, and so little space to do it in. It would be fatuous to suggest that all this doesn't matter, but the fact is that it doesn't seem to matter all that much. Take a walk around its older quarters (Spaccanapoli), making sure to leave your camera equipment at the hotel), and you'll start to see what we mean.

Useful Addresses

EPT Office: At the Stazione Centrale, opposite track 22. If you're staying 3 days or more, you get a book of tickets good for free or reduced admission at city museums, concerts, plays, and special events, on excursion boats, and so forth.

Post Office: Piazza Matteotti, not far from via Roma.

American Express: C/o Airontour, via Santa Brigida, 68.

Banca d'America e d'Italia: Via Santa Brigida, 10. Telephone 325-470. You can obtain cash on presentation of a VISA card.

To report a stolen car (it does happen): Telephone 31-31-31.

U.S. Consulate: Piazza della Repubblica. Telephone 660-960.

Where to Sleep

• *Near the Station*

The first 3 are all on via Milano, the fourth street on the right as you leave the station:

Albergo Milano: At No. 82. Telephone 51-83-73. Perfectly okay.

Albergo Vittorio Veneto: At No. 96 (second floor). Telephone 20-15-39. Same as the above.

Pensione Fiore: Up on the fifth floor. Cheap. The shower is out in the corridor.

Take your first right off via Milano (via Firenze). You'll find 4 or 5 more in the same price range, including *Albergo Zara* at No. 81 and *Hotel Primus.*

On via Spaventa, the first street on the left as you leave the station:

Hotel Gallo: At No. 9. Relatively expensive but very quiet. The rooms have private baths.

Albergo Odeon: At No. 29. Some basic format, but a little less expensive.

• *Further West*

Ostello della Gioventu: Salita della Grotta, 23. Telephone 68-53-46. Take the *metropolitana* from the central station to Mergellina station; take a right and then another right. A modern 200-bed hostel with cafeteria. Curfew is 11 P.M.

Camping Solfatara: From the station, take the No. 152 (Pozzuoli) bus. An immense, well-maintained campground with pool and good, inexpensive eats. Impressive special effects that are provided gratis: pervasive odor of brimstone, sulfurous vents and fissures right on the campsite, and eerie nocturnal glows and flashes. While you're here you might as well make it out to *Pozzuoli,* just another 2 kilometers. Near the harbor is the magnificent ancient Temple of Serapis, an imported Egyptian deity, with its columns about hip-deep in the bay. Pozzuoli is also the girlhood home of Sophia Loren, who might very well be running a *tabaccheria* today if Carlo Ponti's car hadn't happened to break down one day in this very spot. So who says there's no such thing as Fate?

• In Santa Lucia (near the water and the Castel dell'Ovo

Albergo Teresita: Via Santa Lucia (third floor). Schlocko decor but spacious rooms. A little expensive. The *Astoria* (second floor) is a little more expensive but otherwise comparable, and the *Hotel Castello,* up on the fifth floor, is nice and quiet.

Hotel Rex: Via Palepoli, 12. Telephone 41-63-88. In a very old building whose interior has recently been restored; on a fairly quiet street by the water. Well maintained. A step up in class and price from the foregoing.

Where to Eat

Ristorante Avellinese: Via Spaventa, 35, off to the left as you leave the central station. A popular neighborhood place famous for its seafood.

Da Luciano: Piazza Capuana, 11, off to your right as you leave the central station. A typically Neopolitan atmosphere and bill of fare, including fish, octopus, choice crustaceans, and excellent clams.

Da Marino: Via Santa Lucia, 118. Not far from the Castel dell'Ovo. A very popular seafood place (notably with U.S. military personnel), specializing in pizza and *zuppa di pesce.*

Da Michele: Via Pietro Colleta. Succulent pizzas, for which you may have to stand in line.

Remy Gelo: Via Galiani, right on the water. Great *gelato.* Closed on Monday.

• Upscale

La Bersagliera: Next to the Castel dell'Ovo. One of Naples' most famous restaurants. Has a gigantic neon sign outside and painted bas reliefs on the ceiling. Great spaghetti with clams *(alle vongole)* plus a fried seafood assortment.

The Sights

Piazza Municipio: Historic center of the city. Sums up the city's maritime career and its predilection for bombastic public buildings at a glance. Right next door, stroll through the *Galleria Umberto,* a nineteenth-century shopping arcade; very ornate and very lively. Further down toward the water is the enormous *Castel Nuovo,* built by Chalres of Anjou (c. 1280), who made Naples his capital after the

Corsica

Civitavécchia

ROME

Latina

Pto Tórres
Olbia

Sassari

Núoro

SARDINIA

Oristano

TYRRHENIAN   SEA

Iglésias
Cágliari

Trápani

Egadi Islands

Marsala

SOUTHERN ITALY

0   100 km

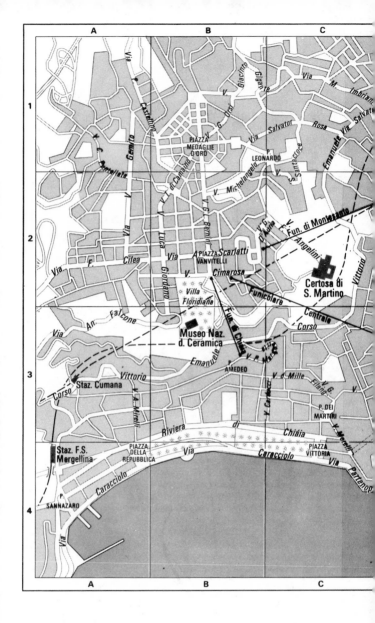

NAPLES

0   200   400m

French were chased out of Sicily. Recalls (perhaps coincidentally) the moats and massive turrets of the castle of Angers in Charles's homeland. Via Toledo is the main shopping drag.

Spaccanapoli: From piazza Nuovo walk as far as the Church of Santa Chiara, though a neighborhood of narrow streets, old houses (including an occasional down-at-the-heels palazzo), and all the other classic components of outdoor Neopolitan life: wash hanging on a line, intimate private conversations bellowed across the courtyards, and forlorn little wayside Madonnas on certain corners, feebly illuminated and universally ignored. *Santa Chiara* has a lovely cloister, miraculously remote from all the above distractions and adorned with beautiful blue-and-yellow faïence.

Castel dell'Ovo: On the water. A castle built by the Normans (who followed the Romans, Byzantines, and Saracens, and preceded the Angevins, Aragonese, Hapsburgs, and Bourbons as rulers of Naples). On the site of an ancient villa owned by Lucullus, celebrated Roman bon vivant. Now in the most sedate part of the city, filled with upscale tourist hotels (most of them a little bit past it). The atmosphere is remarkably stodgy after dark.

National Archeological Museum: At the end of via Toledo (D1 on map). Perhaps Italy's most astounding collection of classical sculpture and decorative art, though part of the museum is still closed for restoration after the 1980 earthquake. After the Romans conquered Greece, Greek sculptors began to specialize in turning out museum-quality replicas of earlier masterpieces for the benefit of wealthy collectors abroad; for example, the exquisite marble copy of Polyclitus' *Doryphorus* (Javelin Bearer), the bronze original of which has long since vanished. In another room there's another famous Roman copy of a lost original, the so-called *Farnese Bull;* this large sculptural group (over 12 feet tall) has come down to us from antiquity, retrieved from the ruins of the Baths of Caracalla; it later served as an inspiration for much of the farm-animals-in-crisis imagery in Picasso's *Guernica.*

The collection of classical mosaics from Pompeii and Herculaneum is immensely more interesting than it sounds; the colors are still remarkably bright and fresh, and the figures, in spite of the stylized format, are still remarkably vital. The standout masterpiece of this collection is a good-sized mosaic called the *Battle of Alexander,* from the Casa del Fauno in Pompeii; this depicts the climactic moment in the battle in which 2 opposing commanders come face to face, Alexander flicking his chariot reins aggressively, Darius and his Immortals shrinking back in disarray. The murals from Pompeii and Herculaneum give us a rare opportunity to see some nonsculptural Roman art, remarkably modern in its use of color and perspective and its realistic treatment of figures and landscapes. In the ceramics collection, the room containing the erotic vases, sculpted phalluses, and so forth—in which the well-known Roman tendency toward the grandiose and the monumental generally wins out over the merely realistic—was regrettably closed in 1982 due to earthquake damage.

Museo e Gallerie di Capodimonte: In the park of the same name (north of D1). Best known for its roomful of Titians (gallery 19). Also features *the* masterpiece by Masaccio (not counting the Brancacci Chapel in Florence, of course), another roomful of Raphaels and Michelangelos, miscellaneous Mannerists (gallery 12), a few Brueghels, and 2 dynamite El Grecos.

Catacombs of San Gennaro: On the way back from Capodimonte toward the city center. Open from 9:30 to 12:30 on Saturday, Sunday, and holidays *only.*

Hitching Out of Naples

Toward Rome: No. 14 bus.

Toward Salerno: The highway on-ramp is just about 350 yards from the Stazione Centrale.

The Outskirts

Caserta: 17 miles northeast of Naples. Site of the "Italian Versailles," built in 1751 for one of Naples' lame Bourbon rulers. Contains 1,200 rooms, 34 staircases, and 143 windows on the main facade. Closes at 3. There's also a lovely park with waterfalls, fountains, statuary, and 7 kilometers of shaded alleys and promenades.

POMPEII

Nowadays called Pompei for short. Take the Circumvesuviana (train) from the central station in Naples and get off at Villa dei Misteri (not Pompei). There's a train every half hour (Inter-Rail and related railpasses are not valid for this ride).

Where to Sleep

As with many uninhabited ancient cities, there isn't a wide choice of accommodations. The 2 campgrounds are both well run, convenient to the site, and very crowded in the summer.

Camping Sparticus: Via Plinio, 177. Groceries, pizza, and other edibles cooked over a wood fire. When the ground rumbles, that probably means there's a train going by (and not that you're about to be buried beneath an asphyxiating blanket of volcanic ash).

Camping Pompei: Right next door. Bigger.

Hotel Vittoria: Across the road from the preceding and 5 minutes from the ruins. A handsome old building in the middle of a grove of trees. Generally not many vacancies, and a bit out of our normal price range.

The Sights

As you may have heard, the city and several thousand of its human and animal residents were buried by an extremely vigorous eruption of Mount Vesuvius on August 24, A.D. 79, giving us an opportunity to walk the streets and explore the houses of a prosperous Roman suburb just as it was in the days when the Empire was at its greatest.

You'll find that many of the buildings are locked; the guard who has the keys may or may not be in evidence. Accordingly, a personal tour might well be worthwhile (especially with the cost split 3 or 4 ways); cheapos will attach themselves unobtrusively to a large lecture tour in the language of their choice. Open from 9 to 7 (until 6 in the off-season), plus evening visits from 10 to 11 between June 1 and

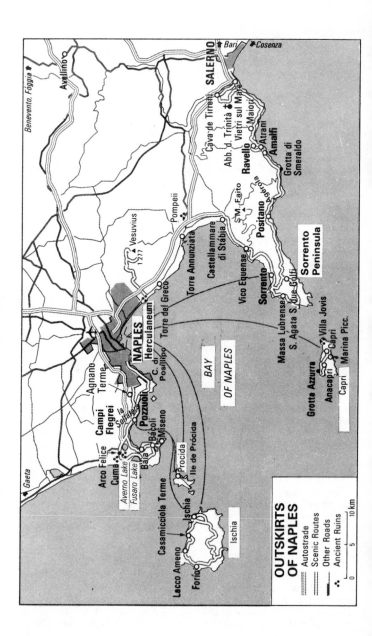

OUTSKIRTS OF NAPLES

	Autostrade
	Scenic Routes
	Other Roads
∴	Ancient Ruins

0   5   10 km

SALERNO

Bari • Cosenza

Cava de' Tirreni

Abb. d. Trinità

Vietri sul Mare

Maiori

Ravello

Atrani

Amalfi

Grotta di Smeraldo

Pompeii

Vesuvius 1277

M. Faito

Positano

Sorrento Peninsula

Torre Annunziata

Castellammare di Stàbia

Vico Equense

Sorrento

Torre del Greco

Herculaneum

NAPLES

C. di Posillipo

Massa Lubrense

S. Agata S. due Golfi

Villa Jovis

Capri

Marina Picc.

BAY

OF NAPLES

Agnano Terme

Campi Flegrei

la Solfatara

Pozzuoli

Bàcoli

Capo Miseno

Baia

Grotta Azzurra

Anacapri

Capri

Arco Felice

Cumà

Averno Lake

Fusaro Lake

Procida

Ile de Prócida

Casamicciola Terme

Ischia

Lacco Ameno

Ischia

Forìo

Avellino

Benevento, Fòggia

Gaeta

September 30 (great when there's a full moon). Sometimes closed on Monday; make inquiries locally. After you go in by the porta Marina, you'll come to (in order of appearance):

The Forum: The main piazza, with adjoining law courts, temples, and other public buildings. Unlike many of its kind today, it was closed off to wheeled traffic by a row of dragon's teeth set into the pavement. Take a walk down via dell'Abbondanza, one of Pompeii's main streets; note the raised pedestrian crosswalks.

Teatro Grande: Take a right off via dell'Abbondanza. In the Hellenistic style; not as well preserved as its smaller neighbor, the *Odeon.*

House of Loreius Tibertinus: Toward the end of via dell' Abbondanza. Had been owned by a patrician family. With an ornamental pool to catch rainwater *(impluvium)* in the inner courtyard. Delicate frescoes in the inner rooms and a network of fountains and canals in the garden.

The Amphitheater: The oldest of its kind still standing. Seating capacity of 12,000.

Terme Stabiane: Back down via dell'Abbondanza, toward the Forum and to the right. Public baths, the best preserved of several such establishments in Pompeii. The layout is much the same as in a modern Turkish bath, with a locker room *(vestiarium),* a fountain (rather than a shower) for one's initial ablutions, warm and hot baths *(tepidarium* and *caldarium,* respectively), and separate facilities for men and women (the latter being somewhat fewer in number).

The Lupunar: Right next to the baths. The brothel consists of 2 floors of little cubicles, some decorated with frescoes that clients must have found both stimulating and instructive. Named for the resident *lupae* (she-wolves), disciplinary types whose specialty was snarling and howling at their tricks. Some prostitutes were slaves, some volunteers, and others were nonaffiliates who worked the necropolis outside town.

Casa dei Vettii: Head north from the Forum and then turn right after the restaurant. Famous for its frescoes, which are delicately rendered scenes from Greek mythology for the most part (that is, not counting the industrial-strength Priapus on the right-hand side of the entry hall, said to be effective as a charm against the evil eye). Less spectacular features of the villa include the garden (accurately reconstructed from traces of the original roots left in the soil) and the lead-lined gutters in the street outside.

Casa del Fauno: Right near the preceding. As noted, the original home of *The Battle of Alexander.* The villa was named for the delightful bronze statuette of a dancing faun that was discovered in one of the *impluvia.*

Terme del Foro: To the west. Its interior rooms are quite well preserved, as are the 2 petrified Pompeiians on display within.

Villa dei Misteri: Out at the edge of town. About a 15-minute-walk down a handsome paved street lined with tombs and porticoes, something like the Appian Way and with fewer tourists than downtown Pompeii. Don't throw away your ticket of admission because they'll want to collect it from you at the villa. A sort of chapel used by devotees of the Dionysian mystery cult, one of the largest and best preserved villas on the site. The famous frescoes depicting the rites of Dionysus are in the room at the right front corner of the villa and are definitely not to be missed.

HERCULANEUM

As before, take the Circumvesuviano from the central station in Naples; the station is Ercolano. Before the catastrophe the town was right on the bay. It is somewhat smaller and a bit more exclusive than Pompeii, but, as they say in the real estate game, location is everything. Its buildings were buried under a very dense layer of volcanic mud rather than volcanic ash, and thus they are better preserved than Pompeii's. Nevertheless, Herculaneum doesn't seem nearly as nice, perhaps because there's less of it and there's nothing growing there. As at Pompeii, the houses are now equipped with locked gates, and you have to ask the guards to take you around. You approach by means of a causeway built by Mussolini that gives you a great view of the entire site.

Casa del Tremezzo di Legno: The *tablinum,* the room where the family accounts and records were kept, is partitioned off with wooden paneling, pierced by 3 doors, and is still in very fine shape.

Casa di Nettuno e Anfitrite: The first floor is a wine shop with a counter, measuring cups and other utensils, and shelves laden with amphorae. The proprietors evidently lived behind the store in a house with some very nice mosaics in its little courtyard.

Casa dei Cervi: Easily the most impressive building on the site. Built around a very attractive courtyard decorated with famous frescoes of a stag hunt, hence House of the Stags. There's an amazing statue of a drunken Hercules. The villa was built right on the water and is now backed up against an imposing wall of lava.

MOUNT VESUVIUS

Not dead but merely sleeping. The last major eruption was in 1944, the same day that U.S. forces began the offshore bombardment of the city. More impressionable members of the U.S. invasion task force immediately dropped to their knees and repented when Vesuvius (presumably as a sign from God) started to return their fire. People ashore in Naples could have told them that *both* of these deplorable things had happened because the city's annual miracle of the liquefaction of the blood of San Gennaro had unaccountably failed to take place that year.

If you're driving, get off at the Ercolano exit, then follow the signs (Vesuvio) for another 8 miles (13k). By train, get off at Ercolano station, then take the bus to the foot of the volcano; check the schedule to see when the last bus heads back to the station. Take the chairlift or the convenient cinder track; it's 30 to 45 minutes on foot up to the crater; be sure to wear a sweater or a warm jacket. The crater is very impressive, containing as it does a number of sinister crevices with vast clouds of brimstone billowing forth (what your doctor refers to as a *fumarole*). The view out over the Bay of Naples is even more impressive.

CAPRI

Here is a suggested itinerary for Naples and environs: Take the train to Pompeii, then come back to Naples and take the ferry out to Capri (one way); take a different ferry to Sorrento (see map). Ferries leave for Capri quite frequently from the Calata Beverello, right near the Stazione Marittima. The trip takes about 90 minutes. Forget about the hydrofoil *(aliscafo),* which is faster but more expensive and not as much fun—you have to sit in an enclosed cabin. You'd do better to set out early in the morning. The last boat back to Naples leaves Capri at 5:30 P.M.

Capri is a little island about 2 miles by 4, commonly represented in fiction as a place for people with more money than good sense (for example, the odious Emperor Tiberius in *I, Claudius* and the dopey American film director in Godard's *Contempt).* Still, if you happen to recall the beautiful azure seascapes and the incredible villa (in real life, the Villa Malaparte) in that very same film, you'll understand why we decided to go ahead and take a look, suspecting all the while that it wasn't for the likes of us (with infinitely less money than good sense). Capri admittedly has its bad side (unaffordable hotels, multitudenous tourists, terminal chic, and super cleanliness) as well as its good side (the aforementioned, plus rocky slopes covered with vineyards and villas surrounded by pine trees, half-buried in arbutus). The former are admittedly hard to overlook, and the latter are fortunately impossible to ignore. Even if you don't enjoy it all that much, you can at least be spoiling it for someone else.

• *Marina Grande*

Where the boat gets in. There's a baggage check near the ferry landing, so you can rush right over and buy your tickets for the Blue Grotto. Microbus tours of the island also set off from here.

• *La Grotta Azzurra*

The Blue Grotto. Astounding lighting effects are caused by the refraction of sunlight through the water; the narrow mouth of the grotto allows very little direct sunlight to enter. At their best between 11 and 1. The white sands along the bottom impart a lovely silvery sheen to anything in the water, and the water itself is a most amazing blue. The effect is so enchanting that old Tiberius had a little pleasure dome (perhaps euphemistically referred to as a "bridal chamber") scooped out for himself from one side of the grotto.

Your visit is actually a 2-stage operation and, in fact, this whole grotto-excursion business is simply called by the islanders the *operazione.* A powerboat picks you up at the marina and drops you off at the entrance to the grotto. A rowboat takes you through the grotto for which there's a separate charge; if you forget, your boatman will remind you, and if he's feeling especially expensive, he may sing you a little ditty, just like a gondolier except with lyrics in Neapolitan rather than Venetian. There's generally a long wait for the rowboats in the summer; cheapos and diehards can skip the powerboat stage and take the bus (on the road to Anacapri). If you're feeling venturesome, you can go out on your own outside business hours and take a swim, being careful to observe all the normal rules of water safety.

• *The Town of Capri*

The funicular from Marina Grande whisks you up through the vineyards in a matter of minutes to the tiny capital city of the island. No cars are allowed, and the streets that converge on piazza Umberto are as lovely as you can find anywhere in the Aegean. The crowds of tourists and rootless sophisticates that prowl these same streets may not be quite so much to your liking.

There aren't many affordable places to stay. Try *Pensione Terminus,* via delle Grazie, 3, not far from piazza Umberto. A staircase leads up to the balcony and a little courtyard. Everything is white and clean and perfectly shipshape. Another possibility is *Pensione Belsito,* via Matermania (on the way out to the Arco Naturale). Telephone 837-09-69. An old white building with a spectacular view. Kind of expensive. Outdoor types will want to try camping out in the fields around the Arco Naturale. There is a high incidence of grass fires in the summer, so cigarettes and campfires are definitely out.

Settiani, in back of piazza Umberto, is one of the cheaper restaurants, with decent food, a great view, and an interesting collection of *paparazzi* photos of 60s celebs, including Orson Welles (surprisingly svelte), Jean-Paul Sartre (pop-eyed and bilious), and Princess Grace (lovely). There are also some grocery stores in town.

The Garden of Augustus is about a 10-minute walk from town. It has a splendid view out over the water, including the 2 famous rocks known as the *Faraglioni.*

• Villa Jovis

The walk from piazza Umberto is one of the nicest the island offers, past gardens and olive groves, with a spectacular overlook of Marina Grande. Takes about an hour. The villa was Tiberius's general headquarters, though only one of a dozen he maintained on Capri. (For details, consult the astounding description of his activities in Suetonius's *Lives of the 12 Caesars.*)

• Anacapri

4 kilometers west of Marina Grande. Walk or take the Microbus. Not as many international fun seekers as in the town of Capri. The *Villa Michele* is delightful and provides another spectacular panorama of the sea and the golf course. Plus, you can stop at the above-mentioned Grotta Azzurra on the way.

THE AMALFI COAST

If you decide to skip Capri, we suggest you take the Circumvesuviano out to Pompeii, then take another train down to Sorrento (see map, Outskirts of Naples). Along the coastline between Sorrento and Salerno you'll find a series of little towns perched up on the rocks overlooking the sea and linked by an elegant road that runs along the edge of the peninsula. Very popular with British summer visitors in the old days; they found them as little fishing villages and left them as natty little resorts. As with the Saracens, Byzantines, and other foreign overlords, a few traces of their occupancy still remain: an occasional shabby palace along the coast, a placard outside a restaurant offering "4 O'clock Tea," and deck chairs and umbrellas by the hundreds in numerous public places, just like at Brighton or Bournemouth (the main difference being that here the water, the sky, and the landscape are all absolutely gorgeous).

• Sorrento

Was the center of all this activity in prewar days; it still remains quite active (lots of noise, cars, and exhaust fumes). If you change your mind about Capri, you can catch the ferry down at the harbor.

Youth Hostel: Via Capasso, 5, about 250 yards from the station.

Pensione Mara: Via Rota, 5, not far from the above.

Camping Campo Gaïo: Out on the little cape of Sorrento (not to be confused with the tip of the Sorrento peninsula, which is about 10 miles down the coast). Exceptional location: set on sloping terraces amid the olive groves. Perfect view of the cliffs and town of Sorrento, from the upper stories, at any rate. Also groceries, snack bar, pool, and a private shingle beach (that is, rocks and stones). Our rating is 4 stars. Almost deserves to be as expensive as it is.

• Positano

A semiretired fishing village turned chic international resort. The cliffside houses of the year-round residents have a kind of Middle Eastern look. Its cafés and luxury hotels attract a more discerning brand of rootless sophisticate than is to be found on Capri.

• Praiano

5 miles west of Positano. The transitional fishing village has fewer unaffordable hotels, and its tourists are not quite so stunningly dressed. Similarly situated halfway up the side of a mountain. Our favorite on the Amalfi Coast, in fact. Has lots of relatively reasonable priced *pensioni* and a campground 1 kilometer out of town, toward Amalfi.

Youth Hostel: Overlooks the sea. At the other end of town, toward Positano.

About 2 miles further on, toward Amalfi, is *La Grotta di Smeraldo,* the Emerald Grotto. Recommended for those who have not already undergone the *operazione* on Capri.

• Amalfi

One of the 4 ancient maritime republics, along with Venice, Pisa, and Genoa, and the only one to have shrunk considerably in size—perhaps due to the natural limitations of its snug little rocky harbor. The mariners of Amalfi are credited with being the first to use the magnetic compass, by the way (the Chinese having already thought of using it on land). Next to piazza del Duomo there is an interesting little labyrinth of medieval streets and stairways, vaulted passages, and miniature piazze with softly murmuring fountains. *Hotel Capuccini,* a former monastery, has a nice thirteenth-century cloister (okay to look at, too expensive to stay in). A less deluxe establishment, the *Hotel Luna,* occupies a former convent.

SALERNO

A good-sized seaport. The evening promenade *(passeggiata)* along the water, formerly a major event, is not nearly as enjoyable as it once was; when you get near the water, you'll know why. Recommended for a brief stopover, nothing more. You might want to walk around the old city for a while, notably along *via dei Mercanti,* next to the Duomo, a kind of twisting and elongated Oriental bazaar with lots of colorful retail activity. The *Duomo* itself, built by a Norman, seems partly Moorish and partly Byzantine in inspiration, with a vast colonnaded inner courtyard just beyond the main entrance.

If you're driving south, be advised that there are no tolls on the *autostrada* down through Calabria, but you'll also miss out on a whole string of great little villages if you take it.

Ostello per la Gioventù: Lungomare Marconi, 34, south of town. Telephone 35-73-62. A decrepit old house on the water. The beach is very dirty, but there's a spectacular view of the entire Amalfi Coast. There are also lots of *pensioni* along corso Vittorio Emanuele (first on your right as you leave the train station).

PAESTUM

About 25 miles south of Salerno (10 or so trains a day, plus frequent buses), 2 miles from the water. One of Italy's greatest classical sites, frequently bypassed by overefficient sightseers. This is a serious blunder. Paestum was an important Greek colony back in the days when southern Italy was known as Magna Graecia (Big Greece). Surrounded by impressive fortifications (some of them still visible), which of course didn't prevent the Romans from taking over when the time came. The site is very beautiful in its own right, and the architecture is just about unsurpassed (the *Temple of Neptune,* along with the Parthenon, is generally ranked somewhere in the classical top 2).

Where to Sleep

The *hostel* near the train station was recently closed. Bungalows at *Camping Hera Argive,* about 2 miles from the site, are supposed to fill in as temporary replacements. It's best to inquire on the spot. The bungalows in question, though very tiny, are right on the water.

With a maximum of 35 rainy days a year (all during the off-season), almost 10 miles of beaches and pine forests adjacent to a world-class tourist attraction, Paestum has naturally evolved into the sleeping-bag capital of southern Italy. There are about a dozen campgrounds, all characterized by your basic carefree European holiday-camp atmosphere (perhaps in a slightly more exuberant form than elsewhere in Europe). *Ulisse, Athena Mare* (in a pine forest; tents only), *Mare Pineta,* and *Nettuno* all have direct access to the water. Great places to stay for a few days, especially if you're traveling with younger kids who can enjoy all sorts of wholesome activities on the beach (sandcastles, splashing contests) while parents slump into postures of vigilant supervisory idleness.

The Sights

Open from 9 until 2 hours before sunset. Closed on Monday. Free admission on Sunday.

Temple of Neptune: A copy of the Temple of Zeus at Olympia, which, as you'll recall, was one of the 7 wonders of the Ancient World. Noted for its stylish golden-section proportions (in this case, approximately 2 across the façade by 5 along the sides). A slight thickening of the columns in the middle (called *entasis*) makes them look straighter from far away and pleasingly bloated from up close.

The Basilica: An earlier temple, archaic in style and not nearly as well preserved.

It's quite enjoyable just to wander around the site, which is studded with columns, tombs, and other ancient structures strewn over a vast and very lovely terrain overgrown, in part, with wild roses (in season).

The Museum: Across the road from the archeological site. An agreeably spacious and uncluttered display of friezes, sculpted capitals, and so forth, from Paestum and environs. A notable collection of archaic temple friezes (the *metopes of the Thesauros*—ask for them by name), among the most remarkable sculptures produced anywhere in the Hellenic world; they were upstaged by a remarkable discovery made in 1968—an underground rock tomb at Paestum, the *Tomb of the Diver,* which dates from the fifth century B.C. and is decorated with wall paintings (the only examples of classical Greek painting of any kind that have turned up thus far). The paintings, on 5 different limestone slabs, are almost perfectly intact; the colors are very bright and, as in Etruscan tomb paintings of a somewhat later period, the decedent and his drinking buds seem to be having a good time. Open only from 9 to 12:30 (1:30 on holidays). Free admission. Closed on Monday.

SCILLA

A pleasant seaport town about 15 miles north of Reggio de Calabria. Home of the rock (or, as some would have it, the 6-headed monster) Scylla, wisely avoided by Odysseus and other ancient mariners. Later the site of a fortress that was turned into a *youth hostel* a couple of years ago. (Scylla's mythical partner, Charybdis—voracious imaginary monster and real-life treacherous tidal vortex on the other side of the Straits of Messina—has never been converted to any other use.) The hostel is an almost compulsory stopover. Its setting is unsurpassed, and the town itself is very pretty and not much frequented by tourists (thus, no campgrounds and very few hotels). Right down from the fortress there's a nice stretch of beach.

Also at the foot of the rock is the old fishermen's quarter of Chianalea. Swordfish, which in these waters frequently attain a length of 15 feet and weigh almost 1,500 pounds, are the fishermen's principal quarry; they're still hunted with harpoons, and as the fishing boats sail out of the harbor, you'll note that some of them have a lookout stationed in the foretop (or the maintop really, since these boats are only equipped with a single aluminum mast).

Ristorante Vertigine: Down from the piazza. A few outdoor tables with a great view of the water and little plaster gnomes, which are closer to hand but not nearly so attractive.

REGGIO DI CALABRIA

Right across the straits from Sicily. The town has been leveled by earthquakes several times, so current architecture tends toward the squatly functional. Still worth a visit, if only for the sake of the bronze Riace Warriors in the National Museum.

Where to Sleep

Albergo Noel: Via Zerbi, 13, 5 minutes from the museum (head toward the water). From the central station, take the little shuttle train that runs along the beachfront to the Stazione Lido. Moderately priced. Some of the rooms have balconies.

Camping degli Ulivi: North of Reggio, on a hill overlooking the city and the sea. Has a pool.

Camping Internazionale: By the water, in Marina Gallico.

The Sights

Museo Nazionale della Magna Grecia: Viale G. Amendola. Open from 9 to 1 and from 3:30 to 5:30 (in the summer), 9 to 1 on Sunday. Closed on Monday. Like it says, works of art that originated in the numerous ancient Greek settlements in southern Italy. Check out in particular the terra-cotta votive tablets and marble sculptures from Marasa and the terra-cotta statue of the young man on horseback from the Temple of Zeus. There's also an extensive collection of ancient coinage.

But, as noted, the 2 stars of the collection are the *Riace Warriors.* In 1972, at a depth of about 20 feet off the coast of Riace in Calabria, a diver came upon 2 bronze statues entombed and protected from corrosion by some 2,300 years' worth of vigorous marine growth, from which only the arm of statue B protruded. The various sediments and secretions in which the statues were embedded were removed very carefully, and after a lengthy conservation process, the 2 bronze warriors were put on public display (mounted on special shock absorbers to protect them from seismic tremors). Artistically, both are of exceptional quality, ranking with the greatest classical bronzes that have come down to us (the Charioteer of Delphi, for example).

Statue A, over 6 feet tall, weighing in at 550 pounds, is the more impressive of the 2, a defiant young warrior who appears to be squaring off against an unseen adversary. This work has been attributed by some to Phidias, the foremost sculptor of antiquity. Statue B, slightly smaller, is most notable for the realistic treatment of the musculature of the back and torso—on that account he's been variously attributed to Polyclitus and to a certain Pythagoras (not the mathematician) who worked in Reggio (Rhegium) during the fifth century B.C. and is mentioned by Pliny as the first sculptor to portray such anatomical niceties as the veins beneath the skin.

THE SOUTHEAST

Surrounded by a vast and uninteresting expanse of low-cost housing developments and famous for an earlier experiment in low-cost housing—the *sassi,* or troglydyte dwellings, which once housed a population of several thousand. These were natural or artificial caves or clefts in the rock, generally provided with a front wall of unmortared stone—the same basic principle as the ancient Anasazi cliff dwellings of the American Southwest—and an all-purpose aperture that served as door, window, chimney, and so forth. Each of the *sassi* was normally occupied in the good old days by an entire extended family, plus domestic animals. One of the kids hanging around piazza Pascoli will be your unofficial and highly conscientious tour guide, making sure you don't miss any of the highlights of this strange subterranean city, including a number of rock chapels built by monks, some decorated with frescoes in the Byzantine style.

The *Albergo Roma,* via Roma, 62, is a very nice non-troglodyte dwelling. Very reasonably priced.

TARANTO

The old city is built on a little island in the harbor; it has at one time or another been sacked, besieged, bombarded, or destroyed by practically everyone who ever ruled the waves from the Carthaginians to the British (during World War II); its scrofulous stone walls continue to exude a certain charm, perhaps reminiscent of the mustier parts of Venice. The modern city, on the mainland, has gone in mostly for industry and suburban sprawl.

Where to Sleep

Albergo Sorrentino: Piazza Fontana, 7. Telephone 40-74-56. In the old city, by the harbor. Most rooms have a balcony with a view of the water. Not very expensive.

Albergo Ariston: Piazza Fontana, 15, right next door. Expect to be awakened in the morning by the chuff-chuff-chuffing of the fishing boats in the harbor.

Hotel Miramare: Via Roma, 4. Telephone 228-54. On the mainland, but only about 3 minutes from the old city. The rooms face the sea and are cleaner than in the other 2 places. An elevator building. A little expensive.

Where to Eat

Pesce Frito: Largo Pesceria, 42, on the harbor of the old city, by the dock where the fishing boats unload the day's catch. Specializes in very fresh fish.

Ristorante la Barbaccia: Corso Due Mari, 22. In the new city, opposite the island. The dining room has an enormous vaulted ceiling (unwisely painted green). Great regional dishes. Renowned for its seafood but not really all that cheap.

The Sights

The Old City (Città Vecchia) occupies the site of ancient Taras/Tarentum. The Duomo, at the heart of the usual medieval maze, is a Byzantine-style cathedral for the most part with a Baroque façade and a crypt decorated with frescoes.

National Museum: Features a magnificent collection of ceramics and jewelry recovered from ancient tombs of Magna Graecia vintage.

LECCE

Sometimes called by its inhabitants the Florence of the South (in case you might have overlooked the resemblance). Actually a very lovely city with a high concentration of Baroque buildings character-ized by a highly ornate and truly astounding decorative style. The façades of the churches, the palazzi, and sometimes just ordinary houses are positively crawling with apes, eagles, and dragons, plus bizarre mutant foliage and all manner of mythical and Biblical celeb-rities. The warm, golden-white local building stone makes it all seem charmingly inventive rather than merely silly and overwrought. If your tastes run to something a little bit more austere, you might want to skip Lecce altogether.

Where to Sleep

Ostello per la Gioventù: In San Cataldo. A little seaside resort about 7 or 8 miles from Lecce. Telephone 65-00-26. A modern 65-bed hostel surrounded by pine trees; right on the beach. Bus service. There's also a *campground* nearby.

Albergo Patria Touring: Piazza Riccardi, 13, next to the Church of Santa Croce. A nice old hotel that boasts an authentic Baroque fa-çade and a lovely sort of stained-glass awning (a *marquise* to the initiated) over the front door. Fairly expensive, however.

Locanda Fiaggiano: Via Cavour, 4. One of the cheapest places in town but not without reason.

The Sights

Piazza San Oronzo: Center of outdoor social life in Lecce. The Roman column in the middle of the piazza was one of 2 that marked the end of the Appian Way; the other one is back in Brindisi, where it belongs. The saint on top is a later addition, as you might have guessed. There's also a Roman amphitheater on the piazza, and it is still in very good shape.

Piazza del Duomo: Our favorite. Surrounded on all sides with goofy Baroque façades. The Duomo, with its 5-story campanile, is on one side; on the other is a handsome loggia that runs the full width of the bishop's palace. Old-fashioned streetlamps provide a nice at-mospheric evening glow; less picturesque by day when it's used as a parking lot.

Santa Croce: Flagship example of the Leccese decorative style.

Has some nice humorous touches including dwarfs staggering beneath the weight of an enormous balcony, a bevy of strikingly butch caryatids, cherubs practicing juggling with wreaths of kudzu, and a highly disrespectful rendering of the Roman she-wolf totem—all to be found on the façade of this remarkable building.

OTRANTO

A lovely city that awakens from its slumbers every summer when the ferry starts making the weekly run over to Corfu. The old city is still protected by a handsome set of medieval ramparts, with a nice view of the water. The cathedral, built by the Normans in the eleventh century, has a beautiful rose window.

Where to Sleep

Camping Hydrusa: On the right just before you get to the harbor. Nice and shady.

Alternatively: Go on into the harbor. When you get to the water, make a right and follow the road that cuts right into the rock. It leads to a vast and uninhabited stretch of shoreline where you can pitch a tent, spread out a sleeping bag, or what you will.

BRINDISI

Has always been a terminus of one kind or another; in classical times it was a terminus of the Appian Way. (The mate of the Roman column in Lecce still occupies its original location by the harbor.) It is also the port from which Hannibal sailed home to Carthage, after stomping up and down the Italian boot for many years, and the one from which Jules Verne's Phileas Fogg took ship for Suez in *Around the World in 80 Days* (an episode regrettably deleted from the movie). Today, piazza Vittorio Emanuele serves as a kind of outdoor waiting room for the ferry to Corfu and points south. The cheapest of the ferry lines, *Libra Mare,* goes directly to Patras on the Greek mainland without stopping at Corfu. There's a student discount, but also a fairly hefty embarkation tax.

Where to Sleep

Benches in the piazza are the most popular place by far, which is okay as long as your belongings are reasonably secure. There's a *diurno* at the foot of the steps below the Appian Column, right on the harbor. The facilities are clean but kind of expensive.

Ostello per la Gioventù: Via Nicola Brandi, 2. Telephone 424-24. About 2 miles from the ferryboat dock, way over on the other side of the inlet. A modern building surrounded by trees, with a peaceful atmosphere and an excellent view of some kind of Fascist triumphal column down by the water. Kitchen privileges. Take bus No. 3 or 5.

Hotel La Rosetta: Via San Dionysio. In a quiet little street about 5 minutes from the ferryboat dock. Reasonably priced.

Camping Internazionale: In Mater Domini, about 3.5 miles north of Brindisi. In a stand of pines right by the water and not far from the airport; air traffic is minimal, however.

Where to Eat

Pizzeria l'Agnoletto: Via Pergola, a little street off corso Garibaldi. A little place with 2 or 3 outdoor tables. The food is quite decent.

The Sights

Once you've seen the Appian Column and explored the old city (fairly picturesque but limited in its extent), you've pretty much seen it all. There's a huge commemorative tablet in honor of Mussolini down by the harbor, below piazza Santa Teresa)—possibly inspired by the bronze tablets that Hannibal caused to be engraved with an account of his exploits and dropped off at a local temple. No subsequent administration has gone to the trouble and expense that would be involved in prying it loose and throwing it in the drink, though the inscription is routinely defaced with hostile and derisive graffiti.

To get out to the beach, buy a bus ticket at a *tabaccheria* and catch a No. 4 on piazza del Popolo.

OSTUNI

On the road to Bari, 27 miles north of Brindisi. An amazing little city built on a headland surmounting a plain covered with olive trees. The houses are little white cubes stacked on top of one another like Lego blocks or (perhaps a more decisive cultural influence) like the buildings in an Algerian casbah.

ALBEROBELLO

About 20 miles north of Ostuni but further inland, on the road between Bari and Taranto. A fair-sized town best known for the *zona trulli* (plural: *trulli;* singular: *trullo*), a collection of traditional stone houses of bizarre conehead design, located on a hill to the south of town. The cylindrical lower part of a *trullo* is built of big stone blocks mortared together; the conical roof is made of flat stones stacked up concentrically, whitewashed, and embellished with curious signs such as a cartoon wizard's hat, a solar wheel, an Akhnaten cross, a menorah, and a Sacred Heart inscribed inside a triangle. There are a number of multiroom *trulli* in which each room occupies a separate cone. The *zona* is now classed as a historic monument and is very well maintained, though if you want to see *trulli* in slightly more authentic surroundings (without the sleazy souvenir stands), look in back of the cathedral.

Where to Sleep

Pensione Cucina da Miniello: Via Balenzano, 14, across from the *zona trulli.* Single rooms and doubles (a little expensive). Restaurant on the ground floor.

Hotel dei Trulli: Via Cadore, 35. Telephone 721-130. Purists may find fault, but every room of this unique and rather expensive tourist hotel consists of a remodeled and lavishly appointed *trullo,* like a little bungalow surrounded by luxuriant foliage. Right in the midst of the *zona.*

BARI

The old city, now surrounded by a vigorous and expansive modern seaport, was the traditional point of embarkation for Crusaders and pilgrims bound for the Holy Land, and the shipowners of Bari, though not as aggressive as the Venetians, did very nicely for themselves in the long-haul charter-party business.

Where to Sleep

Go straight as you leave the station, then make a left onto via Crisanzio:

Pensione Romeo: At No. 12. Take the elevator to the third floor. Right on the main piazza. Plenty of action at night. In the same building is *Pensione Giulia,* but the hotel on the fourth floor is expensive.

Locanda Robinson: At No. 18 (third floor). Same prices. At No. 26 is *Locanda Maria.* 3 of the rooms have beautiful stone balconies overlooking the piazza.

Less centrally located:

Ostello per la Gioventù: Via Nicola Masaro, 33, in Palese, a little seaside resort about 4 miles north of Bari. Telephone 32-02-82. Right on the water; the beach is rocky, but there's a good place to go swimming about 10 minutes to the north. Recently built, though already getting a little dog-eared. From Bari, catch a No. 1 bus outside the Teatro Petruzelli on corso Cavour; it's a 20-minute ride.

Camping San Giorgio: Strada Adriatica, 5 miles from Bari on the highway to Brindisi. Pool and bungalows available.

Where to Eat

Vini e Cucina: Strada Vallisa, 23 (old city), behind the fish market. Complete authenticity is assured. By the door is an interesting device for tapping winecasks. Home-style cuisine, *"la cucina della mamma,"* in the troglodytic dining area downstairs.

Trattoria al Pescatore: Piazza Federico II (old city), near the castello. One of the city's best known fish restaurants. Not exactly cheap but decidedly worth the money.

Ristorante Porta d'Oro: Via Argiro, 90, in the modern city. Good food. White-collar clientele. Pleasant atmosphere, but the neon is perhaps overly scintillating. Try the *zuppa di cozze* (mussels) *crostino.*

The Sights

The Old City: Of Byzantine origin, one of the very best of its kind in southern Italy. You should enjoy slinking around its exceedingly narrow streets, something like those on Mont. St. Michel except with more real-life inhabitants and fewer tourists.

The Castello: Consists of a palace—occupied during their respective centuries by Emperor Frederick II and Lady Bona Sforza of the Milanese warlord family—surrounded by bastions, barbicans, and other serious fortifications.

The Duomo: The spareness and simplicity of the interior decor is very appealing. Light slanting down through the clerestory windows above the nave gives the impression of great purity and delicacy.

Basilica di San Nicola: Not far from the Duomo. This is the shrine of St. Nicholas, who became patron saint of children (and, eventually, Santa Claus) after resurrecting 3 of them who had been murdered and dismembered by an evil innkeeper and were already marinating in a pickle barrel by the time the case was brought to his attention. Superb carvings, with figures of lions and elephants over the central doorway out front. Just to the right of the left-hand doorway you can still make out a graffito (a cross) scratched into the doorframe by a passing Crusader.

SICILY

Sicilians like to be told their island is "nothing at all like Italy," even though the place they're really in competition with is Greece—same climate, same blue Mediterranean, same warmhearted hospitality, same Greek temples—though of course they don't make nearly such a big deal of it. When was the last time you heard someone mention "the glory that was Sicily, the grandeur that was Syracuse"? Their history has been characterized by alternating waves of invasion and immigration, which makes them distantly related to almost all other nations. They like Americans, for example, because they have even more second and third cousins in Boston and New York than first cousins in Turin and Milan. They even like the French because of all that Norman blood coursing (or they like to imagine coursing) through their veins and because they're both so much more proficient at swallowing final vowels than the Northern Italians.

Climate

There's always an offshore breeze, and the climate is roughly comparable to that of California (or North Africa, if you prefer). Green in the spring, with plenty of flowers and foliage, and lots of little green oranges on the trees; yellow or brown in the summer and not much in the way of foliage. Clearly you're going to have to make 2 trips (or not go home at all) in order to get the full effect.

Getting Around

By Train: Cheap but not very fast (gives you lots of time to admire the landscape). In the countryside, stations are very frequent, and you can always check your stuff and fill up on drinking water.

By Bus: Often cheaper and faster than the train. Especially useful for getting to some of those hard-to-reach places in the center of the island. Actually an institutionalized form of hitchhiking, since bus routes and schedules seem to be almost entirely at the discretion of the driver. Still, you should be able to get anywhere you want to go very cheaply by means of a judicious combination of trains and buses, bearing in mind that very few of the latter keep running after 8:30 P.M.

Hitching: Quite easy if you stick to the main arteries. Can be something of an ordeal in the summer. The larger cities are both populous (Palermo, 800,000; Catania, 500,000; Messina, 250,000) and sprawling, so the familiar technique of taking a bus out to the city limits is recommended.

Where to Sleep

Campgrounds are pretty rare except on the eastern coast. Hostels aren't all that common either, but there are many inexpensive hotels in the old quarters of the larger towns and in the villages. Cheapos will prefer to sleep in the train stations, which are none too shabby as a rule.

Interruption of Vital Services

Sicilians are famous for their piety, which means, among other things, that everything shuts down on local religious holidays *(feste)*. As elsewhere, midday closing hours for stores and museums are religiously observed, though this has nothing to do with conventional piety.

Churches do not normally stay open all day, and there's nothing more frustrating than walking up the steps of one to find it *chiusa* after you've made a special trip to see the Byzantine mosaics, Van Dyck altarpiece, and so forth, that's locked up inside. The best way to avoid this is to show up in time for daily mass, that is 7 to 8:30 A.M. on weekdays and occasionally on Sunday, sometimes after 5 P.M., frequently between 6 and 7 P.M., and usually between 9 and noon on Sunday. Bear in mind that these hours are typical but by no means universal. *Buona fortuna.*

How to Get There

There are several departures every hour from *Villa San Giovanni* and *Reggio di Calabria.* Fares are the same in either direction. No charge to holders of Inter-Rail/Eurail passes.

The *Tirrenia* ferry line has at least one departure every day from Naples to Catania or Palermo. It's an overnight trip; 30 percent discount available to holders of Inter-Rail/Eurail passes.

Sicil-Ferry has 4 boats a week from Genoa to Palermo. The crossing takes 23 hours.

The Sicilians

We didn't mean to imply earlier on that merely because of certain shared genetic and linguistic peculiarities the Sicilians are anything like the French. (For example, they couldn't reasonably get upset at anyone for mispronouncing their language because they're constantly doing it themselves.) However, it is true that the somewhat operatic exuberance of the mainland Italians is replaced with an attitude of diplomatic expectancy, with the possibility of real (as opposed to superficial) warmth if you turn out to be all right after all. The natural Sicilian tendency to assist helpless strangers is powerfully tempered by the desire to avoid the appearance of condescension at all costs. We recall one instance where we had stopped to ask directions in the midst of a hopeless Byzantine labyrinth. A young fellow volunteered to show us the way out; he hopped into his car and drove off at top speed, threading his way through the oncoming traffic with the skill and insouciance of an Olympic slalom racer. To have done any less would have been tantamount to implying that we weren't together enough to get in our car and drive out of town like a normal person.

It has to be admitted that after so many millennia of being oppressed and imposed on by other nations the Sicilians have forged a national consciousness that is stubbornly independent but not the least bit straightforward. Failure to take this into account could mean the difference between a merely idyllic circuit of the island (with postcards to prove it) and a series of truly memorable encounters with its people. In this connection we should perhaps repeat our earlier highly qualified warning against pickpockets, bag snatchers, and so forth. Your best approach is to avoid an ostentatious display of your holdings; however, free-floating, generalized paranoia is sure to be detected and resented by all those who are *not* pickpockets, bag snatchers, and so forth. Remember that these people are professionals, and there's sure to be somebody else around who is richer than you are.

In traditional Sicily, as in nineteenth-century North America, sex is kept pretty much under wraps (see below, Passeggiata), whereas death is right out in the open. Apart from the omnipresent old women in black, there's the only slightly less conspicuous custom of placarding every available inch of urban wall space with obituary notices of roughly the same size and density as rock concert and movie posters in North American cities. Often richly illuminated and in extreme cases (by richer families in Agrigento, Taormina, and Syracuse) adorned with a full-color picture of the Holy Face these announcements are put up not only by the bereaved family but also by the neighbors or co-workers of the deceased, burial societies, soccer clubs, and so forth, and are frequent updates expressing the family's grateful thanks, the first or second anniversary of the death, and so on.

Murder and vendetta are of paramount importance in the Sicilian mythology of death, and the famous Sicilian fatalism—dismissed as laziness by some—has been described by no less an authority than Giuseppe di Lampadusa in *The Leopard* as "the yearning for a state of voluptuous immobility, simply another form of the desire for death." The combined legacy of all their foreign occupiers has left the Sicilians with a variety of deep cultural wounds, exotic monuments, and curious customs, but the Sicilian philosophy of fatalism —"the tragic sense of life," as the Spanish gentleman said—still insists on a certain dignity and style, and may even require considerable audacity and enthusiasm, to put it into practice.

Passeggiata

In the rest of Italy this is a prominent part of urban life, but in Sicily it is a sacred rite. It provides an immediate index of cultural change in a given village or town. In its classical form only the men turned out for the evening grand promenade, dressed in their nattiest dark suits and with pointed shoes glistening. After a time women were permitted to join in as well, adding variety to the color and texture of the human stream that flowed through the corso or the piazza between the hours of 6 and 8 P.M. every evening; adolescents circulated in single-sex packs, fraternization between them being conducted exclusively through the medium of eye contact so that an especially burning glance was regarded as a binding proposal of marriage (witnessed, of course, by the entire community).

Today things are not what they were, and you may actually see a teenage girl walk up to a boy and start talking to him, bold as brass, in some of the more culturally damaged communities. After everyone has exchanged a few conventional words of greeting, it is suddenly 8 o'clock; mother, father, and children are reunited, and it's time to go home.

The Mafia

We thought it best to mention it since Sicily and the Mafia seem to be closely linked in the popular mind, as your dentist or dry

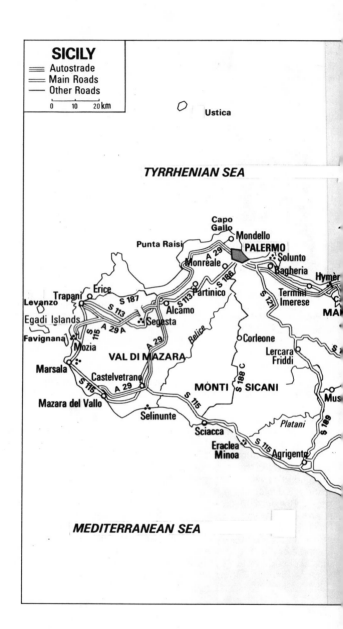

SICILY

- ═══ Autostrade
- ══ Main Roads
- — Other Roads

0   10   20 km

Ustica

TYRRHENIAN SEA

Capo Gallo
Mondello
PALERMO
Punta Raisi
A 29
Monreale
Solunto
Bagheria
Hymèr
S 186
Termini Imerese
Partinico
Erice
S 187
Trapani
S 113
Alcamo
Levanzo
S 113
Segesta
Egadi Islands
A 29 A
S 115
Balice
MA
Favignana
Mozia
Corleone
Lercara Friddi
VAL DI MAZARA
A 29
S 1
Marsala
Castelvetrano
S 115
A 29
MÓNTI SICANI
S 188 C
Mazara del Vallo
Mus
Selinunte
S 115
Platani
S 189
Sciacca
Eraclea Minoa
S 115
Agrigento

MEDITERRANEAN SEA

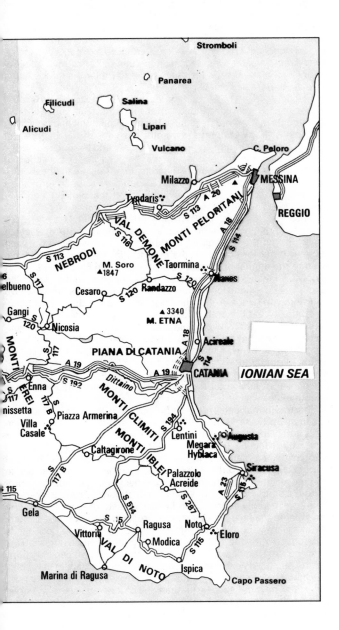

Stromboli

Panarea

Filicudi

Salina

Alicudi

Lipari

Vulcano

C. Peloro

Milazzo

MESSINA

Tyndaris

S 113 A 20

S 113

MONTI PELORITANI

A 18

REGGIO

VAL DEMONE

NEBRODI

S 116

M. Soro
▲1847

Taormina

A 18

S 114

elbueno

S 117

Cesaro

S 120

Randazzo

S 120

▲3340
M. ETNA

Naxes

Gangi

S
120

Nicosia

Acireale

MONTI

S 117

PIANA DI CATANIA

A 18

A 19

S 114

CATANIA

IONIAN SEA

Enna

S 192

Dittaino

A 19

S 117

nissetta

S 117 B

Piazza Armerina

Villa
Casale

MONTI CLIMITI

S 194

Lentini

Megara
Hyblaea

Augusta

Caltagirone

MONTI IBLEI

Palazzolo
Acreide

Siracusa

A 23

S 115

S 115

S
117 B

Gela

S 514

Palazzolo
Acreide

S 287

Vittoria

S 5

Ragusa

Noto

Eloro

Modica

S 115

Marina di Ragusa

VAL DI NOTO

Ispica

Capo Passero

cleaner is sure to remind you when you mention where you're thinking of going for your vacation. According to tradition the Mafia arose as a kind of shadow government of the Sicilian countryside, a natural counterbalance to the corruption, callousness, and incompetence of foreign rule (the Normans, Spanish, Neapolitans, and the French under Napoleon are variously cited as the corrupt foreign incompetents in question). The word itself is said to be a popular corruption of the Arabic *mûafat,* which meant something like "courageous protectors"; in later years its members came to prefer the term *onerata società,* "honorable society."

As a government of, by, and for the submerged Sicilian peasantry, the society naturally depended on at least the tacit support of its constituents in the struggle against the cruel but bumbling Bourbons (or whoever they were); thus, the notorious code of silence *(omertà)* that the society enjoined on both its members and the public at large. Later on, after the society had further evolved into a collection of feuding extortionists and brutal bandits, the principle of "hear nothing, see nothing, give nothing away" continued to be in force, now chiefly for reasons of self-preservation rather than enlightened self-interest.

Since 1981 the Corleonesi (from Corleone, which is a real place and not a figment of Mario Puzo's imagination) and a rival crime family that controls certain neighborhoods in Palermo have been slugging it out for control of the drug traffic. The day we arrived in Palermo the annual body count stood at 79 (with 6 more added that day); by the time we left it had risen to 88. Apart from the screaming headlines in *ORA,* the local tabloid, which specializes in investigative reporting, you're not likely to hear too much about this sort of thing, the doings of the honorable society not being regarded as a fit subject for casual *trattoria* conversation. The few people willing to venture an opinion may tell you that it has all been downhill for the Mafia since they got involved in drugs and the criminal element took over —what might be thought of as the straight *Godfather* line, a kind of ancestral memory of the days when the Mafia really was regarded as a dispenser of justice for the poor and a ferocious settler of scores other than its own.

The traditional centers of Mafia activity are (or were) Palermo, Alacamo, Corleone, Gangi, Villalba, and Catania. *Villalba,* for example, a little village on the main road between Palermo and Caltanissetta, still living by the leisurely agrarian rhythms of the Sicilian countryside, was famous during the 30s, 40s, and 50s as the rural seat of *Don Calogero* (Don Carlo), who died peacefully in his bed in 1954, never having been convicted of any criminal offense. According to his obituary notice: "With the skill of genius, he increased the fortunes of a noble house . . . and was a benefactor to the land . . . He was great in the face of persecution, greater still at the hour of combat, ceaselessly doing good." Numerous attempts have been made to dispense with the services of such public benefactors as Don Calogero over the course of the last century or so; we can only hope that the one that is currently in progress (which appears to have lined up a number of especially courageous prosecution witnesses) will turn out to be more successful than any of its predecessors. A great book on the subject (that is, one not necessarily written for the purpose of a quick-and-dirty movie sale) is *The Sea the Color of Wine* by Leonardo Sciascia.

City Driving *alla Siciliana*

Driving, even in Sicily, is nothing more than a sequence of learned behavior patterns. In order to be able to do it in a relaxed and confident manner, what has previously been learned (for purposes of surviving in a less exacting cultural context—for example, almost every other country in the world but Mexico) must now be unlearned. In short, you must either learn to obey the Sicilian code of the road or somehow compel the Sicilians to start obeying yours. This is a question on which there can be no compromise, and when in Rome . . . though as far as driving is concerned, you'll recall that we strongly advised against any attempt to do as the Romans do.

If a stop sign in other cultures can be likened to the period at the end of a sentence, then a stop sign in Sicily is more like a comma; it indicates a pause but not enough of one to seriously disrupt the flow. Similarly, there is no such thing as a "right" of way; it's purely a question of evaluating the physical constraints on your freedom of action as a driver in certain situations and of not attempting to exceed them—in other words, of acting decisively but not without prudence. With practice, anyone can learn to do it.

The rearview mirror is a largely useless accessory. Your responsibility as a driver extends only to what is directly in front of you and maybe a little bit to each side. The horn, as you'll discover, can be used to convey a wide variety of emotions, though rarely irritation or impatience. If a Sicilian driver sees you pausing for too long at a stop sign—acting indecisively or in some other manner not conducive to the common good—then he may give you a gentle bleat of the horn to call this to your attention.

You'll find parking is not nearly so easy as driving. Every town, village, archeological site, and so forth, possesses its own more or less official parking lot. When the attendant approaches you, hand over the few hundred lire that he asks for with a brisk and confident gesture, as if to say that you're familiar with the customs of the country and you fully expect to find your car still there, in whole *and* in part, when you come back. If you come back more than an hour later, you can also expect to hand over a few more hundred lire.

The basic principle involved in parking in Sicily is that of the optimal use of space. You'll note that in an unsupervised setting, on the street, cars normally are parked in a close-formation herringbone pattern (at an acute angle to the curb), with both front wheels well up *over* the curb and onto the sidewalk. You can readily see how, in this context, any driver with your profligate notions of "parallel parking" and keeping the leading edge of the vehicle a good 6 inches/13 centimeters *away* from the curb will (a) be perceived by other drivers as acting in a manner entirely detrimental to the common good and (b) will never get a parking place.

Motor scooters, minibikes, and the like, may take some getting used to; the same basic principle applies here—optimal use of available space, which generally means papa, mamma, and baby are all aboard, with maybe a cat or 2 perched on the handlebars. (The wearing of helmets is regarded as unsportsmanlike.) These brave little crafts, frail and vulnerable though they may seem, are still entirely capable of taking care of business. In this respect, an even more basic principle applies—every man for himself, and God looks after all. You may be surprised by how few accidents (even including the gentlest of collisions) actually occur on Sicilian city streets, but when you stop to consider the principal components of this sublime vehicular anarchy—altruism and good fellowship rather than aggression and "defensiveness," a realistic acceptance of the immutable laws of physics, and a humane consensus rather than slavish obedience to an incomprehensible "code"—it may not seem so surprising after all.

We hope you learn to appreciate and take advantage of the greater freedom from unnatural constraints (including seatbelts) that the Sicilian system confers upon you as a driver, and also the highly decorous manner in which it thumbs its nose at all authority. The Sicilian traffic cop, like the U.S. Supreme Court, is only prepared to intervene in the most consequential cases, and he watches the most critically overpopulated Vespas whiz by without so much as the flick of an eyebrow. He has no intention of making your life more difficult than it already is.

Study the Sicilian traffic cop; study the Sicilian driver; study their serenity and supreme indifference in the face of anything less than certain death. Learn to override your uptight Anglo-Saxon attitudes and foibles. Study the code of the road, and make it your own; enshrine its principles in your heart. And let us know how you make out.

PALERMO

Capital of Sicily. If you're driving (see above), the late-morning traffic on via Roma may be your first real exposure to the code of the road. Even before the thrillingly anticlimactic moment when you succeed in parking your car, you may not like the look of the place; basic prejudices (regarding noise, dirt, confusion, chaos, and decay) may have already come into play. It may take you some little time before you begin to appreciate Palermo as a city of almost limitless visual resources, a city of many surprises and a study in glaring, unsubtle contrasts. We freely admit that the esthetic appeal of the latter is often overestimated by travel writers but not, we assure you, in this particular case.

Apart from the artistic and architectural interest of its various monuments, Palermo is primarily an atmosphere—magnificent churches alongside the sleaziest and most dilapidated tenements, and beautiful abandoned palazzi face to face with the ugliest and most uncouth of postwar buildings. Without trying to paint an overly sentimental picture of the culture of poverty (like the ones of those bright-eyed Neopolitan waifs, of which you may already have seen one or two by now), we'd still like to suggest that what is likely to provide your most enduring impressions of the city is the popular culture of Palermo—which seems to flourish even in the streets where the garbage is piled highest and in the grungiest back alleys, where the kids invent at least one new game every day. This is almost likely to be your first encounter with the incredible *niceness* of the Sicilians, something else that fortunately will be remaining with you for at least the duration of your stay on the island.

Palermo, once properly appreciated, is never likely to be forgotten—any more than you could forget your first date, your first car, your first [you fill in the blank with an appropriate peak experience].

Useful Addresses

EPT Office: Piazza Castelnuovo, 34. Telephone 58-38-47. There's another one out at the airport (telephone 29-18-86), with a very efficient, friendly staff, and lots of literature.

Airport: At Punta Raisi, 19 miles (31 k) out of town. Frequent buses run to Palermo between 6:30 A.M. and 10:10 P.M. You can also take a taxi (price to be negotiated in advance).

Train Station (D4 on map): Has a currency exchange that is open on Sunday and past regular banking hours. Also has an information booth, long-distance telephones (on the piazza), and trains to just about every place on the island.

More *telephones* can be found on piazza Ungheria.

U.S. Consulate: Via Vaccarini. Telephone 29-15-32.

Central Post Office: Via Roma, 319.

American Express: c/o Ruggeri, via Amari, 40. Open until 1, then between 4 and 7.

Where to Sleep

• *Hotels*

They are nearly all clustered around the train station, many occupying a floor in a déclassé palazzo or large private house.

Albergo Sicilia: Via Divisi, 99 (intersection of via Maqueda, not far from the station). Telephone 28-44-60. A clean, hospitable establishment in a handsome building with an enormous staircase. The rooms on via Maqueda may be a little noisy. The owner has just repainted and raised his prices, but they are still tolerable. Upstairs, *Albergo Alessandro;* same basic deal.

Albergo Firenze: Via Candelai, 68. Telephone 58-08-69. A handsome palazzo-type building with a sculpted facade and wrought-iron balconies located on a quiet street in a working-class district. Rooms with or without private bath. Clean and scarcely more expensive than most.

Albergo Vienna: Via Roma, 188 (fourth floor). Telephone 32-99-69. Family atmosphere. The owner speaks English. The premises are unattractive and none too clean. A double room (no bath) is fairly cheap. Lockup is at 11:30 P.M.

Albergo Piccadilly: Via Roma, 72 (third floor). A little expensive. The owner is very nice and thoroughly honest. Don't get a room that faces the street.

Hotel Petit: Via Pipe di Belmonte, 84. Clean and fairly inexpensive. A nice location.

Hotel Odeon: Piazza Ruggero Settimo (B1 on map). Quiet, fairly inexpensive (showers included).

Albergo Orientale: Via Maqueda, 26. Telephone 23-57-27. On the second floor of a Renaissance palazzo. Handsome exterior but the insides are a little murky. Hospitable and reasonably priced.

Albergo Verdi: Via Maqueda, 417. Telephone 58-49-28. Not so near the station but still quite centrally located. Clean, hospitable, fairly inexpensive but a little noisy.

Albergo Rosalia Conca d'Oro: Via Santa Rosalia, 7 (fourth floor). Telephone 23-35-43. The nearest to the station. A bit expensive. No private baths; archaic plumbing.

PALERMO

0   100   200m

- P. XIII VITTIME
- V. F. Patti
- Via Francesco Crispi
- V. Meli
- P. CARBONE
- della
- Emanuelle
- Cala
- Foro
- Foro
- V. Butera
- PIAZZA MARINA
- Vittorio
- GIARDINO GARIBALDI
- Pal Chiaramonte
- S. Francesco d'Assisi
- Lungarini
- Alloro
- Pal Abatellis
- Umberto
- V. N. Cervello
- Italico
- To
- Via
- Paternostra
- Alloro
- L. Castrofilippo
- V. Spasimo
- Lincoln
- Via
- P.D. REVOLUZIONE
- La Magione
- Via
- VILLA GIULIA
- Roma
- Garibaldi
- Lincoln
- Via
- ORTO BOTANICO
- Maqueda
- Via
- Corso
- dei
- Mille
- Archirafi
- V. Tiro a Segno Naz.
- kory
- P. GIULIO CESARE
- Stazione Centrale

Hotel Pretoria: via Maqueda, 124. Telephone 23-18-05. Faces a courtyard. Clean and reasonably priced.

• *Campgrounds*

Internazionale Trinacria: Via Barcarello, in Sferracavallo, about 8 miles out of town. Telephone (091) 53-05-90. Right on the beach. Nice facilities. Open all year. Somewhat expensive. Take a No. 28 bus from piazza Verdi or a No. 16 from the station.

Club dell'Ulivo: Via Pegaso, also n Sferracavallo. About 600 yards from the water. Open all year. If you're staying at either of these places, be sure to try the *spaghetti alle vongole* at *Il Delfino,* right in the middle of the village. A warm welcome is guaranteed to all.

The next 3 are in or near *Isola delle Femine,* about 8 miles to the east of Palermo:

Pepsi Cola: Via Spaggia, in Pozzillo, about a mile from Isola delle Femine (follow the signs from the highway). Telephone 67-76-54. Family atmosphere. Well maintained. On the water, but there's no beach and the water is kind of foul. Open from April to early September.

La Plaia: Lungomare dei Saraceni. Telephone 67-70-01. On the water. Open year round.

La Scogliera: Via Palermo, 20. Telephone 67-73-15. Close to but not actually on the water. Bar and cafeteria. Open from June 1 to September 30.

Where to Eat

Natale Osteria con Cucina: Via Francesco Matera, 2, opposite Cala basin, near piazza Fonderia. A popular, moderately priced seafood place located on a peaceful little piazza. Has a terrace and a nice relaxing atmosphere. Snails available in season (August to September). Closed on Sunday.

Trattoria Johnny: Via Sperlinga, 57, near the Teatro Massimo. Telephone 33-46-78. Forget about the jive-turkey decor and concentrate on the food. Excellent Sicilian specialties at a very reasonable price; gastronomic adventurers will want to try the *rigatoni maneggiati* and the *involtini alla siciliana.* Very hospitable. One of our best addresses in Palermo.

Shangaï: Vicolo Mezzani, 34, near the intersection of corso Vittorio Emanuele and via Roma. Telephone 58-95-73. On a second-floor terrace, right in the middle of the Vucciria market. When they run out of something in the kitchen, the proprietor lowers a basket over the rail. Definitely not to be missed. Specializes in seafood and has a few inexpensive entrees. The service is pretty sloppy.

Ristorante Pizzeria Bellini: Piazza Bellini, 6. Telephone 23-04-13. A great location (see below, Quattro Canti. Reasonable prices, considering. The fairly ordinary pizza is to be consumed on the terrace (very nice), at the counter, or out on the piazza. In any case, an after-dinner stroll around Quattro Canti is obligatory.

Antica San Francesco: Piazza San Francesco (take via Paternostro off corso Vittorio Emanuele). An old tavern with marble tables and kind of an old-fashioned ice cream parlor decor, not counting the enormous cast-iron stove. A simple daily entree and a couple of different cheeses. Recommended not so much for the food as for the neighborhood atmosphere and the beautiful church outside (see below).

Da Leonardo: Via Gorizia, 19, third on your right as you head down via Roma from the station. Checkered oilcloth on the tables and a family atmosphere. Inexpensive *menù.*

Tu . . . e basta: Via Giorgio Castriota (corner of via Enrico Albanese). A great restaurant that specializes in meat dishes with raw materials lovingly selected by the owner. Reasonably priced, considering both quality and quantity; we've never seen anyone actually clean their plate, and not from any lack of trying.

Il Brodo: Via Discesa dei Giudici, 24. Telephone 23-75-20. If you're not familiar with *brodo,* you'll see several enormous pots of the stuff simmering on the stoves by the door.

Pizzeria Le Caprice: via Cavour, 42. Expensive but worth it.

Via Filippina: 17. A budget eatery with an affordable one-price menu, specializing in stuffed slices of fresh tuna. Copious portions.

Vino Locale

Just as the Vikings called northern Canada "Vinland the Good," the Greeks called Sicily *Oinotria,* "Wineland"—the main difference being that the Greeks seem to have had some idea of what they were talking about. You'll come across lots of little *osterie* all over Sicily with good local wines right out of the cask. In Palermo:

80 via Divisi: The casks are truly enormous. The white is a little cloudy, but it goes down quite smoothly all the same. Closes fairly early.

26 via Maqueda: The casks are painted with little scenes, emphasizing a grape-picking motif.

Maxim's Bar: Via Vigo, 3. Fairly inexpensive. Also a good place for breakfast (solid food is also available, that is).

There are lots of other nice places like these in Palermo; we leave the task of locating and evaluating them as an exercise for the serious student.

The Sights

• The Main Attractions

Quattro Canti: Intersection of via Maqueda and corso Vittorio Emanuele. So-called because each of the *quattro canti* (four corners) of the intersection is adorned with a clump of Baroque statuary. The 2 adjacent piazze are very lovely: *piazza Pretoria* with a large, graceful fountain at its center and Palazzo del Municipio along one side, and *piazza Bellini* which is surrounded by a number of interesting churches, including *Santa Caterina, La Martorana* (great mosaics), and *San Cataldo* (with its 3 little red Moorish domes).

Duomo: On your right as you head up Vittorio Emanuele. Basically in the Arabo-Norman style (attractive regional blend of Moorish and Romanesque) with numerous additions and subtractions by later regimes. The long amber-colored façade with its crenelated roof (since the Arabs and the Normans didn't get on all that well) is especially well proportioned. You'll find some interesting stuff inside including the *treasury.*

Palazzo dei Normanni and *Capella Palatina:* Not to be missed on any account. Go up the staircase on your left, just before Porta Nuova (an arch with a ceramic-tile roof). The Palazzo has a beautiful interior courtyard with loggia (if that's the word we want—balconies with a colonnade on every floor). The *Capella* is another Arabo-Norman dazzler, featuring Norman vaults, Moorish carved wooden ceilings, and a few other inspired eclectic touches: Roman columns and Byzantine mosaics, including the overwhelmingly majestic *Christos Pantocrator,* "Christ the Ruler of the Universe." Note that women wearing T-shirts, dresses with shoulder straps, and so forth, are not admitted to the chapel. The Palazzo is currently the seat of the Sicilian parliament; no visitors are allowed when the latter is in session.

San Giovanni degli Eremiti: Via dei Benedettini, right by the Norman Palace. A delightful Norman church with Moorish domes and a lovely cloister, half swallowed up by the aggressive foliage of the garden. An ideal rest stop.

• By the Harbor

The harbor area still hasn't fully recovered from World War II: bombsites, parking lots, and ugly modern buildings alternate with shabby old working-class neighborhoods and beautiful parish churches. Right around piazza Kalsa and vie Torremuzza and Cervello is a neighborhood full of little fix-it shops, good-smelling bakeries, and countertop restaurants specializing in *trippa alla palermitana.*

Giardino Garibaldi: Piazza Marina. A wild and weirdly overgrown public garden (a state that has been reprovingly noted by the guidebooks for many editions now) furnishes one of Palermo's more interesting contrasts: The park is filled with portrait busts of eminent men you never heard of, cutthroat card games surrounded by cheering crowds of spectators, and a number of exotic banyan trees (Indian ficus), a kind of giant magnolia with aerial roots that sprout high up on the trunk and slither through the air for several yards before burying themselves in the ground. Nearby is the elegant *Palazzo Chairamonte* and the *Marionette Museum,* in the Palazzo Fatta del Bosco, piazza Marina, 19. The latter houses a magnificent collection of *pupi* (large-size Sicilian marionettes). Open only from 5 to 7 P.M. on Monday, Wednesday, and Friday.

Opera dei Pupi: A stately, chivalric Sicilian version of Punch and Judy, with themes and characters (Roland and Reinaut, Princess Angelica, and the wicked Gano) drawn from *Orlando Furioso* or other romances and medieval Sicilian history. It's more enjoyable if you understand Italian but, as with real-live opera, the settings and situations are highly conventionalized (the Christians always enter from stage left and the Saracens from stage right), so usually you can follow right along in any case. It's also nice to go with Sicilians, just to make sure you'll be able to find the theater; this also decreases the chances that somebody will go through your pockets during the performance (no fooling). Present-day *pupi* performances sort of straddle the boundary between an authentic popular art form and touristic hokum. In Palermo, the theaters are located at via del Pappagallo, 10; vicolo Ragusi, 6; via Bara (all'Olivela), 95; piazza Luigi Sturzo, 4, and via del Medico, 6. The first show generally starts at 6 P.M.

National Gallery of Sicily: Via Alloro, 4, just minutes away from Giardino Garibaldi. A great museum. The collection is housed in the elegant arcaded galleries of the Palazzo Abatellis, which is very beautiful in its own right. On the ground floor is an interesting jumble of Arab decorative woodcarving and ceramics, works by the Renaissance sculptor Gagini, and an extraordinary fifteenth-century fresco, *The Triumph of Death.* Upstairs you'll find Sicilian paintings from the twelfth to the sixteenth centuries, with emphasis on *Antonello da Messina.* If you're very lucky, his touching and dramatic *Annunciation* won't be off somewhere with a traveling exhibit. Our personal favorite is a triptych by a non-Sicilian, Jan Gossaert van *Mabuse,* called *Virgin and Child with SS. Catherine and Dorothy*—a masterpiece of northern Renaissance hyperrealism. Check out the little rustic Flemish scenes in the background, doubtless painted with a brush made out of a single hair (2 at most). Open from 9 to 1:30 (1 on Sunday) and also from 3 to 6 on Tuesday and Thursday during the summer, but don't count on it. Closed on Monday. Free admission on the first days and the second and fourth Saturdays.

Museo Archeologico: Next to the central post office. Installed in a former convent. To be perfectly candid, once we got past the airy little cloister by the main entrance with its fountain and semitropical foliage, our attention started to droop a little bit. Fans of the Doric order will want to see the famous *metopes from Selinute,* and there are a few nice bronzes upstairs, but we'd suggest you concentrate on the National Gallery instead.

• *Some Nice Churches*

Santa Maria della Catena: Near the Giardino Garibaldi. You can visit it if you find it open.

San Francesco d'Assisi: Nearby, at the intersection of vie Merlo and Paternostro. A beautiful fourteenth-century Gothic façade with a rose window—most impressive at night. Has a richly decorated Renaissance/Baroque interior.

La Magione: Near the station (E4 on map), 5 minutes from San Francesco d'Assisi. On your way here you'll pass the site of the famous Sicilian Vespers of 1282, when the Palermitans rose up against their hated Angevin overlords and slaughtered most of the French population of Palermo (many of whom are buried beneath the piazza). The uprising is said to have broken out after a French soldier made a naughty gesture at a local woman after church (hence, "Vespers"); the conspirators who planned it chose the word *cicere* (chickpeas) for their password since the French have always had trouble with the *ch*'s.

Oratoria de Santa Cita: At the end of via Valverde, back near the central post office. Lavishly decorated by Serpotta, the eighteenth-century stucco king, who went in for chubby cherubs, stately allegorical females, and startlingly flexible-looking stucco flowers and foliage. Doesn't quite attain the heights of goofy Baroque but still pretty astounding—so much so, in fact, that we completely forgot about *San Domenico,* right next door. Walked right past it and everything. Sorry.

• *Markets*

Vucciria: The original. Starts at piazza San Domenico, runs along via Maccaronai to the little piazza with the fish market (very lively and colorful), and then on down to the harbor along via Argenteria. Specializes in both the redolent (herbs and anchovies) and the succulent (ices, cheapest in town).

Via Agostino: Between via Maqueda and via Porta Carini. More typical of Palermo. Not so many foodstuffs but lots of clothes, little trinkets, and knickknacks, plus vendors selling mackerel cooked over the coals for just a fistful of lire.

Via Papireto: This street is just to the right of the Duomo. Lots of furniture. Probably not so many great finds unless you're looking for a deal on an authentic Sicilian oxcart.

• *The Modern City*

Most of Palermo is residential with fairly standard architecture (a glance at the apartment buildings along via della Libertà gives you an upscale example of the basic pattern). The older public buildings in this part of town tend to reflect the artistic tastes of Dickens's Mr. Podsnap (the stuffier upper bourgeoisie of the previous century, in other words); see the *Teatro Massimo* and the *Politeama Garibaldi,* which now houses the museum of modern art.

The Outskirts

Museo Etnografico Pitré: In the Parco della Favorita, west of the city. Has an interesting collection of antiques, spectacular painted carts, folk art of various kinds, and *pupi,* with a free *pupi* performance every day at 4 P.M. Open from 9 to 1 and from 3 to 5.

Convento dei Cappuccini: Via Cappuccini, which runs parallel to corso Calatafimi. A catacomb containing about 8,000 mummified Palermitans, reasonably well preserved and dressed in the fashion of the 1850s; they are hung up on full-length display, like unclaimed coats in a cloakroom. A highly decorous spectacle; relatives used to come and change the mummies' clothes for them when they were starting to get a little shabby. Not especially creepy, and regarded by Sicilian kids with signs of polite interest.

Cathedral and Cloister of Monreale: 5 miles south of Palermo. A highway provides a panoramic view of the Conca d'Oro, the shell-shaped crescent of fertile land between the mountains and the water. This one, unlike the preceding, is a compulsory attraction, or in the words of a local proverb: "Whosoever comes to Palermo and not to Monreale arrives a jackass and departs a donkey." Catch a No. 8/9 bus on piazza Indipendenza.

The cathedral represents the greatest artistic achievement of the Normans on the island, though its fortresslike exterior hardly prepares you for the incredible richness of the interior: 6,340 square meters of mosaics, ceilings adorned with painted beams or Moorish "stalactite" carvings, another impressive Pantocrator, marble chapels, and much, much more. The cloister is another Arab-Norman co-production, with arcades, lush greenery, flowers, fountains, slender Moorish double columns embellished with mosaics, and Norman columns with intricate sculpted capitals—highly compact little scriptural scenes intended for the instruction of the ignorant and the idolatrous. It certainly deserves as close an examination as time permits. The cathedral is open every day from 7 to 12:30 and from 3 to 5. The cloister is open from 9 to 4:30 and from 9 to 1 on Sunday and holidays. Closed on Monday.

Mondello: 7 miles northwest of Palermo. A former fishing village that now serves as Palermo's official beach. Catch bus No. 14 or 15 on via Roma. This could turn into an expensive little outing, but the water contains several shades of blue not normally found in nature, and the beach is very nice as well (though note that a lot of it seems to get into the little cabanas where you leave your clothes).

Villas of Bagheria: About 9 miles east of Palermo, in the direction of Cefalu. Recommended only to those who are very fond of villas and apocryphal villa stories. *Villa Palagonia* is famous for its 60-odd statues of grimacing grotesques commissioned (according to the apocryphal villa story) by the jealous husband who built the place for the purpose of terrifying his helpless young wife. The interior decor, very little of which remains, is said to have been conceived along similar lines. Paid admission. Open from 9 to 1 and from 5 to 7. *Villa Valguarnera* is a big Baroque horseshoe of a place, much admired by Stendhal and still very well thought of in architectural circles. Frankly we'd put it somewhere in the bottom quartile of the Sicilian Baroque division. Don't forget that Stendhal spent the best part of his adult life in Italy; if you only have a few days to see Sicily, there are a lot better places than this (of which more anon). So it shouldn't be a total loss, however, there's a great restaurant in town: *Trattoria Santo,* via Fuxa, 6. It has excellent meat dishes.

Monte Pellegrino: The scenic route to the village near the top is full of exciting hairpin turns. The village of Santa Rosalia, which is quite small, has steps instead of streets. Further up, the *sanctuary of Santa Rosalia,* a beautiful little church hollowed out of the living rock, contains statues and reliquaries (in the treasury) of the local saint.

SEGESTA

An ancient site between Palermo and Trepani, just 2 kilometers from the nearest train station. There's a nice panoramic view of the valley from the *theater,* at the edge of the ancient city. The *temple,* left unfinished in antiquity—with no roof or interior walls—and seemingly destined to end up as a beautiful Doric ruin, sits off by itself in splendid isolation. The site would still be pretty nice without the temple; there's not even a village nearby (hence, the guy who *pretends* to be the parking lot attendant performs no useful function and should be severely ignored). The train station is very clean and is suitable for sleeping. Pack provisions; there's a bar nearby but no grocery store. Another possibility is:

Hotel Mille Pini: Right behind the church in Calatafami (you'll see plenty of signs). Quiet, friendly, and a great view of the mountains. Puts you within striking distance of Segesta, Trapani, and Erice.

TRAPANI

Called Drepanum, "the Sickle," by the Romans, it is actually located on a long tongue of land shaped more like a chisel—which you may not see the point of until you get past the postwar building boom all around its base and out to the old city at its very tip. You'll find an old harbor, Baroque churches, a palazzi, whitewashed fishermen's houses, and other good stuff. There's also a ferry to Tunis every Wednesday; the fare is about half of what it costs from Palermo.

Useful Addresses

Tourist Office: Piazzetta Saturno, in the old city. There's a competent staff and plenty of literature.

Post Office: Piazza V. Veneto.

Where to Sleep

Pensione Messina: Corso Vittorio Emanuele, 87. Telephone 21-19-8. A former private town house with an arcaded courtyard in the heart of the old city. Run by a charming family, its rooms get lots of light and are fairly inexpensive.

Pensione Macotta: Via degli Argentieri, 4 (third floor). Telephone 284-18. On a very noisy intersection. For the heavy sleeper.

Miramare: Via Vulpia, 4, right by lungomare Dante Alighieri (northern edge of the sickle) and 10 minutes from the station. A modern hotel with a restaurant. Well run but a little expensive.

Moderno: Via Genovese, 20, between via Libertà and corso Vittorio Emanuele, in the old city. Reasonably priced.

Sole: Piazza Umberto I, 3, opposite the station. Telephone 220-35. Tolerable and fairly inexpensive (but try all the others first).

Vittoria: Via Crispi, 4. Telephone 272-44. For the young sophisticate.

The next 3 are campgrounds on *Favignana,* the largest of the Egadi Islands (see below, Outskirts).

Egad: At a little place called Arena, right outside the village of Favignana. Telephone (09-23) 92-15-55. Comfortable. There's a store and a little restaurant nearby. A few bungalows are available.

Camping Miramare: In Casticella, 1 kilometer outside Favignana. Telephone 92-13-30. Has a little spot set aside for cooking.

Quattro Rose: At Mulini, about half a mile from Favignana. Telephone 92-12-23.

Where to Eat

La Bettolaccia: Via Fardella, 25. On a little street in the old city. A pleasant setting (the premises date from 1613). Reasonable prices. Seafood is a specialty. If eels are currently on the menu, your choice is already made. Service is extremely slow. Bring a book.

Felice: Via Staiti, 45. A very nice, inexpensive place on the harbor. Fish *couscous* (spelled *cuscus* around these parts) is recommended.

Pizzeria Calvino: Via Nasi, 73. Booths. Popular with the younger crowd. Pizza to go or to be devoured on the spot. Chicken and lasagne are also available. Inexpensive.

Trattoria Fontana: Via S. Giovanni Bosco, 22/26, near the station. Telephone 240-56. Warmly recommended by local informants.

Trattoria Giovanni: Corso Italia, 61. Big portions. Fairly inexpensive.

The Sights

The Old City: The church of *Sant'Agostino,* on piazzetta Saturno, still has its original fourteenth-century façade, with a rose window and a splendid carved doorway. On corso Vittorio Emanuele, the main pedestrian throughfare, is the beautiful church of the *Collegio,* as Baroque as they come, and farther along the cathedral of *San Lorenzo,* which is very pretty when the porch is lit up at night. Even if you include the *fish market* at the northern end of via Torrearsa you can take it all in in the course of a morning or an afternoon.

Museo Pepoli: Via Conte A. Pepoli, in the modern city. Starting at the gardens of the Villa Margherita, take the via Fardella as far as Martiri d'Ungheria (the big intersection). One of the most beautiful museum collections in Sicily, it is attractively presented and remarkably comprehensive as far as the folk art, popular art, and religious art of the region is concerned. You'll see magnificent panel paintings and altarpieces of the fourteenth and fifteenth centuries, liturgical vessels, painted terra-cotta statuettes of local occupations and "types," coral sculpture, and an astounding eighteenth-century Nativity scene made entirely out of seashells (a regular tour de force). The building itself is a former Carmelite convent notable for its lovely cloister and spectacular marble staircase. Closed on Monday.

L'Annunziata: Next to the museum; look for a little door after you come to the piazza. The silver- and gold-encrusted marble chapel of Maria Santissima, patron of the fishermen of Trapani, is not the kind of thing you normally associate with humble fisherfolk. There's also a statue of the Virgin by the Tuscan artist *Nino Pisano* and a sturdy sixteenth-century bronze grille. The humbler element are in fact represented by the usual strange collection of ex-votos by the main entrance. There's an impressive sacristy with a high, vaulted ceiling, frescoes, and carved wooden cupboards (conspicuous against the basic all-white decor).

The Outskirts

Favignana: Noted for its annual tuna roundup, the *mattanza,* in which the fish are herded into shallow water, Polynesian-style, and bloodily dispatched. The island has several campgrounds and a few nice beaches. Bicycle rental can be had in the village. There are several crossings a day from Trapani, ferry or *aliscafo;* the trip takes about 20 minutes.

Levanzo: Smaller than Favignana. Quiet—no cars. Has some caves with prehistoric paintings. Several restaurants on the island serve good food, though it's advisable to ask the price of everything in advance. Local residents advertise rooms for rent in the summer. *Paradiso* (telephone 921-580) is an inexpensive *pensione.*

Marettimo: Rockier and more remote than the other 2 Egadi. It has a beautiful little harbor and great hiking trails, and there are no cars. The ferry leaves Trapani every morning at 8:30, with additional crossings during the summer.

San Vito lo Capo: Sicily's northwestern tip—for fans of Land's End, Cape Finisterre, Tierra del Fuego, and other terminal spots. A toothy stretch of coastline about 20 miles north of Trapani, with extensive beaches and beautiful clear water. San Vito was chosen as the site of the first international underwater photography competition in 1978. The town of San Vito is very pleasant, and before you know it, you're out on the beach again. There are 3 organized campsites (*El Bahira,* 2 miles outside town, and 2 more in San Vito) and a virtually infinite number of unorganized ones.

Perched high atop a little nubbin of rock (at 2,300 feet). The road that leads up to it provides an excellent view of Trapani. Erice is the ancient *Eryx,* a religious sanctuary of the Phoenicians, Greeks, Cartheginians, and Romans, and then became merely a stronghold of the Arabs and the Normans. Nothing remains of the earlier tenants except the giant stone blocks (fifth century B.C.) that provide the foundations for the Norman ramparts. The town itself is primarily (in fact almost entirely) medieval; perhaps the first thing that strikes you when you get up here is the silence, a silence that can still be heard above the ordinary noises of an Italian village and the sounds of the wind whistling along the stones. Cable-car service from Trapani was recently interrupted (perhaps indefinitely). It's best to inquire.

The Sights

It is worth spending at least a morning in a reconnaissance of the tiny streets and *cortiletti* of the town, perhaps initially noting the different varieties of paving stones: polished beach-type cobbles and smallish squares to fill in the gaps between the long, flat flagstones that are laid down in a zigzag pattern, in alternating courses of black and white, to make the stairs (with a smooth, immemorial gutter running down the center of each stairway). Streets of this kind generally have a worthwhile destination—a flowery patio or a little courtyard shaded by a mossy archway.

You may end up skipping one or two of Erice's churches, but *San Pietro,* on via Filippo Guarnoti, should definitely not be missed. At the Porta Trapani, the *Duomo* is notable for its rose window, arcaded porch, and free-standing Tuscan-style campanile. The little *Museo Comunale* is on piazza Umberto I; just past the church of San Giuliano, on via Roma, you'll come upon the ruins of *Castello Pepoli* and, a little farther on, those of *Castello di Venere,* which date from the twelfth century.

Where to Sleep

No cheap hotels. The town's spectacular sunsets are chiefly reserved for the affluent.

Communal Campground: The path to the campground leads off from the road that turns to the right (uphill), 2 kilometers before you get to Erice. No lavatories or running water. No charge. Not much room, but it has a great view of the valley.

Hotel Edelweiss: Piazza Santa Domenica. Telephone 869-158. Great location. Hot showers. A bit expensive.

Where to Eat

Pizzeria Ulisse: Via Chiaramonte. A very nice location. Cheapest in town.

Ristorante Erice: Via Vittorio Emanuele. Telephone 473-61. Reasonably priced in spite of touristy surroundings. Delicious *antipasto alla siciliana.*

Fork and Knife: Down the street. A self-service restaurant with an attractive setting. Much cheaper than it looks. Excellent fish *cuscus.*

MARSALA

Once past Trapani the coast is heavily built up and not terribly interesting. Marsala, a famous name in high-class cooking sherry and heavily engaged in the wine trade, is no exception. There's not all that much to see and no cheap places to stay. If you're in any kind of a hurry, we suggest you press on immediately to Mazara del Vallo.

Camping Villa del Sole: Lungomare Mediterraneo, 63. Telephone (09-23) 95-15-93. Keep heading south until you're out of the warehouse district (many of them heavily fortified, you'll observe). Recommended only as a last resort, in case you get stranded. The campsite is surrounded by a high wall; the water, on the other side of the wall, is not too inviting.

MAZARA DEL VALLO

One of Italy's greatest fishing ports, it leaves you with the impression of a forest of masts a very great distance along the banks of a canal, plus a permanent tang in the air of salt, fish, and tar. The old city is very charming, and though most of its principal monuments were constructed by the Normans, it still bears traces of an earlier Moorish occupation. "A splendid city," wrote the Arab geographer El-Idrissi, "superb.... Merchants and travelers come from all directions to bear away with them the abundant products of our bazaars." Today Mazara is especially conspicuous as a transshipment port for the distinctive fat white raisins that are produced on the island of Pantelleria.

Tourist Office: Piazza della Repubblica, 9.

Where to Sleep, Where to Eat

Hotel Mediterraneo: Via Valeria, 36 (runs perpendicular to corso Armando Diaz), not far from the cathedral. Telephone 941-465. The building is nondescript. The rooms are clean and quiet. A little expensive.

Pizzeria la Scoiattolo: On the waterfront. Our favorite. Nice decor and very cheap.

The Sights

Duomo: Built during the eleventh century; substantially remodeled during the seventeenth. The absidal chapels around the back (go under the porch) are about all that remain of the original Norman structure. The interior has a number of interesting features—there's a list posted by the door that mentions 28 of them specifically— including a series of not very convincing frescoes painted in trompe l'oeil, some statues by the prolific Gagini, a painted thirteenth-century crucifix, and (outside, above the doorway) a sculpture of a Norman knight (dates from 1584, long after the fact) trampling an Arab beneath the hooves of his charger. Bare legs and shoulders are not permitted inside the cathedral.

Piazza della Repubblica: Near the cathedral. Scene of a very intense *passeggiata* that might readily be mistaken for some kind of civil disturbance or spontaneous political rally (as we did on our first evening in Mazara). The square itself boasts a number of attractive buildings, including the former *seminary,* with a portico *and* a loggia, and on the other side, *Palazzo del Municipio* and *Palazzo Vescovile,* plus a number of statues (exemplarily unaffected by automobile exhaust).

Next, take via XX Settembre and piazza Plebiscito to the *Jesuit college,* which has a beautiful inner courtyard with a portico. The *municipal museum,* via del Carmine, once the local headquarters of the Knights of Malta, is full of amphoras and ancient coins, the kind of thing you normally walk right past to get to the good stuff.

On the waterfront (piazza Mokarta), the remains of a *castello* built by the Norman king Roger Guiscard can still be seen. We suggest you make a right (facing the water) and take a stroll among the palm trees; Villa Garibaldi now contains a collection of stuffed birds (not reviewed by us). Further on, by the harbor, there's a *Norman church,* a hardened site, as we'd say today, with 3 fortified chapels out back. Mazara was an important stopover on the main pilgrimage route to the Holy Land, which means that Romanesque churches are only slightly less common than raisins. It's best to restrict your intake to no more than 5 or 6 a day.

CASTELVETRANO

A country town of some 30,000 inhabitants. At some earlier stage in their history Sicilian peasant farmers decided they would rather take their chances and live in large fortified towns and get up earlier to get out to their fields than live in small, unprotected villages that were closer to their fields. Thus, the Sicilian farmer became a commuter, and the oxcart (now supplanted by the tractor) came to assume an enormously important role in rural life. Castelvetrano is one such huge overgrown village (specializing in fruit and other perishables), perhaps most famous in its own right as the place where the bandit *Salvatore Guiliano* met his end (in cortile di Maria, in the middle of town). Mostly of interest to us as a convenient jumping-off place for the incredible classical site of Selinunte.

Useful Addresses

Tourist Office: In a little courtyard near the post office.

Post Office: Via Vittorio Emanuele, 64.

Buses to Selinunte: Piazza Regina Margherita, near the church of San Giovanni. At 8:25 A.M. and 4:15 P.M.

Where to Sleep

Impero: Via Vittorio Emanuele, 7. Kind of old and dingy but centrally located and fairly cheap.

Pensione Ideal: Via Partanna, not far from the station. Telephone 442-99. Also quite cheap.

Camping Sombrero: In Tre Fontane, outskirts of town. The facilities are quite decent.

Camping La Palma: In Menji. Quiet, shady, and inexpensive. Hot showers, first-class facilities, an enormous beach, a restaurant, and a place to buy groceries.

Where to Eat

La Lanterna: Via Gioberti Vincenzo, 7, cantone della Balaliscia. Good pizza. A nice little spot.

Pizzeria Golden: Viale Roma, 231, on the outskirts of town. A big neighborhood restaurant on the highway to Palermo.

The Sights

La Chiesa Madre: Piazza Garibaldi. A very pretty church with a richly sculpted doorway. The campanile overlooks a handsome fountain (1615).

Mario Puzo fans will want to stand on the very spot where *Giuliano* breathed his last. The exact location is available from numerous local informants.

The Outskirts

Limestone quarries at Cusa: 7.5 miles to the southwest, on the other side of Campobello di Mazara. It looks as though Selinunte was in the midst of an ambitious building program at the very moment that it was destroyed by the Carthaginians (c. 400 B.C.; thus you'll notice the roughed-out capitals and drums of columns and various pieces of entablature lying around all over the place or just barely beginning to emerge from the rock. An interesting warmup for the visit to the archeological site; you get the definite feeling of a work in progress, as if the masons and quarrymen had just knocked off for a siesta or perhaps a wildcat strike.

SELINUNTE

Accessible by bus and train from Castelverano (6 departures a day). Extensive and impressive remains of one of Sicily's most important Greek cities. It was founded about 650 B.C. and finally succumbed to the combined might of Segesta (in spite of all appearances, the more formidable of the two) and Carthage, after being shaken up a bit by some earthquakes. The site's principal challenge for the amateur photographer consists of catching the last dying rays of the setting sun between the columns of the most substantial of Selinunte's many temples and thus preserving forever "their splendid patina of amber, of honey and burnished gold" (in the words of an obscure poet of our acquaintance.

The temples are designated by letter, since we no longer have any idea what their original names were. As you come onto the site you'll see on your left the fairly vigorous ruins of temple E (notable, under certain conditions, for its patina of amber, and so forth) with a little museum next to it. Temple G, to your right, now little more than a heap of rubble, is thought to have covered about 3 times the surface area of the Parthenon and to have taken at least 70 years to erect. There's a small admission charge to see the bases of the columns on the acropolis which can still impress by their diameter, if no longer by their height. A dozen of the columns of temple C have been put back up on their feet again; they are also the source of the above-mentioned Doric metopes in the archeological museum in Palermo.

Where to Sleep, Where to Eat

Marinella: A pleasant little resort nearby. It has a number of friendly and inexpensive restaurants plus a few disturbing signs of overdevelopment. Their friendliness and inexpensiveness may be less apparent during the tourist season; it's advisable to get out here early in the day.

Albergo Lido Azzurro: Via Marco Polo. Telephone 460-57. Our best bet in Marinella. Quite hospitable, especially if you neglect to mention that you'll be staying only the one night. A good restaurant.

John Bua: Near the station as you come into town. Clean but not particularly friendly. Recommended only if all the places down by the water are full.

Up to the right of the acropolis as you face the water you'll notice a vast beach of fine white sand stretching off into the distance. The dunes are highly suitable for camping out especially under the pine trees, where you'll get a little shade. There's even a shower and a toilet, both badly in need of restoration.

The Outskirts

The Enoagri Museum, on the road out to Selinunte, consists of a sign and a little exhibit of farm implements and other *vino locale*-related items put together by an enterprising wine merchant to attract tourists. Each visitor is entitled to a little taste of the product as well.

Porto Palo: A few kilometers out of Selinunte toward Sciacca. A nice beach with an adjoining *taverna* and a small campground, on the left before you get to the shore.

Camping Hawaii: In Triscina, 7.5 miles from Selinunte (you'll see lots of signs). The beach is very lovely and very clean.

SCIACCA

Said to be the world's oldest thermal spa, it is now almost entirely paved over and encased in cement. The town is not so hot, and the beach fairly decent. The old harbor, which may seem a bit self-consciously picturesque in the midst of its new surroundings, becomes the scene of furious animation during the *mercato ittico,* the auction at which the fishermen dispose of the day's catch. Further on, *Seccagrande* offers a not very tempting shingle beach, a bunch of crummy-looking new buildings, and miscellaneous flotsam of the rising suburban tide.

Where to Sleep

Camping delle Mimose-Al Mare: Contrada Foggia, as you come into town from Selinunte (or, alternatively, as you leave town, coming from the direction of Agrigento). It's the one in back. The owner maintains an excellent stock of local wine, and the proprietress is adept at cooking up little snacks to help you make it through the night.

The Outskirts

Caltabellotta: A very pretty town perched on a little spur of rock. In the wake of the Sicilian Vespers, and so forth, it was here that the treaty of peace was signed confirming the ignominious departure of the French and the succession of the Aragonese as the overlords of the island. You'll find a lovely original Norman church, the ruins of an Arabo-Norman castle, and a splendid panoramic view.

ERACLEA MINOA

The first reasonably acceptable beach in quite some time: a wide expanse of fine white sand at the foot of a step cliff, bordered by a kind of tufty scrub-pine vegetation, but unfortunately not too clean. There are some nice places for camping out—as far as possible from the entrance to the beach.

Camping Eraclea. Decent facilities. Numerous signboards that instruct you not to do this or that are kind of annoying.

The *ruins* of Eraclea Minoa, the former colony of Selinunte that was wiped out by a landslide during the first century B.C., are not nearly as interesting as those of the mother city: a few sections of the city wall, foundations of houses, and a theater, the latter preposterously encased in plastic. There's a nice view of the beach and the cliffs.

AGRIGENTO

You'll see striking signs of change along the road to Agrigento, but they may possibly be a case of two steps forward and one step back. The new *autostrada,* propped up on the massive concrete pillars, can now leap whole valleys at a single bound so that some villages in its shadow, with their tortuous mountains roads now clear of long-distance travelers, may find themselves sinking even further back into their immemorial isolation. Agrigento, which at first glance could almost be mistaken for Albuquerque or some other ungainly exurb in a picturesque setting, has a real heart-of-gold Sicilian city buried somewhere beneath its uncouth concrete exterior; it has wonderful churches and opportunities for some great excursions among its furtive stairways and flavorsome [a euphemism for funky-smelling] passageways.

Most important of all, from any reasonable vantage point in the city you can look down on the incredible Valley of the Temples in which the only hint of intrusive modernity is supplied by a twelfth-century church (not counting the spotlights that beautifully illuminate the valley at night, a sight that causes even the most frivolous traveler to pause for a brief meditation on the beautiful and the good). On a more prosaic note: The train from *Syracuse* takes 7 hours, with a change at Gela. The bus takes only 4 hours, with one leaving every hour.

Useful Addresses

Tourist Office: Piazzale Roma. Telephone (0922) 204-54.

Azienda autonoma ... : Piazza Vittorio Emanuele. Telephone 203-91.

Post Office: Piazza Vittorio Emanuele.

Where to Sleep

Pensione Gorizia: Via Boccerie alla Discesa Gallo, opposite via Atenea, 283. Telephone 201-05. Nothing luxurious but very friendly and the cheapest in town.

Albergo Atenea: Cortile Pancucci, 15, opposite via Atenea, 90. Still less luxurious, rather noisy, and quite cheap.

Belvedere: Via San Vito, 20 (off piazza Vittorio Emanuele). Telephone 200-51. A handsome, modern hotel. Clean. A bit expensive. It is so-called because some of the rooms have an astounding view of the valley.

Bella Napoli: Piazza Lena, 6. Telephone 204-35. A great location (old city) and all the comforts.

Camping San Leone: In San Leone. Telephone 449-12. A beautiful spot on the water, underneath the sheltering pines. Get a bus at the station out to San Leone, the same one that you take out to the archeological site), then be prepared for a 2-mile (3-k) walk to the campground. The scenic route along the shore is recommended. In the summer, when the place is generally packed, they sometimes run some buses directly to the campground; ask the bus driver.

Where to Eat

Trattoria Akragas: Via Matteotti, 27 (head down via Bac), opposite Bella Napoli. A very nice neighborhood place with a family atmosphere. Simple and delectable: *primasole* (local cheese) and *manzolesso* (very tender boiled beef). Should be sampled in quantity. Open until 10:30 P.M. Closed on Sunday.

All'Impero: Via Giambertoni, 2, opposite via Atenea, 144. A reasonably clean little eatery; the food is simple enough (we suggest you stay away from the fish) but kind of expensive.

Trattoria Atenea: Via Ficani, 32, opposite via Atenea, 106. Quite acceptable.

• Upscale

Villa Athena: 2 kilometers out of town on the road to the archeological site. A very classy joint attached to the poshest of the tourist hotels in the valley (right at the base of the Temple of Concord). It should provide you with plenty of imperishable Proustian memories of Sicily (that is, every time you bite into a succulent morsel of *ihuoltini alla siciliana*). Taking quality into account, the prices for both the Sicilian and the basic International-style specialties are really quite reasonable. Your plate of *antipasto alla siciliana* (inexpensive) will be liberally replenished when the time comes. You may want to dress up a bit for this one, as for a big-time *passeggiata* or a diplomatic reception hosted by a medium-sized country. Closed on Sunday.

La Tavernetta: On a little street (with a staircase) off via Atenea. Watch for the sign. The proprietor, a retired ship's navigator, speaks several languages and has a vast fund of nautical anecdotes.

Pizzeria Venta Vecchia: Via Teneres. The proprietor speaks every known language and defies you to eat everything on your plate.

The Sights

• *Valley of the Temples*

An astounding array of Doric temples and other ancient monuments set against a unique landscape. An especially fit subject for contemplation at sunset.

Temple of Concord: The best preserved of all the temples. It was consecrated as a church by Christian priests and thus saved from destruction at the hands of the iconoclastic mob . . . admittedly at the price of a few little monkish cloisters hacked out of the side walls of the temple at a later date. Take a walk down to the *Temple of Juno,* which is not quite so steady on its pins but affords an entirely different view of the valley.

Temple of the Olympian Zeus: On the other side of the road. In its prime this was the largest temple in Sicily and the third largest in the Hellenic world. Present ruins give some idea of its horizontal dimensions. Its roof was supported by giant atlantes ("atlases" that is, male caryatids), a replica of which can still be seen on the premises (the original is in the museum). Further down is the *Temple of Castor and Pollux,* as featured on the postcard of choice for most of Agrigento's summer visitors; it now has just one little corner peeking out of the substrate.

Museo Archeologico: Features the *Ephebus of Agrigento,* a young man of classical proportions, plus statuettes and some beautiful pottery, painted bowls, and domestic implements.

The remains of the *Greco-Roman city,* opposite the museum, give you a good idea of contemporary notions of urban design.

There are 2 more interesting structures on the way back (toward the city cemetery); the *Church of San Biagio,* a twelfth century Norman church superimposed on the foundations of a classical temple, and a rough-hewn *sanctuary of Demeter,* goddess of fertility, the harvest, and so forth. A local classical scholar and modern linguist (self-taught) often turns up on the site and treats visitors to his own highly personal commentaries on Agrigentine antiquity.

• *The Old City*

One of the best. All of its funky stairways, picturesque little plazas, and many delightful churches are conveniently arranged athwart the long and tortuous main street, *via Atenea.*

Duomo and environs: From piazza Lena, on via Atenea, take the little stairway to the left, which should bring you to the twelfth-century church of *Santa Maria dei Greci,* down the street from the Duomo, its handsome Gothic portal coyly visible amidst the foliage of a little garden. The place is looked after by 2 charming sisters who are pleased to admit visitors at any time after 2 P.M. This church was also built on the foundations of a classical temple. Bases of a number of the original columns are still to be seen, plus Byzantine frescoes on the right-hand wall; columns are in the basement.

Head down via Alfonso to the *Duomo,* pausing to admire some handsome eighteenth-century houses along the way. The Duomo is still undergoing restoration in the wake of the 1966 earthquake. A broad staircase leads up to the Norman façade, surmounted by an imposing fourteenth-century campanile and a decorative set of Catalan Gothic windows. Sculptures over the doorways are skillfully carved but badly eroded; as with most of the old buildings in the neighborhood, lightly scratching one finger along the stone will release a little rivulet of beautiful golden sand. Maybe it's best just to take our word for it.

To get inside the Duomo, try the middle door at the head of the double staircase on the side, which is sometimes left open for the workmen. If not, ask one of the neighborhood kids (while significantly flashing a banknote of low denomination) to take you to find the *custodia.* You're sure to find the neighborhood kids very personable and outgoing and even if your efforts are not rewarded with success (as ours weren't; we arrived at via del Duomo, 135, only to be told that the good lady was out shopping—not advisable to try this maneuver during siesta time either). The Duomo is said to contain some lovely Baroque stucco, a carved wooden ceiling, nice frescoes, plus interesting Greco-Sicilian remnants (of a former temple subsequently annexed by the cathedral). Remember that in a case of this kind, if you're really dead set on seeing the interior of a church, the best chances of finding it open are generally between the hours of 6 and 7 P.M.

Santo Spirito: Take the labyrinthine sequence of stairways and passages of your choice back down to via Atenea; head over to *Chiesa del Purgatorio,* down the street, which contains a number of stucco sculptures by the inimitable Serpotta. Take via Fodera (right next to the church) to the *Convento del Santo Spirito.* At the time we went the *custodia* just happened to be there, and another small-denomination banknote changed hands, as is the custom. Inside are more Serpotta stuccos, doors with painted panels, a Madonna by Gagini, the cloister, and traces of the original building (thirteenth century). Nuns specialize in little homemade *dolces,* the best in Sicily (and we've tried them all). They're an excellent gift idea, though they don't always travel that well (there may be none left by the time you get home). Ring at the doorway on the right.

Lastly, there's *piazza del Municipio,* with the *Palazzo del Municipio* and the *Church of San Domenico,* which you've probably been by a dozen or so times already. This time, examine it closely.

Fans of *Luigi Pirandello* may wish to pay their respects at his former home, now a museum. He's buried beneath the pine tree down by the water, where he once sought inspiration while gazing out over the sea (roughly in the direction of Tunisia).

FROM AGRIGENTO TO SYRACUSE VIA THE COASTAL ROUTE

• *Palma di Montechiaro*

Home of the novelist *Giuseppe di Lampedusa,* a Sicilian nobleman who wrote only one book but made it a good one: *The Leopard,* one of the best Italian novels of the twentieth century, the story of a Sicilian aristocrat of an earlier generation (c. 1860) coming to grips with the problems posed by modernity, democracy, and social change. Made into a memorable film by Milanese aristocrat L. Visconti (starring Burt Lancaster and Claudia Cardinale, it has been recently rereleased in the U.S. in its original uncut version).

In town, *Chiesa Madre,* at the head of a stairway lined with old houses, has an interesting Baroque facade.

Licata

Has a beautiful beach with lots of tourists. Those desirous of a little more privacy would do well to pass it by and continue a few kilometers down the road to Gela.

Eurocamping 2 Rocche: Telephone (09-22) 86-15-87. Quiet, clean, and a few yards from the beach. Few amenities, and the barbed-wire fence may give you the impression that you've been taken prisoner. The proprietor also runs a pizzeria with a reasonably priced *menù.* The beach is nice, with practically no traces of modernity.

Falconara

A beautiful beach at the base of a castle, bounded by an impressive stretch of prickly pear, plus no shortage of foreign visitors.

Gela

Agrigento (ancient *Akragas*) was founded by colonists from Gela. Not very much remains of the original city except for a tiny chunk of the acropolis (posed against a post-modern petrochemical backdrop). Not too interesting. The archeological museum has been shut down permanently after thieves made off with most of the good stuff. It is permissible to shoot through without stopping; if you want to stop over for any reason, the *Hotel Leone,* near piazza Umberto, is adequate.

FROM AGRIGENTO TO SYRACUSE VIA THE INLAND ROUTE

In the heart of the heart of the country (though recently bisected by the quadruple bypass of the Palermo-Catania *autostrada,* which is mostly what makes your journey possible). This route is totally lacking in the artificial Club Med overlay of the southern coastal route and in our view is much more interesting besides. It abounds in amazing wild landscapes and leaves a poignant impression of a country too beautiful to leave and too harsh and unforgiving to survive in (which, unfortunately for many of its inhabitants, is a critical real-life dilemma rather than just a fleeting poetic insight).

CALTANISSETTA

The largest town in the interior of Sicily. Primarily modern, with some older quarters and splendid Baroque churches tucked away here and there. Basically drab and workaday in appearance, with none of the mellow golden-ochre tones of the coastal cities. Caltanissetta also presents a curious contrast with the dusty, sunbleached hills and valleys of the countryside in the summer, a contrast that habitués of Fresno or Glendale should be familiar with).

For many years sulfur-mining was the principal activity of the region, but the last mines were worked out in 1975. Extraction of saltpeter and other minerals has recently started to take up some of the slack. One of the more interesting products of this much-abused and long-suffering landscape is an herbal liquer called *Amaro Av-*

erna, one of the gentlest and most flavorful of Italy's many, many regional liquers. It's an excellent gift idea.

Useful Addresses

EPT: Corso Vittorio Emanuele, 109. Telephone (09-34) 217-31 Very friendly and very knowledgeable concerning the entire province. Can help you find a place to stay in town from a very limited selection or plan your itinerary for the region.

Post Office: Piazza Marconi, between the station and piazza Garibaldi.

Where to Sleep, Where to Eat

Europa: Via Gaetani, 5, near piazza Garibaldi. Telephone 210-51. Quite inexpensive.

Albergo Moderno: via Mangione, 2, near the Palazzo Moncada. Telephone 262-40. Also inexpensive.

Diprima: Viz Kennedy, 16. Telephone 260-88. A modern hotel, centrally located. On the expensive side.

Gallo: Via Gattuso, 10 (fourth street on your right as you go up corso Umberto). A family-run *taverna.* Simple and good-tasting fare in a nice atmosphere, and inexpensive.

Trattoria Pace Rosario: Contrada Serrapantano, 2 miles outside town in the direction of Gela (by way of via Napoleone Colajanni). Upscale in manner and appearance. Somewhat inaccessible, but the food is very good and relatively cheap.

Pasticceria Romano: Piazza Garibaldi, at the beginning of corso Umberto. Best pastries and *dolces* around these parts. If you're too proud to point, ask for them by name: *Torrone, pasta di mandorla, rollo, taralli bianchi e neri. . . .*

The Sights

All within easy walking distance.

Duomo: Piazza Garibaldi. Ceiling frescoes that ascend the most dizzying heights of the Baroque, the work of an itinerant Netherlander by the name of *Borremans.* Note also the amazing Baroque organ with its decorative wooden panels, plus 2 major works by a late-model Florentine called *Paladini.*

Chiesa Sant'Agata: Corso Umberto. A little bit like a geode you might pick up on the beach, with a nondescript gray exterior and full of all kinds of shimmering delights: the high altar adorned with multicolored marble inlays and the altar of Sant'Ignazio Loyola. Defies description. Don't miss it.

Palazzo Moncado: Via Matteotti. A beautiful stone façade adorned with grimacing statuary. One of the few secular buildings in the Sicilian Baroque style.

Convento del Santo Spirito: About 2 miles (3 k) out of town, in the direction of Enna. Worth the detour. This abbey was founded by the Norman king Roger Guiscard to commemorate his victory over the Arabs. (*Quick quiz:* What century? Answer below.) There are 3 Romanesque absidal chapels by Roger (the ones in the back); the rest of this little church dates from a later period. Contains a nice medieval *baptistery,* a fifteenth-century Pantocrator fresco, and a confessional that looks something like a highly customized sedan chair.

The interior is highly conducive to meditation on higher things but is accessible only by means of the guided tour conducted by the caretaker, a very scholarly type, at 5 P.M. every day. Free admission, but please observe the sign by the entrance to the choir: "To admire is not enough." (*Answer to quick quiz:* twelfth century!)

Archeological Museum: At the corner of vie Cavour and Napoleone Colajanni. Objects unearthed in the course of recent digs in the area, notably a handsome bronze warrior's *helmet.*

Mineralogical Museum: Via della Regione (edge of town, in the direction of Agrigento). Take the No. 1 bus from the center of town. In the basement of the school of mines. Has an extensive collection of minerals, Sicilian and worldwide, plus photos and other documents relating to the local mineral-extractive industries, which we found interesting and which shed considerable light on yet another harsh and forbidding aspect of rural Sicilian life. For lovers of natural beauty for its own sake: some very attractive $CaSO_4 \cdot 2H_2o$ crystals, plus allomorphic forms of sulfur (which you may recall from high-school chemistry class). Open from 9 to 1 every day.

The *Castello di Pietrarossa* is totally in ruins and not worth the detour.

Holy Week

The ritual commemoration of the Passion, which involves nearly the entire city both as spectators and as participants, is perhaps not the most picturesque or esthetically pleasing of its kind in Sicily, but it is certainly one of the most affecting.

Festivities begin on Wednesday morning with a costumed parade of the city's ancient workers', merchants', and craftsmen's guilds, called the *reale maestranza,* followed by the procession of the Blessed Sacrament, which begins at the cathedral and winds its way through the streets of the old city. The evening procession, the *variæde,* is basically a dress rehearsal for the events of the following day. On Holy Thursday, the *vare,* sculpted scenes from the Passion drama, are retrieved from the museum and borne through the streets in procession, each preceded by the members of the religious confraternity that has traditionally been associated with it. The processional hymns are solemn and resonant, almost anguished, and full of truly passionate intensity.

That evening, solemn high mass is celebrated in front of the cathedral, followed by a second illuminated procession with the *vare* (some of which are fairly tacky in conception and execution, though this is not at all true of the highly expressive grouping of the *Deposizione*). The procession continues until around midnight when it's time for the *spartenza,* "the disappearance," when the *vare* are borne off suddenly into the night—a great moment that is highly charged with emotion.

The Holy Week ceremonies conclude with the procession of the *Cristo Nero,* led by local representatives of the civil administration, *carabinieri,* clergy, and other local notables.

The Outskirts

If you're coming from Agrigento, don't forget that *San Cataldo* is the lace capital of Sicily and is noted for a variety called *ricamo al tombolo,* which is made on a special wooden frame.

Mussomeli: A typical Sicilian village somewhat overshadowed by the impressive *Castello Chiaramonte,* only one of a very great many castles to be seen throughout the province. The Sicilian dialect (or language, if you prefer) is especially pronounced among its inhabitants.

Mazzarino: A bit out of your way, admittedly. If you're coming from Gela (or if this is at least your fifth visit to Sicily), you might want to stop and admire the *Chiesa dei Cappuccini.* The high altar, with its marble inlays and other Baroque wimwams, is the work of a Capuchin artist called Gagliano. There's also a castle and additional churches (notably San Domenico) containing some interesting paintings by the aforementioned Filippo *Paladini.*

ENNA

The "navel of Italy," as it is sometimes called, dominates the region from a height of 2,890 feet. It is surrounded on all sides by fertile plains, with the golden-brown foothills of the Madonie mountains just visible to the northwest. Look to the northeast at sunrise for a fairly astonishing view of Etna's smoky crest. There isn't much in town to compare with it, since Enna has very little to show for its long and tangled history.

It started out as one of the principal settlements of the *Sicani,* an agricultural people who worshipped a goddess of the harvest (later appropriated by the Greeks as Demeter and by the Romans as Ceres) and peaceably coexisted with the neighboring *Siculi* (hence, Sicily). Then came the Greeks, who taught the native Sicilians how to appreciate the finer things in life (and how to work for long hours in the hot sun for practically no pay). Ownership was later contested by the Carthaginians and Pyrrhus of Epirus (of Pyrrhic victory fame) who fought a battle nearby that resulted in an unaccustomed Pyrrhic defeat.

Finally, along with the rest of the island, Enna fell under the domination of the Romans, who treated their Sicilian serfs and slaves so wretchedly that a revolt broke out in 135 B.C. The rebel leader *Euno* managed to keep the Romans at bay for 2 years (about as long as Spartacus and friends held out in a more widely publicized incident about 60 years later) and gave his name to the modern city, Enna. The Romans were followed by the familiar sequence of conquerors and invaders—Vandals, Byzantines, Saracens, Normans, Swabians (Emperor Frederick II and company), Aragonese, Spaniards—which, as far as Enna is concerned, pretty much brings us right down to the present.

Useful Addresses

Tourist Office: Piazza N. Colajanni. Telephone 261-19. You can obtain a free city map plus a list of the cheaper inns.
EPT Office: Piazza Garibaldi, 1. Telephone 211-84.
Post Office: Via Volta, near piazza Garibaldi.
Telephones: Piazza Umberto.

Where to Sleep

Not a wide range of choices:

Belvedere: Piazza Crispi, 2. Telephone 210-20. A hotel of 30s vintage with a fancy Deco decor and a faint aroma of mildew sometimes about the halls. A great location: Most of the rooms (without bath), for all their faults, give you a view of the sunrise behind Mount Etna.

Grande Albergo Sicilia: Piazza Colajanni, 5, the little square before you get to the Duomo. Telephone 211-27. Modern and as depressing as a day without a song.

• If there's nothing for you in Enna, you might try the village of *Pergusa,* 5 or 6 miles to the south. According to legend it is where Persephone, daughter of Demeter and goddess of spring, was raped by Pluto, an alleged Underworld figure.

Miragolo: Telephone 362-72. Fairly cheap.

Pergola: Telephone 360-47. More cheap rooms without bath.

Villagio Turistico Garden: Telephone 361-96. A mite expensive.

Where to Eat

Ristorante Familiare: Via Santa Agata, 123. *Familiare* means familial, not that some guy holding a blackboard is going to come up to you and say, "Hi, I'm Giuseppe, your waiter." A homely family-style place with thick frosted-glass windows and none of the old *mangia, mangia* tourist-trap decor; Serves great food: delicious antipasti and some inexpensive daily specials.

Ristorante Centrale: Via Repentite, 10. Centrality seems to be its outstanding virtue. Humdrum but inexpensive.

The Sights

Duomo: Piazza Mazzini. One of the best. Begun during the twelfth century. The apse is original, the facade dates from the fifteenth century, and the campanile is from the seventeenth. On the left is a beautiful sculpted doorway and inside you'll find a row of black basalt columns with Corinthian capitals (the ones directly behind the font are by Gagini), a marble pulpit in the familiar polychrome mix 'n' match style, a carved wooden organ loft (fifteenth century), and some interesting paintings by Borremans (the one who did the amazing ceiling frescoes in Caltanissetta), Paladini, and de Gangi (known as Zoppo). A very harmonious ensemble.

You might also want to take a peek at the handsome cupboard in the sacristy and the iron grille in front of the baptistery, said to have started out as a harem gate during the old Moorish days. Finally, note the Gothic doorway that is completely sealed up—so it wouldn't be profaned by the feet of the ungodly after the pope walked through it one time back in 1447. (A similar relic is said to exist in an English country house somewhere—a chair with a glass cover over the seat to preserve the irreplaceable imprint of Queen Victoria's backside.) The cathedral *treasury* contains a number of interesting items, including the *Madonna's Crown,* a delicate tracery of gold, enamel, and precious stones. Opening hours for the Duomo and treasury are highly irregular and unpredictable.

Museo Alessi: Next to the Duomo. An interesting collection of Greco-Sicilian and Roman coins, classical vases and statuettes, and magnificent paintings and icons of the Byzantine school. Complements the cathedral treasury. The schedule is somewhat erratic; we suggest you make careful inquiries.

There are at least a dozen other churches in town, including *San Giuseppe* (has a silver-chased altar) and the campanile of *San Giovanni,* both off via Roma. Also *San Francesco* (which has an original fifteenth-century campanile and a painted crucifix), piazza Vittorio Emanuele, plus 3 more on piazza Neglia alone.

Castello di Lombardia: An enormous castle built by Emperor Frederick II: Of its original 20 towers, 6 survive. One of its courtyards is big enough to contain an 8,000-seat outdoor theater (a modern addition). Advice to the indolent: There are those who'll tell you there's a really great view from the top of *Torre Pisano,* the tallest tower, but it's essentially the same one you get from the bottom of Torre Pisano.

Piazza del Belvedere: Very nice and cool in the evening. You'll find an impressive fountain and a bronze copy of Bernini's *Rape of Persephone;* here's where you get a view of the Madonie mountains to the west.

Holy Week

On Good Friday, each of the city's 15 religious confraternities leads a procession from its parish church to the cathedral, each wearing its own (surprisingly colorful) penitent's costume. A nice combination of the transcendental and the picturesque. Later there's a procession with the *Madonna dell'Addolorata* and a disturbingly lifelike image of the dead Christ (reposing in a glass coffin). There's also a very beautiful ceremony on Easter Sunday.

The Outskirts

Calascibetta: 3 or 4 miles to the north of the city. In 951, the Arabs were settling in for a lengthy seige of neighboring Enna and decided to make themselves truly at home by building a little town. This is it. Points of interest include the *Chiesa Madre,* in the upper part of the town, the *Chiesa dei Cappuccini,* with its beautiful altarpiece *(Adoration of the Magi),* and the 300 ancient tombs in the Sicel (native Sicilian) necropolis.

Leonforte: 9 miles north of Enna. A very lovely little place with a first-rate church, to your left as you come into town from the direction of Enna, and a monumental Baroque fountain (1651) with water spurting out of 24 little gargoyle faces.

PIAZZA ARMERINA

Best known for the astounding Roman mosaics in the *Villa Casale,* this town has a couple of downtown attractions of its own: Its houses cling to the slopes of a steep hill crowned by the *Duomo,* which has a campanile in the Catalan Gothic style (as was the rest of the cathedral at one time) and a carved doorway flanked by delicate Moorish-style columns, plus, in the interior, a Baroque altarpiece and baptismal fonts (school of Gagini). Also worth a glance: *San Pietro,* with its intricate coffered ceiling, and a couple of palazzi, to be sought after along many of the town's narrower streets.

Useful Addresses

Tourist Office: Piazza Garibaldi, 1. Telephone 812-01.
Post Office: Via S. la Malfa.
Telephones: Via G. lo Giudice.

Where to Eat, Where to Sleep

There's no campground and no really affordable hotel.
Albergo Paradise Park: Near the villa. A little expensive, but it's a peaceful spot with plenty of trees and no other buildings about.
Ristorante Centrale Da'Toto: Via Mazzini, 29. Basic Formica decor. Decent food at reasonable prices.

The Sight

Villa Casale: About 3 miles south of town, in a pleasant little valley at the foot of Monte Mangone. A Roman villa built during the fourth century and rediscovered in 1929; its amazing collection of mosaics was not fully uncovered—hence, not properly appreciated as one of Sicily's greatest art treasures—until 1954. We have no idea who built the villa, possibly a wealthy merchant, probably someone with a highly developed sense of his own importance (considering the enormous size of the place), most definitely someone with excellent taste (or who was merely incredibly lucky with his interior decorator and subcontractors).

The mosaics cover a total area of over 8,000 square feet, but the layout of the villa enables you to orient yourself and to grasp the thematic connections between the various rooms and corridors quite readily. Some of the colors are still very bright, others a little faded; virtually all of the mosaics are very original in design and brilliantly skillful in execution. The 2 most famous sequences are to be found in the Bikini Room, a group of frisky young women in 2-piece bathing suits (who look as though they should be playing volleyball), and along the Corridor of the Hunt, an astonishing variety of African animals being rounded up for the Roman arena (the rendering of the rhinoceros compares very favorably with Dürer's of about 1,200 years later). The hunt sequence is almost 250 feet long and over 700 square yards in total area. The owner's bedroom contains a touch of soft-core eroticism (on account of a peplum—a tunic, that is, that has worked a little bit loose from its moorings). The villa is open for inspection between 9 A.M. and an hour before sunset.

The Outskirts

Archeological dig at Morgantina: A pre-Hellenic site located in a fairly rugged terrain near the town of Aidone. There's an excellent view from the surrounding hills, which gives you a very good idea of the original extent of the town.

FROM CALTANISSETTA, ENNA, OR PIAZZA ARMERINA TO SYRACUSE VIA CALTAGIRONE

We recommend this itinerary very strongly to those who want to see a little bit of the Sicilian back country. Rather than getting on the main highway for Caltagirone, your interim destination, the idea is to take the long way around by first making for *Aidone* or *Raddusa*, then bushwhacking over the local roads in a basically southerly direction. Not many of these roads are paved, and the ones that are are rarely the better for it. We suggest that you set out early in the morning, and make sure your car is fully operational before doing so. Raddusa is a quiet little town, undisturbed by the seasonal fluxes of the tourist trade and wholly typical of the region. The café on the central piazza (coming from Catania, it's on your left) makes the best cappuccino in Sicily. The only hotel in town has inexpensive rooms with basic amenities and meals on request (tasty family-style cooking).

On the back roads, a cruising speed of about 10–15 miles/20 k per hour is recommended—all the better to admire the landscape, which is splendid, very lonely and wild. Plenty of deserted farmsteads can be seen; the little round dovecotes out front with the red roof tiles always seem particularly poignant. The sign for Caltagirone as you head out of Aidone or Raddusa is the last of its kind you're going to see for some time. Your chances of getting lost are excellent, and before too long the sight of a lonely but still inhabited farmhouse or a farmer on his donkey will take on a special significance out of proportion to its ordinary importance, like a clothesline thrown to a drowning man. When you're back on the track again, you may almost regret it, for after a couple of hours of wandering around getting your brains baked by the relentless Sicilian sun—"the rain of fire," as they call it around these parts—you finally link up with the *nazionale* that runs between Caltagirone and Catania (see highway map of Sicily). The valley just this side of Caltagirone is irrigated and fertile, which makes the contrast even more striking, almost brutal.

CALTAGIRONE

Gets its name from the Arabic *kalaaat*, fortress; its nickname, Queen of the Mountains, seems especially appropriate. The city, with its stairways, vast terraced shoals of tile roof, and all, sits very compactly on 3 hills. Its principal products are pottery and ceramic tiles, which are to be found all over the city—on the walls and bridges, churches and public buildings; the stuff in the stores tends to be kind of expensive, though the colors (blue, brown, and an occasional streak of yellow) are very appealing. Luigi Sturzo, founder of the Christian Democratic party, is Caltagirone's most famous native son.

Where to Sleep

Casa Donato: Via San Paolo, 24. From the intercity bus stop, walk past the hospital and the only starred hotel in town, then about 120 yards past the latter. Family-run, very clean, and rather inexpensive; the shower is out in the hall.

The Sights

Ceramics and Pottery Museum: In the "Villa," a big public garden. An interesting collection of vases, terra-cotta, enamelware, and tableware from the Bronze Age to Microwave cultures. Closed on Sunday.

Piazza Umberto I and environs: Might as well start with the *Duomo,* next to the Bank of Sicily, which has some nice ceiling frescoes. A little farther on is the *Palazzo della Corte Capitaniale,* now a showcase for potters and other local artisans (with many items offered for sale). The handsome staircase that starts in front of the palazzo dates from 1506, with majolica decorations supplied by 2 local residents, c. 1960. It leads to the upper city, where those who are especially sound of wind and limb might care to admire the *Church of Santa Maria del Monte* and its thirteenth-century *Madonna dei Comadomini,* object of local veneration and star of the annual *festa* (May 20–31). On the way back down toward piazza Umberto, check out the *Chiesa del Gesù,* which has a very fancy marble-inlay decor and a couple of interesting paintings.

FROM CALTAGIRONE TO SYRACUSE VIA RAGUSA, MODICA, AND NOTO

Takes a little time but hits most of the high spots:

• *Ragusa*
(Not to be confused with Raddusa, on the other side of Caltagirone.) A handsome provincial capital also built on 3 hills; overlooks a primarily agricultural landscape that slopes down in terraces toward the sea. You'll find some splendid palazzi and Baroque churches in Ragusa. *Donnafugata,* 7 miles to the south, has one of Sicily's most impressive medieval castles.

• *Modica*
Clings bravely to the side of an enormous rocky outcropping. Climb a staircase of 250 steps to examine the *Church of San Giorgio,* which, fortunately, is one of the most beautiful Baroque churches in Sicily. It has a handsome facade and a luxuriant interior with paintings, a richly decorated organ case, and so forth. About 7–8 miles in the direction of Noto there's a Sicel *necropolis* (plus trogolydyte dwellings and an Early Christian catacomb) in a notably rugged terrain. Makes for a nice walk.

Albergo Minerva: Via San Domenico, 71. Telephone 941-249. Fairly cheap. The proprietor is friendly.

Pizzeria Italia: Via S. Grimaldi, 15. Quite decent food. Inexpensive. Art gallery decor.

• *Noto*
See below, right after Syracuse.

FROM CALTAGIRONE TO SYRACUSE VIA GRAMMICHELE, VIZZINI, AND PALAZZOLO ACRIEDE

A somewhat less leisurely route that takes you through the forbidding mountain landscapes of the *Iblei,* a frequent refuge from foreign intruders in ages past. The roads are narrow and winding, and are lined with extensive stands of prickly pear, which (as in Mexico) plays an important part in the local cuisine. *Palazzolo Acreide,* a little market town that hasn't changed much since the eighteenth century, is worth a modest detour. There's also an archeological site, with a Hellenistic theater (third century B.C.) remodeled by the Romans, and *latomiae* (quarryings used as prison cells, a common practice in classical times) which became catacombs in the Christian era. A very beautiful place a bit off the beaten path. Take the *strada panoramica* for an interesting view of the whole ensemble.

Note that this route will take you about 4 or 5 hours at night, as opposed to 2 or 3 if you go by way of Catania, plus you won't get to see much of anything anyway.

FROM CALTAGIRONE TO SYRACUSE VIA CATANIA

Use this route if you're in any kind of a hurry or have to make the drive by night. It may look longer on the map, but it isn't. You'll pick up the highway to Syracuse right before you get to Catania.

SYRACUSE

Really *Siracusa,* of course. Once you get past the industrial rough edges and the modern city to the delightful little offshore island of *Ortigia* (classical Ortygia), your only regret will be that you don't have more time to spend here. The island has barely enough room for all the treasures that it contains. The Baroque churches have an especially Spanish look to them; the Duomo, when you look at it from the side, seems more like a Greek temple (and with good reason); and the palazzi squint at you through harlequin Catalan Gothic windows. The modern city on the mainland, though less uniformly charming, includes the site of ancient Neapolis and a number of interesting archeological attractions.

Syracuse was by far the most important of Sicily's Greek cities, one that inflicted the decisive and humiliating defeat on the Athenians (as readers of Thucydides will immediately recall) that broke their power forever. By the end of the reign of the tyrant Dionysus (367 B.C.), Syracuse was undoubtedly the richest and most powerful city of the Hellenic world. A later tyrant, Hieron II, managed to stave off the Roman threat with adroit diplomacy, but his successors made the mistake of picking the Carthaginians over the Romans and soon found themselves blockaded by the Roman fleet.

Archimedes, the greatest inventor and mathematician of antiquity (though not, as many people believe, the inventor of the bathtub), luckily happened to be a resident of the city. He created a battery of highly effective shore-to-ship weapons, including catapults and, perhaps apocryphally, a kind of giant burning glass that focused the rays of the sun on the sails of the Roman ships until they burst into flames; this held them off for another 3 years. Finally, in 212 B.C., Syracuse was captured and extensively pillaged, an event that was very important in developing the Romans' insatiable appetite for Hellenistic art treasures. The Roman general made his troops promise beforehand that they wouldn't kill Archimedes, but one of them forgot. . . . The rest of Syracuse's history is essentially that of the island as a whole, passing from the hands of one foreign empire to another (Byzantine, Muslim, Holy Roman, Spanish Hapsburgs, plus the lesser kingdoms of the Norman, Aragonese, Neapolitans, and so forth).

Useful Addresses

Tourist Office: Via Maestranza, 33 (Ortigia). Telephone 669-32.
Post Office: Piazza della Posta (Ortigia).

Where to Sleep

Albergo Gran Bretagna: Via Savoia, 21 (Ortigia). Telephone (09-31) 687-65. Our best address in Syracuse. An adorable family hotel with a romantic threshold, an atrium full of green plants, and a first-rate atmosphere. The rooms are light, spacious, and incredibly clean but without bath, and there's a fairly substantial surcharge for hot showers. One of the rooms has frescoes on the ceiling, and the ones on the courtyard are very quiet.

Milano: Corso Umberto, 10 (5 minutes from Ortigia on the mainland). Telephone 669-81. A handsome facade but a less well preserved interior. Fairly noisy, but one of the cheapest places in town.

Albergo Centrale: Corso Umberto, 141, near the station and about 10 minutes from Ortigia. Telephone 605-28. Clean but without character.

Pensione Gelone: Via Epicarmo, 36, at the corner of via Gelone. In the Achradina section of the city, a very *populare* residential district about 10–12 minutes from Ortigia. Telephone 624-72. Inexpensive. Lockup is at 11:30.

Albergo per la Gioventù: About 4 miles out of town, near the Castello Eurialo, right off the highway to Belvedere. Telephone 711-118. Frequent buses arrive from Syracuse. Not an official hostel (no card required) but very nice all the same: inexpensive and copious portions at mealtime, though there's not always enough hot water.

• *Campgrounds*

Fontane Bianche: in the town of F.B., 10–12 miles out of Syracuse (catch a No. 34 bus on piazza della Posta; the last one leaves at 8:15 P.M.). Telephone (09-31) 79-03-33. Nice facilities. Access to a very nice private beach. Open from April 1 to October 31.

Agritourist Rinaura: On the SS 115 highway to Ragusa, about 4 kilometers out of Syracuse. Telephone 72-12-24. Take the No. 34 bus from piazza della Posta. A campground with bungalows about a mile from the water. Very well maintained. Has a grocery store, but staple foodstuffs are a lot cheaper in town. Open year round.

Ognina: A little town on the water before you get to Fontane Bianche. Just past the harbor at the base of a great big rock and a ruined fort there's a stretch of rocky shoreline that's entirely suitable for camping.

Where to Eat

Trattoria Vecchia Guardia: Via dei Mergulensi, 1, near piazza Archimede (Ortigia). A pleasant atmosphere and a very peaceful spot. The terrace is overlooked by the handsome (Catalan Gothic) windows of the Palazzo Montaldo. Great fish dishes. Highly recommended.

Trattoria Ortigia: Via XX Settembre, 37 (Ortigia). A popular restaurant that serves good pizza in a nice setting. Remember the price of everything you eat, however, and check the mathematics (we hesitate to call it addition) on your tab.

Spaghetteria Russo: Via Scinà, 11–18, a little street between piazza Archimede and via Cavour. A nice place. Inexpensive menu.

Trattoria do Scoggliu: Via Scinà. Pasta *modo nostro.* A very nice place. Very popular, so it's best to go early.

Don Jose Pizzeria: Via Filisto, next to the Park Hotel. To the north of town (complicated directions follow); only worth attempting by those with a car and a city map: Head down viale Teocrito, turn left at the new museum onto via Augusto von Platen, then take via Tica, via Damone, via Tista, and via Pitia. Has a nice terrace and an extra-friendly manager. The pizza *speziale casa* is what brought you all the way out here in the first place.

The Sights

• *Ortigia*

Set aside a full day for the old city, where just about every building has something interesting; there's an especially amazing sequence of beautiful facades and carved balconies along *via Vittorio Veneto.*

Temple of Apollo: Piazza Pancali, right after the bridge as you come onto the island. A couple of columns are pretty much all that remains of Sicily's earliest Doric temple.

Piazza Archimede: About 100 yards from the Tourist Office. Numerous palazzi.

Duomo: Wears its 2,500-year history on its face, particularly the north one, which consists of a kind of homemade neoclassical portico (that is, 10 genuine Doric columns with the spaces between them filled in with medieval masonry; the effect is a little strange but basically quite attractive). Inside is mostly Byzantine with Romanesque vaults; when the Norman façade collapsed after an earthquake in 1683, it was replaced by a full-scale Baroque prosthesis. Most of the other buildings on piazza del Duomo are Baroque through and through, such as the *Archbishop's Palace,* the *Palazzo Beneventano,* and the *archeological museum.*

Fountain of Arethusa: This is a freshwater spring a few yards from the saltwater inlet that separates the island from the mainland. In classical mythology, Arethusa was a nymph who was pursued by Alpheus, whom she didn't much care for. One day he finally caught her, and Arethusa appealed to the goddess Artemis, protector of virgins, to do something in a hurry. Artemis changed Alpheus into a river (over in Greece) and Arethusa into a fountain (on this very spot), but Alpheus figured out a way to bore right through the Ionian Sea and mingle his waters with hers. (Some say that Alpheus was already a river, or a river-god at least, whom Arethusa used to tantalize beyond endurance by taking a bath in him every morning.) If you want to see all this with your own eyes, ask for the *Fontana Aretusa.*

Archeological Museum (Museo Nazionale): Piazza del Duomo. One of the very best of its kind, it has lots of first-rate classical works including the famous *Venus Anadyomene* (Venus Rising from the

Vaves). Its attractive new quarters on viale Teocrito are supposed to be ready any day now. There's a branch office on via Capodieci (*Palazzo Bellomo*) that contains more recent works: medieval and Renaissance sculpture, Byzantine and Slavic icons, and paintings from the fourteenth to the eighteenth centuries.

A very colorful *market* is held every morning near the end of the bridge.

Neapolis

To get to the *archeological park,* take corso Gelone, then turn onto via Augusto.

Roman Amphitheater: One of the largest in Italy.

Altar of Hieron II: Originally measured something like 600 feet by 70; the platform was big enough to sacrifice 100 oxen at a single go, but only the lower part survives. Hieron's abortive attempts to "duplicate the cube" (to build another one *exactly* twice as big) are said to have resulted in the discovery of irrational numbers.

Greek Theater: Like the altar, cut out of the living rock. Could accommodate 15,000 spectators. Aeschylus and Euripides both supervised productions of their plays here; later performances were most probably attended by Plato and Archimedes. Closed on Monday.

The Latomie: Excavations that served both as quarries and slave-labor camps for prisoners. One of the caves is known as the Ear of Dionysus for the special acoustical properties that enabled the tyrant Dionysus to listen in on the conversations of the prisoners in the dungeon; another is known as the Cave of the Ropemakers, an occupation that requires a cool, damp environment. In the cave now known as the *Latomie dei Capuccini* 7,000 Athenian prisoners captured at the disastrous siege of Syracuse were confined and eventually perished.

Catacombs of San Giovanni: Viale Teocrito. Very interesting, even if you've already seen the ones in Rome. To get in, ring for Brother Porter, whose fairly strict ideas of what constitutes proper attire in these sacred precincts (no bare shoulders, and so forth) may happily coincide with your own on how to avoid catching your death in a catacomb.

The Outskirts

Castello Eurialo: About 5 miles out of town on the road to Belvedere. This is the fortress from which Archimedes defied the Romans, though there's some dispute about when it was originally built and by whom (Greeks? Carthaginians?). The exterior is none too impressive these days, but the vast network of subterranean tunnels and galleries—an entire underground city really—is well worth checking out.

Some very pleasant walks can be had along the upper reaches of the *Cyane* river, lined with thick stands of papyrus and once a big favorite with Cicero; especially nice in the late afternoon. If you have a car, you might start by driving in the direction of Ragusa to the river's *source,* which is fairly amazing. Lots of signs to get you there, and foot trails are laid out along the riverbank. There's also an excursion boat that makes the same trip (4 hours both ways). Make inquiries at the harbormaster's office, corso Italiano.

Festa

Not much chance you'll still be here on December 13, which is a shame because that's the festival of *Santa Lucia,* celebrated with tremendous brio by the entire city and featuring a procession of the saint's image followed by an ornate ceremonial carriage, plus consumption of mass quantities of traditional millet cakes called *cuccia.*

NOTO

About 20 miles (32 k) south of Syracuse. After the original Noto was destroyed by an earthquake in 1693, its successor was built on a specially selected site and in accordance with the best principles of contemporary architecture and urban design. This meant Baroque and plenty of it; the soft, warm color of the local building stone, which almost seems at times to be breathing, actually heightens the normal Baroque impression of voluptuous organic forms or, in the words of a modern disciple of Baudelaire and John Ruskin (currently in the employ of the provincial tourist office), "Here and there, the sensual smile of a cherub, the heavy breast of a siren, the grimace of a drunkard, the roaring mouth of a lion, amid delicate wrought-iron traceries and friezes of living foliage in stone. . . ."

The Sights

Mostly to be found in the vicinity of corso Vittorio Emanuele.

Duomo: Approached by a monumental staircase and conceived on very generous lines (not being subject to the normal constraints of an existing classical, Byzantine, or Norman foundation). The interior is vast and luminous, with marble altars, edible-looking columns of streaked and variegated marble with Corinthian false capitals, and quite unlike that of a normal cathedral—the overall effect is that of an immense child's playroom, with its columns, altars, and objects d'art just so many creative playthings. Alleged by the sacristan to be open every morning at 8:30, on Sunday from 9 to 12, and often after 5:30 . . . subject, of course, to change without notice.

Palazzo Ducezio: Opposite the Duomo. Elegant portico. The upper story, a very good imitation of the original style, was added in 1951.

Chiesa del Collegio: Farther down corso Vittorio Emanuele. Dates from 1736. A lovely facade. It now houses a supermarket.

San Domenico: Has a handsome colonnade, a nice garden out front, and antique furnishings within. Keep walking around for a while and you'll come across a number of other churches, monasteries, and palazzi.

Where to Sleep, Where to Eat

Albergo Stella: Via Maiure, 44. Affordable and quite acceptable.

There's a great restaurant down the street from the post office. Look for the sign that says "Si mangia bene, si spende poco." It's true. The owner is young, very hip, and very nice.

Trattoria Figura Severier: Via Ducezio, 9. Good food. The proprietors are also very, very nice.

The Outskirts

Noto Marina: 5 miles away. A beautiful sandy beach that is not a total stranger to development, since you can go swimming here all year round.

Nota Antica: 11 miles from Noto. The ruins of the pre-Baroque original are not terribly interesting.

Heloros: Just a few kilometers from Noto Marina. An archeological site. Get info at the museum in Syracuse beforehand.

CAPO PASSERO

This southeastern tip of the island may be less stimulating to the eye than to the imagination—on the one hand, a few clumps of reeds and rock formations, and very few trees, contrasted on the other hand with the unseen presence of Africa beyond the horizon. Very little recent construction in the area, which is still almost untouched by the outstretched tentacle of tourism.

• *Portopalo:*
A very pretty little town by the tip of the cape. Has a first-rate *vino locale.*

Capo Passero: Telephone (09-31) 84-23-33. A small campground by the water. Quite pleasant. Has a cafeteria and a *tavola calda,* both moderately priced.

Camping dell'Isola delle Correnti: Near the lighthouse that marks the *southernmost* tip of the island (Capo Isola delle Correnti). Located on a lovely little inlet just moments away from a fine sandy beach. (The landscape is slightly disfigured by a bunch of plastic greenhouses, but who are we to complain about a little thing like that?) Run by a very nice, very accommodating gentleman from Florence. A shady spot with plenty of atmosphere and almost unlimited tranquility. Showers (of the outdoor kind), bar, and grocery. Inexpensive. Some little cabanas can be rented as well (may be regarded either as very flimsy bungalows or as very sturdy tents).

The coast between Syracuse and Catania isn't very interesting—a number of oil refineries and gasworks along the way with big fat polychrome pipelines. Recommended only for those who haven't seen the Centre Pompidou in Paris. Might as well take the *autostrada.*

CATANIA

The second largest city in Sicily has recently benefitted from the discovery of substantial reserves of oil and natural gas in the region, though high unemployment and other problems of the collapsed boomtown are still fairly endemic. Currently, Catania is the island leader in armed robberies and crimes against the person—fairly shocking statistics by Sicilian standards, and none too impressive (and readily comprehensible) by American ones. Normal antitheft precautions on the part of our readers should therefore be sufficient (see the intro to the section on Sicily).

The term "mainland Sicilians" is sometimes used to describe the Catanians (usually by the Palermitans, always maliciously), the implication being that they're a degenerate breed who have sold out their Sicilian birthright by allowing themselves to become assimilated into the Italian cultural mainstream. Whether or not this is regarded as a desirable state of affairs, it must be admitted that it is largely true—at least to the extent that you'll be seeing more expansive, Italian-style gestures, fewer teenage girls with their eys downcast demurely, and more couples carrying on in public places with considerably less restraint than in other Sicilian cities.

One final index of social change—death notices in Catania tend to be just discreet little announcements rather than the great brooding manifestoes you're used to seeing in Palermo and elsewhere. No doubt the Palermitans are right and it all has to do with the erosion of traditional family values, plus the Church seems to have lost some of its ancient grip on public mores. On the other hand, this is no reason for the likes of us to avoid Catania, since the old city is pretty terrific and the *fish market* is the liveliest, most colorful, and picturesque in all of Sicily, and it'd be a shame to miss it.

Useful Addresses

EPT Office: Largo Paisiello, 5. Telephone (095) 322-124, plus a tourist information booth in the station.

Post Office: Via Etnea, opposite Villa Bellini.

Where to Sleep

Pensione Duomo: Via Garibaldi, 9. Telephone 34-01-95. Quite in order. Inexpensive. Run by a very nice extended family.

Savona: Via Vittorio Emanuele, 210. Telephone 32-69-82. Centrally located, pretty decent, and inexpensive. If they're full there's another place across the street.

San Giorgio: Via A. di Sangiuliano, 237. Telephone 22-06-41. Centrally located. Maybe a little noisy and not so clean, but one of the cheapest in town.

YMCA: Lungomare Kennedy, 12, on the water, about 2 miles north of town. Telephone 34-61-41. Open all year round.

Pensione Royal: Salita Sangiuliano, 337 (upstairs), right off via Etnea. Telephone 31-21-08. Clean, has a terrace, and is on a pleasant street.

Pensione Continental: Piazza Trento. Clean, with large rooms. A little expensive. Showers are included.

• Campgrounds

Internazionale la Plaia: Lungomare Kennedy, 47, about 2 miles out of town. Telephone 34-08-80. On the water. Bungalows are available. Open all year round.

Jonio: Via Villini, in Ognina, 1 kilometer north of town. Bungalows on the water. Open all year round.

Where to Eat

Trattoria del Forestiero: Via Luigi Sturzo, 70 (near piazza Santo Spirito, which runs parallel to corso Sicilia). Our best address in Catania. A moderately priced neighborhood restaurant that serves excellent Sicilian specialties—*pesce spada alle bracce,* and *salsiccie*

—plus some great cheeses. The atmosphere is very warm and friendly. Fills up pretty early, so it's best to go before 8.

Trattoria San Michele: Via San Michele, 7. Very cheap. Very well run.

Scarletta Giuseppa: Via A. di Sangiuliano, 38. A neighborhood tavern with wine right out of the cask and some foodstuffs. If you order *antipasti* or a main dish, your tab is likely to be a good deal more inflated than the basic tenor of the establishment would suggest. You'll be fine, however, if you check the prices beforehand.

The Sights

A fairly compact grouping, all within walking distance.

Piazza del Duomo: The Duomo has a magnificent facade and is said to have many wonderful things inside (including a Roman sarcophagus and a fresco depicting the eruption of Mount Etna). The problem, as usual, is getting inside to see them. Other interesting buildings on the piazza: the eighteenth-century *Seminario* and the *Palazzo del Municipio.*

Castello Ursino: Piazza Federico di Svevia. A lowering, very well preserved old medieval castle that now houses the municipal museum, which we didn't much care for (heavy on the archaic Greek). En route, check out *piazza Mazzini,* which is adorned with a peristyle of 32 columns scrounged from a Roman basilica.

Museo Bellini: Piazza San Francesco. Birthplace of the composer of *Norma.* Great for fans of bel canto and perhaps others as well. Bellini spent his last years in Paris and died there in 1834; he later had part of a suburb named after him. His memory is more fittingly enshrined in the *Teatro Bellini,* the opera house on piazza Bellini, right here in Catania.

Roman Theater: Via Vittorio Emanuele, next to the old Bellini place. It is now visible thanks to the removal of a layer of lava from Mount Etna and some neighborhood houses that had been built on top.

Chiesa della Collegiata: On via Etnea. The church's interesting concave facade doesn't seem to have suffered from the billowing clouds of Fiat exhaust along Catania's main street, which is especially recommended for devotees of the Sicilian code of the road.

The very *Old City:* Bounded by via G. di Prima on the north and Antonio di Sangiuliano on the south. In 1693, Catania was simultaneously flattened by an earthquake and buried beneath the debris of an eruption; the Catanians moved right back as soon as the dust settled but didn't possess the technical means at that time to dispose of the larger chunks and outcroppings of lava, with the result that they're still there, many of them as tall as a 2-story building. Nowadays the streets around *via del Finanze* and *via Antonio Canciulla*—your typical seedy, rundown late-seventeenth-century neighborhood—frequently turn up some weird Fellinian scenes at twilight (very much like the assertively unconvincing painted backdrops in some of his recent films, plus strange pastel tints and shadows playing on the walls of the buildings, lots of cheap little *tavernas* exhaling the aroma of refried cooking grease, and a mixed assortment of local characters engaged in a furtive *passeggiata*). Great for fans of *Under the Volcano* as well.

Chiesa San Niccolo: Piazza Dante. The architect succeeded in his design of erecting the longest façade in Sicily, but only just. Much remains to be done, and its stumpy little columns still plaintively await their capitals. A great view of Catania and environs from the *cupola,* and the *Convento dei Beneditini* next door has a much more elegantly abandoned look.

• *Miscellaneous, Seasonal*

Fish Market: Fills the narrow streets and ancient archways around piazza del Duomo with live fish, hoarse market cries, and amazing faces. Plenty of activity and indescribable aromas. As noted, absolutely the best of its kind in Sicily.

Piazza Carlo Alberto: At the end of via Pacini. More like what we're used to: fruits, vegetables, old clothes, and curious little items. Also plenty of activity.

Festa: February 3–5. Relics of Catania's patron saint, *Sant'Agata,* are drawn through the streets by devotees dressed in white robes and black skullcaps, followed of course by a procession.

TAORMINA

A kind of landlocked Isle of Capri, just about a mile (2 k) up the hill from the coast road between Messina and Catania. Its reputation as a totally glitzy, French Riviera-type place is by no means undeserved, but you'd be a fool to miss it if you happen to be passing by. The town itself is medieval and overgrown with flowers. It has an incredible view and that same overly clean look as Capri, perhaps as the result of deferentially keeping pace with several generations of the well bred, well shod, well dressed, and not very well behaved. Our advice, as with sinking into a very wide, very soft sofa, is to give in to it—but not all at once and not so much that you can't spring right back up at a moment's notice.

Useful Addresses

EPT Office: Corso Umberto, 144.
Post Office: Piazza San Antonio, at the edge of town.
Telephones: Piazza del Duomo.
Scooter Rental: California, via Bagnoli.

Where to Sleep

In the summer it's generally advisable to book a room 3 months in advance.

Friuli: Corso Umberto, 19. Telephone 253-19. Signora Caterina, the proprietress, is very nice and runs a clean, no-frills establishment. *Pensione Internazionale,* at the same address, is very clean, fairly quiet, but a little expensive.

Pensione Villa Margherita: Via Dietro Capuccini. Telephone (09-42) 238-48. Villa is pretty neat, has a terrace, peaceful location, just a few minutes from the center of town. Studio apartments also available for long-term rental. Reasonably cheap.

Pensione Villa Liliana: Via Dietro Capuccini, 4. Telephone 243-73. A little expensive. The proprietress is quite delightful if a bit loony.

Villa Sonia: Further uphill, right below the village of Castelmola.

Telephone 237-80. A big, ugly building with an amazing view out over the valley.

Panorama di Sicilia: Above Castelmola, on the peak overlooking Taormina. Telephone 223-05. Like it says. A hotel for honeymoon couples who still have a little cache of traveler's checks left. Not too expensive considering the astounding picture-postcard panorama that is involved. The proprietor is very friendly as well.

Finally, if you do turn up in August and everything is filled to capacity, you might try the very nice little old lady who runs the grocery store on *via Guardiola Vecchia* (the cable car runs overhead), who may be able to fix you up with a private room.

• *Campgrounds*

San Leo: In Capo di Taormina, on the SS 114 (road to Messina). On the water. It's the closest to the train station and therefore of interest to non-motorized travelers. Facilities are somewhat limited.

Castello San Marco: In Calatabiano, a few kilometers past Taormina on the road to Catania. Where every prospect pleases and only man is vile. A great location at the foot of a castle. Tents beneath shady trees in a tranquil setting, just moments away from the blue Mediterranean. Also equipped with a cafeteria, bar, and grocery store. On the other hand, it's fairly expensive and facilities are not so splendid and none too clean. Extra charge for showers (which don't always work). The management is pretty fussy and kind of snotty to boot. It's a trade-off. Open all year round. There's a good restaurant nearby (see below).

Almoetia: A little bit before you get to Castello San Marco. Telephone 641-936. Well equipped, but we still prefer the preceding.

Paradise International Camping: On the SS 114. A well-maintained campground with bar, general store, and a shingle beach.

Where to Eat, Where to Drink

Poco Pago: Via C. Patricio, 10, Porta Messina. "I Pay Little" is what it means; in Taormina this is a novel marketing strategy. Pretty good food. Specializes in *capponata* and *pepperonata*. Open only for dinner.

La Venere: Piazza San Antonio. Expensive and pretty fancy. The food is wonderful.

Bar Arco Rosso: Via Naumachia, 7, a little street off corso Umberto. A very nice bar with inexpensive drinks: Sicilian wines and great fresh-squeezed lemonade.

Snack-bar Ceres: Via Timoleone, 14. A low-cost clearing in the touristic jungle.

Pizzeria Ciccino: Via Castelmola. Excellent small-sized pizzas, reasonably priced.

Pizzeria Ruggeri: Via Regina del Cielo, 51, in Fiumifreddo, not far from the Castello San Marco campground. Doesn't look like much but serves gigantic succulent pizzas at ridiculously low prices. The owner is very nice; he lived in Venezuela for 20 years and has a broad international outlook.

The Sights

The Greek Theater: An ideal vantage point from which to look at Etna or out over the Mediterranean—the playgoers of Magna Graecia must have possessed amazing powers of concentration. Exhibits the normal characteristics of Greek theaters on the island—looks like an immense fossil seashell hewn out of the living rock. Remodeled by the Romans who put up a backstop-type proscenium stage, which fortunately has partly fallen down since then and to some extent restored the original view.

Duomo: Ideal for those who have already gorged themselves on Baroque. The fountain out front (1635) leads one to expect the worst, but the façade is quite severe, with Norman-style crenelations, and the interior is positively unassuming.

Palazzo Badia Vecchia: An exquisite medieval building with Catalan Gothic double windows ornamented with sculpted friezes and arabesques, and unusual swallowtail-shaped battlements on top. A number of other buildings of similar vintage can be seen by taking a little walk around the *Torre del Orologio,* notably the Catalan Gothic *Palazzo Ciampoli* (now a hotel).

The Outskirts

Castelmola: The village up on the heights, clustered around the ruins of a castello. Offers the best panoramic view of the region. There is frequent bus service from Taormina between 7:20 A.M. and 8 P.M.

Gorges of Alcantara: On the road out to Francavilla di Sicilia. They don't add up to much by North American standards, plus there's an admission charge!

MOUNT ETNA

One of the world's most beautiful and most accessible volcanic peaks. Until a few years ago, the southern approach was the usual one—by way of Nicolosi and the cable car station at Casa Cantoniera. There was a fair-sized eruption in the spring of '83 that wiped out all the access roads and a number of the pylons that hold up the cables. Service may be restored by the time you get here (so it's best to inquire). Normally the bus leaves from the stop outside the train station in *Catania* at 8 A.M. and heads back (from the cable car station) at 6 P.M. The bus leaves the stop in *Nicolosi* at 8:50 A.M. and gets back at 6:15 P.M.

If service has not been restored, the western approach is the only feasible one these days, which means that if you're driving up from Catania, don't follow the signs that say Etna. Instead, make for Trecastagni, then Zeffarena, and from there to the Sapienza shelter. Minibuses can take you up to the vents from which molten lava and burning brimstone occasionally issue forth.

Camping Panorama: In Acireale, about 11 miles north of Catania. Makes an excellent base for those about to embark on the conquest of Mount Etna. Right on the water and has a splendid view.

The guided tour of the southern face did not take you up as far as the main crater, which you had to get up to on your own and entirely at your own risk. Nowadays, the minibus takes you up to 3,000 meters, and if you want to get out and walk back down—a splendid idea when the weather is good—you only pay half fair. Good sturdy shoes (not necessarily climbing boots) are a must, and some extra sweaters or additional thermal layers may be advisable since sudden and dramatic temperature drops are very common. We caution you not to get caught up on the slopes by a fog or approaching storm; also, the volcano gives off little coughs and sputters from time to time that should not be ignored. Thick black smoke may be regarded as perfectly normal and healthy, while white smoke may be a sign of impending trouble—and a party of 10 tourists who failed to absorb this simple lesson back in 1979 are still unaccounted for.

MESSINA

This slovenly commercial city of 250,000 people may not have much to do with the *National Geographic* Sicily of colorful painted oxcarts and dazzling Baroque cathedrals. Still, it can hardly be blamed for trying to keep a low profile after having been knocked flat by an earthquake in 1783, once again in 1908 (and almost completely destroyed), and then sent reeling onto the ropes once more by Allied bombers during World War II. Notable as the birthplace of Sicily's greatest painter, *Antonello da Messina.*

Tourist Office: Outside the central train station.

Where to Sleep, Where to Eat

Pensione Roma: Piazza del Duomo, 3. Clean and fairly cheap but no showers; not even a sink, for that matter.

Albergo Centrale: Via Cannizzaro. Clean and inexpensive.

Cucina Universitas: Via Venezia. Very reasonably priced. Very few tables, supply being generally exceeded by demand.

The Sights

Duomo: Built by the Normans during the twelfth century and patiently reconstructed by the Messinians after each successive civic disaster. The campanile dates from our own century and it is noted for its astronomical clock, adorned with clockwork representations of various symbolic animals. Worth seeing at noon when they all hit the fan at once (offstage flourishes, lion roars, rooster crows, and so forth). The 3 sculpted doorways date from the fifteenth and sixteenth centuries; inside, the mosaic decorations of the apse and the ornamental woodwork of the choir have been scrupulously restored.

Museo Nazionale: Has only a single painting by Antonello da Messina, fortunately one of the best of the lot: *The Polyptych of St. Gregory.* Also has other works by members of his school, 2 Caravaggios, as well as classical art and archaeology, sculpture, and so forth.

The local *festa* takes place on August 14–15. Notable for a pageant commemorating the Norman conquest of Sicily known as the Parade of the Giants. (Forget about finding inexpensive lodgings during these 2 days.)

Made famous in their respective centuries by Ingrid Bergman and Jules Verne (the spot where his little band of daredevils came back up to the surface in *Journey to the Center of the Earth;* baby-boomers may remember the movie version with Tab Hunter). Part of an extended volcanic belt of which Vesuvius and Etna are the principal ornaments.

The boat trip out to the island and the climb up to the crater are both emphatically recommended. There are 2 ways to get here: by hydroplane from Milazzo (in Sicily), which costs a fortune and doesn't give you much to look at, or by boat, which stops at Naples, Stromboli, Lipari, Vulcano, and Milazzo and is a lot cheaper (showers are included in the fare). 2 departures a week in each direction. For reservations and info, contact *Siramar,* via Depetris, Naples; telephone 31-21-09). There's also an office in Milazzo at via dei Mille, 57; telephone (090) 92-63-81 or 82.

Climb up to the summit of Stromboli toward the end of the afternoon to avoid the fiercest heat of the day. If you start climbing after 4, you have to go up with a tour; otherwise you're on your own. Bring a flashlight, drinking water, and a couple of sweaters, and check out the pyrotechnics. The climb takes 3 or 4 hours, with practically continuous eruptions all night long. If you bring a sleeping bag, sandwiches, and maybe a few more sweaters, you can camp out at the summit; in either case, jeans and serious shoes are recommended for all—though we have seen bemused tourist couples with kids in tow start up the slopes in beach sandals and bathing suits.

The climb is a little rough, we admit, but once it's over with, the view is spectacular in every direction. The major logistical problem is where to leave your backpack, suitcase, and so forth, while you're up there. There's no baggage check on the island, and the one on Lipari doesn't seem to stay open all that much. The solution is to drop into the *pensione*-bar *Roma* on the main street (the one that leads up to the church) on Stromboli, right across from the minimart. With the purchase of an ice cream or something, the owner will cheerfully take all you have to give for a few lire for each item; he's generally up by 5 A.M., so you won't have any trouble reclaiming your stuff in the morning. There's also an observatory at the base of the volcano from which you can watch the eruptions at night. If you make inquiries, you may also be able to make a little offshore circuit of the island in a fishing boat.

Where to Sleep, Where to Eat in Milazzo

Albergo Stella d'Italia: On the harbor. Good eating next door at *La Bussola.*

Ostello delle Aquile: Salta Federico II, in Castoreale, 12 miles south of Milazzo. Telephone 905-247. A youth hostel.

Camping Paradiso: Capo Milazzo. Watch for the signs. Clean, shady, and overlooks the water—a nearby path leads you down to a little inlet. Reasonably priced. Bar and restaurant are nearby.

Ristorante Cambria: Via Giacomo Medici. Locally renowned. Best pizza in Milazzo. The local specialty is *frutta martorana,* fruit with marzipan.

Cucina Casalinga: Via Riccardo d'Amico, 13. No reason to confine yourself to the posted menu; all possible combinations of pasta, fish, and crustaceans are available. Quite reasonably priced.

Where to Sleep, Where to Eat on Stromboli

Prudent campers will bring their own tent and provisions (much cheaper on the mainland).

Pensione di Roma: In the center of the village. Cheapest on the island.

Geo Club: Pietro speaks numerous languages and maintains a spectacular private stock of the local vintage. Barbara is a great hand in the kitchen. Both are highly deserving of your patronage.

The Outskirts of Milazzo

Castoreale Terme: A seaside thermal spa for those in need of a holistic infusion. The *Hotel Belvedere* is modern, comfortable, hospitable, and has some very lovely rooms. Great hikes to be had in the nearby Peloritani mountains.

LIPARI

The largest of the Isole Lipari (Isole Eoli/Eolian Islands). In the town of Lipari is the *Castello,* a natural stronghold reinforced with ramparts. It now also contains a *hostel,* with a campground and public showers adjoining. Affordable lodgings are hard to come by in August. Your best bet may be the *Franciscan nunnery,* where the sisters will put you up in a dormitory room (showers included) for about what you'd pay for a *pensione.* Finally, feel free to camp out about 20 minutes past the first of the signs that says "No Camping on Spiazza Biancha [the beach]."

Points of interest include the *Duomo,* the *archeological museum,* and the *obsidian bed* (black volcanic glass, very pretty). There's another beach with beautiful white sand at *Canneto,* a little before you get to the quarries (commercial source of pumice, in case you were wondering). The island has an efficient bus service, lots of good hiking opportunities, and a *scooter rental* opposite the ferryboat landing.

VULCANO

Another little Æolian Island with lots of tourists and 2 volcanoes, one of which, *Gran Cratere* (500 meters in diameter), can readily be climbed and possesses numerous brimstone fumaroles.

Porto di Levante: A nice little 1-story town with lots of flowers in evidence. Near the harbor. Some underwater fumaroles and a little spa where the afflicted come to steep themselves in volcanic mud, with results sometimes reminiscent of Doré's illustration for the *Inferno.* Even if you don't indulge, there's a self-service right across the street with pastries and delicious *granita de caffè.* There's also a beach with black volcanic sand, a municipal campground *(Sicilia),* and 2 private ones *(Tojo* and *Tojo-Tojo);* the latter 2, run by hungry 80s entrepreneurs, are likely to swoop down on you as you step onto the dock and propel you, practically at gunpoint, into their minibus. There's a great shortage of cold water on the island, but if you want hot water, that's what they've got.

Where to Sleep, Where to Eat

Gabliano Bianco: Via Faravola, 19. A very friendly, reasonably priced restaurant. Very good mussels, with white Piano cheese as an appetizer (on the house).

Vulcanello Sabbie Nera Camping: On the west side of the island, about 15 minutes from Porto di Levante. Telephone (090) 985-22-24. Very basic amenities but has a nice family atomosphere. Popular prices.

PANAREA

A charming little island that is accessible by ferryboat (Tuesday, Saturday, and Sunday). Has about 300 inhabitants and no cars, only a couple of Vespas. Rooms in private houses are sometimes available, but rates are pretty steep since the local homeowners have a pretty shrewd idea of the going rate for a couple of hours in Paradise.

There's a little peninsula on the southwestern edge of the island where the stone foundation circles of a *Neolithic village* can still be seen; makes for a nice excursion. Local fishermen may also be willing to take you out to the tiny uninhabited island of *Basiluzzo.*

MONTI NEBRODI

A very gentle and unforbidding range of mountains to the west of Taormina, a region of wide fertile valleys and extensive commercial fruit orchards. An agreeably scenic road winds through them under the watchful eye of Big Brother Etna.

• *Cesaro* and *Troina:* 2 typical mountain villages along this route. From Cesaro, if you head out along highway 289 (in the direction of Sant'Agata di Militello), stop around Km 17, before you come to the crossroads at the village of Monte Soro, and take a look around. You'll see a very nice *albergo* off to the right, in the middle of the forest. A peaceful haven in a green and very pleasant spot.

• *Cerami:* From the massive *Church of San Sebastiano,* the perfect view of *Monte Soro,* at 5,730 feet/1847 meters the highest point of the Nebrodi mountain chain.

• *Nicosia:* Another very highly placed little town with nothing especially Greek about it apart from the name. The *Duomo,* on the main piazza, has hung onto its fourteenth-century facade. Has a splendid carved portal and campanile, with some of its original polychrome tile decor still in place. Inside, a marble pulpit and baptismal fonts by Gagini. Further uphill, *Santa Maria Maggiore,* with a beautiful carved marble altarpiece tucked away at the back of the choir.

• *Sperlinga:* More or less on the boundary between the Nebrodi range and neighboring Le Madonie, though the 2 terrains are not all that different. The village has an almost vertical cliff face, with a number of houses excavated from the living rock. A series of rounded steps, also carved in stone, leads up to the ruined castello above the town, where the survivors of the French garrison in Palermo took refuge after the Sicilian Vespers massacre of 1282.

LE MADONIE

A splendid mountain chain whose territory is largely delimited by the towns of *Gangi, Alimena, Petralia Sottana, Polizzi Generosa,* and *Castelbuono,* and which presents 2 contrasting faces to the world: Its southern slopes lead down to valleys almost devoid of vegetation and are cut across with occasional watercourses; its northern slopes are almost dry but are covered with thick forests of oak and beech plus dense groves of holly inhabited by foxes, marmots, and wild boar, with eagles, hawks, vultures, and kites still very numerous in the skies.

• *Alimena:* Southern gateway to Le Madonie, a typical village of the region. With the passage of time, the roofs of the houses have taken on the color of the surrounding stones and blend in very successfully and almost imperceptibly with the slopes; unfortunately, some impersonal modern buildings plunked down at the entrance to the village tend to spoil the effect. All of its narrow streets, paved with large flat blocks with gutters cut right down the middle, run straight downhill like rainwater. There's a *hotel* in the upper part of town.

• *Petralia Sottana:* A charming village with an altitude of about 3,100 feet. Facing each other across the main street are 2 old churches, one adorned with a sundial (still in excellent working order), the other with a table of weights and measures dating from 1860 that was intended to help the local farmers get used to the metric system. Further up, the *Chiesa Madre* quite successfully dominates the valley. Built of a lovely gray stone that manages to look both fresh from the quarry and ancient and patinaed at the same time. The campanile has an ogive arch at its base that spans the roadway. The carved church doorway has Gothic stone tracery. There's a cheap *hotel* in town.

• *Petralia Soprana:* Up above the other Petralia, as the name implies, and in fact the highest village in the region (3,555 feet). The church is all white and has an attractive arcaded entryway with a kind of sandblasted look to it.

• *Gangi:* The travel book writers, in their colorful, mindless way, often speak of the houses of a village being "huddled on a hilltop," but the houses in this village really are, like cells in a beehive or kittens in a basket—no exceptions. Whether this is the result of ingrained invasion trauma or just immemorial custom is not clear. Gangi is also notable as the birthplace of a prolific sixteenth-century painter known as Zoppo, (the Lame, in its literal, not its modern colloquial sense). There's a medium-priced *hotel* in town.

• *Geraci Siculo* and *Castelbuona:* The last 2 villages on the way as the northern slope of Le Matanie makes a fast (15-kilometer) break down to Cefalù and the coast. They also represent a way of life that is rapidly dying out. As in many places of this kind throughout the Western world, most of the people you see on the streets seem to be fairly elderly. In Castelbuono, the chapel of *Castello Ventimiglia* was very attractively decorated by Serpotta.

A fair-sized fishing village snuggled down beside a very big rock next to the sea, wtih all 3—the rock, the sea, and the village—in what looks like a very delicate state of equilibrium. Cefalù, a one-of-a-kind attraction as far as Sicily is concerned, is currently monopolized by the Germans during the off-season, which doesn't seem quite right. It's possible to give the place a pretty thorough going-over in just a few hours. There are very nice lighting effects at night when the dim streetlights and the shadows turn every fisherman's house into a little palazzo. You'll also find a great beach with brightly painted fishing boats strung out in a line offshore like marker buoys.

Useful Addresses

Tourist Office: Corso Ruggero, 114. Telephone (09-21) 210-50.
Post Office: Via Matteotti.
Telephones: Corso Ruggero, 78.

Where to Sleep, Where to Eat

Cefalù was caught entirely unaware by the recent influx of summer visitors. When local business interests finally caught on to the fact that the luxury-loving barbarians were at the gates, they stuck up a couple of fancy tourist hotels, but there's not much of what you'd call an affordable infrastructure, except for maybe a few private rooms here and there.

Locanda: Via Umberto I, 24. Cheapest in town. Has very little else going for it.

Santa Dominga: Via Gibilmanna. Reasonably cheap.

Pensione la Giara: Via Veterani, 38, which intersects corso Ruggero and the waterfront. Rooms are rather expensive by Sicilian standards and often booked up due to the *pensione*'s convenient location. The hotel restaurant, open to all, features delicious family-style cuisine at moderate prices; minestrone *de la maison* is not to be missed.

Pensione Germania: Via Bolagnini. Friendly, fairly cheap, but a little noisy.

Camping Costa Ponenete: In Ogliastrillo, 2 miles out of town. Telephone 200-85. Right by the beach. Catch the bus that goes out to Collesano at the train station. Open from April 1 to October 31.

Camping San Filippo: Next door to the preceding. Less modern, more modest, and less expensive.

Bar-Restaurant-Pizzeria Al Bastione: Via Carlo Ortolani di Bordonoro. Nice and fairly cheap.

The Sights

Duomo: Built in fulfillment of a vow made during a violent storm at sea by the Norman king Roger II. Norman on the outside, with the usual Moorish decorative influences inside. It's said that Roger intended his cathedral to rival Monreale, and while it may not surpass it in sheer magnificence or bulk, it is considerably livelier, less solemn, and more human. The carved wooden moldings on the interior doors are deeply wrinkled and burnished with age, like the face of an old Sicilian fisherman. There's a Byzantine-inspired Pantocrator mosaic, of course, and traces of the original painted decor can still be seen on the wooden ceiling. To your right as you come in is an impressive baptismal font (eleventh century) in the form of 4 lions back to back (to back . . .), and the altar in the chapel on the left-hand side is made entirely of silver.

If the cathedral turns out to be closed, there are some places on the piazza where you can console yourself beneath the palm trees with a glass or two of something nice.

Medieval wash basin: In a little alleyway off via Vittorio Emanuele. An interesting relic of communal life in the old days. The time-warp effect of being plunged, so to speak, back into the Middle Ages is especially pronounced at night. Seems sturdy enough, but very few of these have survived the depredations of local town planners and developers, lacking as they do the obvious artistic and patrimonial associations of an altarpiece or a mosaic.

The climb up to the top of the rock overlooking the town takes about an hour. It's a good place to be at sunrise.

The Outskirts

Termini Imerese: A local fair with rides, amusements, and so forth, that goes on all summer. The town is perhaps most notable for the *Gelateria Cicciuzio,* a first-rate *gelato.* Enormous portions—a meal in itself, if not several.

Maremonti: In Pizzillo, between Cefalù and Termini Immerse. A very cute campground about halfway up a mountain and 3 miles from the water. Bar and restaurant.

Himera: At Km 207 on the SS 113 (highway from Messina). Telephone (091) 943-276. Bungalows.

Other books from The Collier World Traveler Series
are available at your local bookstore or from
Macmillan Publishing Company.

To order directly, mail the form below to:
MACMILLAN PUBLISHING COMPANY
Special Sales Department
866 Third Avenue
New York NY 10022

Line Sequence	Quantity	ISBN	Title	Price	Total
1		002097700X	GREAT BRITAIN & IRELAND	$6.95	
2		0020977204	ITALY	$6.95	
3		0020976909	IN & AROUND PARIS	$6.95	
4		0020970404	GREECE & YUGOSLAVIA	$6.95	
5		002097020X	MEXICO, BELIZE, GUATEMALA, & THE FRENCH ANTILLES	$6.95	
6		0020970307	NORTHERN & CENTRAL EUROPE	$6.95	

Please add postage and handling costs--$1.00 for the first book and
25¢ for each additional book--and applicable state sales tax.

TOTAL $ _____

_____ Enclosed is my check/money order payable to Macmillan Publishing Co.

_____ Bill my _____ MasterCard _____ Visa Card # _____

Expiration date _____ Signature _____
--Charge orders valid only with signature--

Lines Units

Control No. [_____]   T-Code [_____]   [____][____]

Account Number/San _____ For charge orders only:

Ship to: _____ Bill to: _____

_____   _____

_____ Zip code   _____ Zip code

For information regarding bulk purchases please write to Special Sales Director
at the above address. Publisher's prices are subject to change without notice.
Offer good January 1, 1986 through December 31, 1986. Allow 3 weeks for delivery.

FC#.207